CITIZENS
IRVING

K.C. IRVING AND HIS LEGACY

CITIZENS
IRVING

K.C. IRVING AND HIS LEGACY

The story of Canada's
wealthiest family

John DeMont

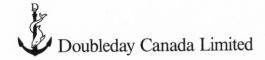 Doubleday Canada Limited

Canadian Cataloguing in Publication Data

DeMont, John, 1956-
  Citizens Irving: K.C. Irving and his legacy

Includes index.
ISBN 0-385-25313-3

1. Irving, K. C. (Kenneth Colin), 1899-
2. Irving family.   3. Industrialists - New Brunswick
- Biography.   4. Capitalists and financiers -
New Brunswick - Biography.   I. Title.

HC112.5.I78D4 1991   338.092   C91-094137-8

Jacket photo by Don Newlands, courtesy Maclean Hunter
Jacket design by Elaine Cohen
Printed and bound in the USA

Published in Canada by
Doubleday Canada Limited
105 Bond Street
Toronto, Ontario
M5B 1Y3

Care has been taken to trace ownership of copyright material
in this book and to secure permissions. The publishers will
gladly receive any information that will enable them to
rectify errors or omissions affecting references or credit
lines in subsequent editions.

CONTENTS

PREFACE

MY EARLIEST encounter with the Irving empire occurred in the early 1960s — or at least I think it did. I was five or six at the time and we were living in Lancaster, a suburb of Saint John. As our family crossed the bridge spanning the Saint John harbour one day I remember a sour, overwhelming smell that seemed to fill our car. I cannot remember if I asked my parents where the odour came from. But at some point I learned that it originated at the Irving Pulp & Paper mill, which, I was told, was owned by a man named K.C. Irving.

There was nothing particularly unusual about my introduction to New Brunswick's first family. Anyone who grows up in the Maritimes, as I did, learns at an early age about the Irvings and their great wealth. It never occurred to me to write a book about them, however, until 1989, when I returned to Saint John to write a series of articles on the family for *Maclean's*. Soon afterwards, I received a telephone call from literary agent David Johnston, who was interested to learn that one of the world's richest families lived quietly in New Brunswick, largely unknown to the rest of the country.

Once my research began I quickly found out how they had managed to remain such a mystery. The Irvings do not like to talk about themselves. K.C. politely refused my written requests for interviews, saying that he "did not want to disturb his retirement." Although his three sons, J.K., Arthur and Jack, had met me for the *Maclean's* stories, they declined further conversations. Their own sons also refused to be interviewed. So did many friends and employees. The experience was the same with competitors, government officials and even outright enemies. In some cases the reluctance of even outsiders to talk about the Irvings stemmed from the natural aversion of Maritimers to invading other people's privacy. Often, though, people simply seemed too intimidated to discuss the family.

Fortunately there were many who did talk to me, although a number insisted that our conversations be off the record. All in all I interviewed more than 150 people. They included family friends, business competitors, current and former employees and officials at all levels of government. I talked to admirers as well as detractors; people were rarely neutral when it came to the Irvings.

While conducting my research I spent three months living in New Brunswick and also travelled to Calgary, Ottawa, Halifax and Charlottetown. I unearthed hundreds of pages of documents involving Irving financial information and read through various court cases and royal commission reports concerning the family. I also relied upon reams of previously published writings, including Russell Hunt and Robert Campbell's 1973 book *K.C. Irving: The Art of the Industrialist*.

Why proceed without the family's cooperation? An obvious answer: the Irvings have built perhaps the greatest fortune Canada has ever known. They are significant public figures — feared as much as admired — whose actions affect thousands of people. Their influence goes far beyond creating jobs. Wealth and power usually have only a remote connection, but their economic power can best be judged by the way they have altered the landscape of New Brunswick and the lives of the people who live there. The Irving story deserves to be told in the fullest fashion possible.

Many people helped with this book. Of the people who can be identified, I am particularly grateful, for the many hours they spent talking with me, to Charles Van Horne, Louis Robichaud, Richard Hatfield, Ray Tanton, Willie Duplessis, Wynton Shatford, Robert Morrissey, Alf Powis, Laurie Boucher, Pat Landers, Fr. Ralph McQuaid, Shirley Morris, Colin Mackay, David Folster, Gary Davis, Jack Abraham, Richard Oland, Chris Morris, Paddy Gregg and Peter Glennie.

I am grateful as well to Phyllis Austin, an award-winning Maine journalist, who conducted interviews and research for the chapter on the Irvings' attempts to penetrate the New England market; Ellen Kierstead of the Saint John Public Library, who assisted with the research on K.C.'s early days in Saint John; Jim Bagnall, Ottawa correspondent with the *Financial Times of Canada*, who supplied important insights into the Irvings' involvement with the Canadian naval frigate program; and Robert Jones of CBC Television in Fredericton, for providing helpful financial information about the Irving companies.

In addition, I would like to thank Philip DeMont of the *Toronto Star*; George Emerson of CBC Radio's *Sunday Morning*; Pierre Cormier of the Musée de Kent; John Edward Belliveau of Shediac, who read various portions of the manuscript and provided valuable comments on content and style; Steve and Lauree Savoie of the Earl of Leinster in Saint John, for their hospitality; and my friends at the Toronto Central YMCA Karate Club, for providing an outlet for my frustrations throughout the run of the project.

My particular thanks go to John Pearce and Barbara Czarnecki, my editors, and David Johnston, my agent, for their help and encouragement; and Kevin Doyle, Robert Lewis and Michael Benedict, my bosses at *Maclean's*, for giving me time away from my regular duties to write this book.

Most of all I would like to thank Lisa, who put up with my long absences and acted as the manuscript's first reader. Her help, patience and encouragement, as much as anything, are responsible for this book.

Halifax
April 1991

PROLOGUE

The Autumn of the Patriarch

*All men dream: but not equally. Those who dream
by night in the dusty recesses of their minds wake
in the day to find that it was vanity: but the dream-
ers of the day are dangerous men, for they may
act their dreams with open eyes, to make it
possible.*

— *The Seven Pillars of Wisdom*, T.E. Lawrence.

THE CITIZENS of Saint John, New Brunswick, call the 13th-storey,
glass-enclosed penthouse over the yellow building on Union Street
"the Bridge." Sometimes, when the sunlight hits its windows just
right, they can see an ancient, lean, hawk-faced man gazing out over
the grimy city below. The old man's bald, gleaming head is trimmed
with a fringe of white hair. His Gothic face is bony, bloodless and
wrinkle-free with a sharp, slightly off-centre nose and thin, firm lips.
Though he was born in the last century, he is still straight-backed
and wears a dark suit that hangs neatly from his spare, angular frame.
But it is the eyes that grab you. Anyone who has ever stared into
those steel-grey, impenetrable eyes — union leaders, provincial pre-
miers, federal cabinet ministers, Bay Street deal-makers, American
oilmen — never forgets them. As he approaches his mid-90s, the
old man's phenomenal mind has begun to be clouded with age. Yet
behind his thick glasses, the lonely eyes still peer back, as calm and
unrevealing as a pair of polished marbles.

From childhood on, Saint John residents are brought up with the
knowledge that Kenneth Colin Irving is there, on the Bridge. Not
because they pass him on the city streets where, until a few years

ago, he liked to take long walks, a blue World War I flyer's beret covering his head. Or because they saw him hunting for bargains at the local supermarket or having his border of hair trimmed at the nearby Dad & Lad's Barber Shop, where only the oldest customers recognized him by sight. They know he is there because the world goes on, life goes on, seagulls circle Saint John harbour and the Irving enterprises hum and churn, clank and hiss. So it was, so it is, and so, if K.C. Irving has his way, it ever shall be.

Officially, he settled into self-imposed exile behind the closed doors of a sprawling Bermuda home a few months before his 73rd birthday. Yet for the past two decades he has spent there only the minimum time necessary to maintain his status as a resident of the tax-free island in the sun. Usually, he prefers passing his twilight days in Saint John, surrounded by his three sons, their wives and his 12 grandchildren. Often he is here, on the Bridge, contemplating the sum of his life's work.

When he peers out from the penthouse atop the Irving Building, K.C. Irving finds many of his prize assets spread before him, most branded with his name. If he looks to the east he sees the sprawling Irving shipyard, with 3,500 workers the country's largest, busy building frigates under a $6-billion contract for the Canadian navy. Further back is the Irving Oil refinery, also the biggest in the land, capable of turning 250,000 barrels of crude each day into gasoline, jet fuel and other petroleum products. Next door is the deep-water port, the first in the western hemisphere, where the fleet of Irving supertankers, each nearly two football fields in length, unload their cargoes of Saudi Arabian crude. Nearby sits his newsprint mill, churning out about 1,000 tons on a good day.[1]

Looking to the west of town, K.C. sees the reassuring clouds of white smoke that tell him that the Irving Pulp & Paper mill is busily transforming logs into pulp for sale throughout Canada and the United States. If he raises his gaze to the horizon, he sees some of the 3.4 million acres of prime timberlands that he owns or leases and that act as a gigantic tree farm to feed his mills.[2] Lowering his eyes, he sees the home of the *Saint John Telegraph-Journal* — the flagship of his newspaper chain, which holds all four of New

Brunswick's English-language dailies — which sits next door to the main studio of CHSJ Television, the centrepiece of his broadcasting interests.

When K.C. Irving shifts his view to the city streets, he sees buses owned by his bus lines. Every so often one of the big yellow, brown or green trucks from his trucking lines rumbles down the street carrying Irving hardware, home furnishings, concrete and steel to their destinations throughout North America and the world. And if K.C. Irving looks directly beneath his penthouse window, he sees one of the 3,000 service stations, all of them emblazoned with the big red-white-and-blue Irving diamond, which started it all, so long ago.[3]

His influence extends into virtually every corner of New Brunswick commerce. Visit a convenience store or a restaurant, walk into a lumberyard or a hardware store, turn on the radio in New Brunswick, and chances are that you make K.C. and his clan richer. The Irvings own a fleet of aircraft, more ships than the Canadian navy and a security company that is thought to be larger than all but two police forces in New Brunswick.[4] Each day his companies make prefabricated homes, office buildings and frozen food. They sell heavy equipment, tires, life insurance, personal computers and translation services. They run tugboats and dredging outfits, apartment buildings, a restaurant chain and a string of home heating companies.

Standing on his summit, the old man must also be content with the knowledge that his power reaches into Nova Scotia, Prince Edward Island and Newfoundland, where his corporate might is nearly as absolute as it is in New Brunswick. His tentacles stretch into Quebec, where his family owns service stations and hardware stores, through Ontario, where a few Irving filling stations sit along the roadside, and as far west as the Alberta oil patch, where hundreds of millions of Irving dollars have gone into petroleum drilling programs over the years.[5]

The Irving name spans national boundaries: in Maine, which is serving as a springboard for the assault on the rich U.S. eastern seaboard — and from there, perhaps, the world — the family holdings include half a million acres of prime forestland, timber mills and the state's largest string of service stations. Overseas, their dredging company cleaned out Saigon harbour after the end of the Vietnam

War. They are said to have mining interests in South America, and their scope is rumoured to extend into Japan, where K.C., who never travels for pleasure, was reportedly making regular excursions in the late 1980s.

Only the patriarch, who has not granted an interview in 30 years, and his three taciturn sons really know the scope of their empire. Indeed, their corporate family tree is so complex that it is virtually indecipherable to outsiders: subsidiaries are owned by holding companies, which are controlled by foreign shell corporations. Ultimately, most arrows point to Bermuda, to a string of offshore holding companies — F.M.O. Co., F.M.R. Co., F.M.W. Ltd., FMI Ltd., FMK Co., FMN Co., FMP Co., FMX S.A., Forest Mere Investments Ltd. — all owned by K.C. Irving. To this day, Irving accountants swear that the balance sheets of the various companies are never consolidated together. Often, the employees themselves don't know who technically owns the company where they work. The ownership can be so tangled that one ship, for example, is owned by several companies (one company holds title to the hull, another the cabin, and so on). The Seafarers' International Union once had to abandon a campaign to organize the crews of six Irving cargo ships because the union couldn't figure out who actually owned the vessels.

Estimates of the Irvings' wealth, however, are possible.[6] When all is said and done, their name is behind at least 300 companies, with assets of nearly $7 billion. If you go by *Fortune* magazine's 1990 rankings of the world's richest people, this makes the Irvings the 10th-wealthiest family in the world. It also may make theirs the largest private Canadian fortune — one that is not based on the gyrating market valuation of a publicly traded company.

Underlying the estimate of the Irving fortune is a refinery worth $1.2 billion, a string of service stations worth $600 million, a shipyard that would fetch more than $500 million and woodland holdings worth $500 million. They have a payroll hovering in the range of 25,000, which means they employ one out of every 12 New Brunswickers.

It is a staggering total, certainly one of the greatest fortunes Canada has ever seen. What makes K.C.'s handiwork all the more amazing is that the Irving empire was forged here — in a province that for the past century has been one of the poorest in the land. The Irvings, moreover, haven't just made incredible amounts of money; they've also managed to hold onto it. While most of the great North American corporate families have watched their wealth dissipate from generation to generation, K.C.'s empire remains as much a tightly private, family-owned-and-run show as it was the day he founded it. Indeed, as the final triumph in his long life, the old man on the Bridge has smoothly passed the running of the empire on to his tough and shrewd sons, J.K., Arthur and Jack, who, in turn, are already grooming their own offspring to be ready for when their day comes.

Their legacy is a degree of unfettered power and influence unheard of in New Brunswick since the 19th century, when an aristocracy of merchant princes controlled the province's trade and commerce and ruled the surrounding land as if it was their own. The Irving family's decisions influence the prices that New Brunswickers pay for everything from gasoline to groceries. They decide which natural resources will be exploited and determine who works, where and for how much. At times they have helped decide who gains political power. If they chose, they could even control the news that people read in the newspapers, hear on the radio and watch on the television. All in all it adds up to a situation that Maurice Mandale, chief economist at the Atlantic Provinces Economic Council, declares is "unique in the industrialized world. You are unlikely to find one family wielding this much power anywhere outside of the Third World."

Make no mistake: there is nothing malevolent about K.C. and his family, who have always thought of themselves as ordinary, Christian folk, doing their part just like everyone else to make New Brunswick a better place in which to live. That the Irvings, on balance, have been good for the province is undeniable; if they had never existed it is doubtful that another group of entrepreneurs would have emerged with the guts and drive to create jobs and enterprise in the barrens of New Brunswick.

All the same, K.C. and his offspring have never been totally benevolent rulers either. When it suits them, they use their corporate might to overwhelm competitors and stare down governments. Other times, their influence is more subtle; an example is the way their newspaper editors choose not to pry too deeply in Irving affairs, even though K.C. and his sons never set foot inside the newsrooms. No matter how they choose to exert their power, the goal is always the same: doing whatever needs to be done to ensure that their companies keep growing. And ultimately, this means that K.C. was forever destined to stand alone on the Bridge, aloof, almighty and as much feared as he is admired.

He had a simple vision, the Man on the Bridge: "You've got to keep going," he said once. "Expansion is the thing." Long ago, when his hair was dark and full and he had nothing but a small Ford dealership and the gas pumps that kept the cars chugging along the dirt roads of his Kent County birthplace, K.C. Irving decided that he would build his own business empire, and he would do it his way. Nothing would be allowed to stand in his path: not harsh landscapes, hostile governments or cutthroat business competitors.

It was a view rooted in the teachings of John Calvin and Adam Smith, his Scots ancestors, and forged by the unshackled capitalism of the early 20th century, a time when businessmen with drive and savvy were coming of age in Canada's embryonic economy. It was all very simple in those bygone days. Find a product or service that people want and will always need, sell it, deliver it and fix it when it busts. When an opportunity arises, seize it, even if it involves taking a risk. That, K.C. understood, was the only way to create wealth in this harsh, thinly populated province in a harsh, thinly populated country.

What K.C. wanted had nothing to do with wealth or power. What he wanted, whether he admitted it or not, was immortality — to live on, through his works, after he had died. That his deeds will outlive him is indisputable. In an era of paper entrepreneurs who are uninterested in projects that add to the nation's wealth, he remains the last great giant of Canadian business. To some, he embodies the triumph of entrepreneurial genius and pure will that has been a motif of North American life since the pioneer days. For as many others he is the archetypical ugly industrialist, destroying anything that stands in the way of his all-consuming passion and, when it no longer suits him, leaving the land that gave him his immense riches. But however he has been viewed — saviour or villain — he certainly has not left New Brunswick the way he found it. His empire, in the end, has become the lengthened shadow of the man, an institution that will long outlast him and perhaps even his sons and grandsons to follow.

What does the old man think as he stands on the Bridge and peers out, stern and unblinking, upon what he has built? Is he proud of what he has accomplished, or does he regret what he has done? Was it worth it — all the work, all the sacrifices, all the battles? Does he see opportunities missed? Or is he just weary of the whole thing? K.C., like his sons and now his grandchildren, has always felt that what he does with his life and his companies is nobody's business. And if, in his twilight, he is remembered as a metaphor for unchecked corporate power rather than as a flesh-and-blood man, a creator of jobs and a business genius, then he is content with the verdict. "I like to see wheels turn," he once said when asked what made him tick.[7] But introspection was never his strong suit. K.C. Irving, if the truth be known, was always too busy considering his next move on the chessboard of commerce to ponder airy questions about motivation. Looking back upon his life he would be no more capable of explaining why he did what he did than he would be able to say why he is six feet tall. That is just the way he was built; it is his nature. And to begin to understand how he came to be such a man you have to go to a place called Bouctouche, where it all began.

1

The Baron of Bouctouche

You gotta shuffle, cut, make a wish. That's it. Cut twice. Any wish you want, that's yer own business. Yer wish, you got it? . . . Okay. Now we're gonna see what life gave you 'n what it has in store fer you.
— *La Sagouine*, Antonine Maillet

"THERE IT IS," cries Laurie Boucher, steering his gas-guzzler through the modest village on the lonely curved New Brunswick bay. With a twist of his head, Boucher indicates a comfortable English-cottage-style home, half hidden among a grove of protective elms and set back from the main road. Its walls are made of white clapboard. Green shingles cover the slanted roof. A pair of white columns support the front portico. The interior is from another, grander time; a white classical mantelpiece tops the imposing living-room fireplace. Framed in heavily carved wood rich with gold leaf, a pair of large Victorian-era oil landscapes bracket the hearth. In the centre of the room sits an elegant French-Empire-style sofa, covered in silk fabric, adorned with woven laurel wreaths. Rich Oriental rugs cover the hardwood floors. When the thick drapes are pulled back, the home's broad front windows and three gables offer a spectacular view of Bouctouche Bay, which served as a safe harbour and refuge for the Acadians who first landed in the village in the late 18th century.

The main street that runs in front of the house is from a simpler era: a pair of restaurants, a couple of service stations, a drugstore, an auto-parts store, a hardware outlet and a barber shop where the local men — the professionals virtually indistinguishable from the farmers and fishermen — gather on Saturday mornings to trade small-town gossip and talk politics. White Victorian homes run out along the line of the bay. At the north end of town sits the cottage where the world-renowned novelist and playwright Antonine Maillet, creator of the Acadian washerwoman "La Sagouine," returns each summer to write in a white, lighthouse-inspired turret. "She has stayed in place," Maillet once wrote about her beloved birthplace, "balanced between two extremes: between a billionaire Irving and a Sagouine on her knees before her scrubbing pail; between the adventurers of the seas and the tillers of the earth; between the wealth of her traditions and her progressive ambitions; between her memory of the past and her dreams of the future."[1]

Each spring, K.C. Irving returns here. His comfortable antique-laden home sits on the very spot where his father, James Dergavel Irving, built his own stately residence more than a century ago. Though he left here for good in 1925, K.C.'s presence is still everywhere in the village: Kent Homes Ltd., his prefabricated-home manufacturing company, is Bouctouche's biggest employer. He holds title to the beautiful 12-kilometre beach formed by the Bouctouche Bar, a sand spit that pushes out into the Northumberland Strait. He donated the carillon that hangs in the steeple of the Saint John the Baptist parish church, the village's tallest building. His name even graces the main street that runs through the centre of town; the two squat white tanks on Irving Street bear the name of the oil company he started there.

"You'll meet him on the street," declares Boucher, a pleasant, open-faced native son who was mayor of Bouctouche throughout the 1970s and '80s. "He visits his old friends." But their numbers are dwindling. By 1990 the only ones still left to reminisce with K.C. about the old days were Clovis King, an Acadian fisherman who turned 104 that year, and Willie Bob Duplessis, who was born in 1898 and spent half a century piloting Irving tugboats along Bouctouche Bay. "Whenever he visits town he comes to see me," whispers Duplessis, who is all springs and sockets, has a face as brown and wrinkled as an apple doll and is fond of showing visitors pictures of himself with his famous former employer.

Bouctouche (population 2,500) is a French village, has been ever since a handful of Acadian families fleeing English persecution arrived in the 1760s.[2] Bearing names like LeBlanc, Bastarache, Babineau, Savoie, Allain, Jaillet and Collette, most of the present-day inhabitants are descended from the early pioneers. They speak a dialect of French that, because of Bouctouche's isolation, still closely resembles the classical language spoken in the old country. It is a rich heritage: Bouctouche gave Acadia its first members of the legislature, not to mention thriving regional theatre, singers, musicians, painters and writers, like Antonine Maillet, whose work is known throughout the French-speaking world.

Nowadays, even by New Brunswick standards scraping out a living can be tough here. Bouctouche has its share of professionals, civil servants and teachers. A few of the local businesses are prospering. The shiny rows of new cars and trucks in the parking lot of the local tavern each Saturday night attest to the numbers of local business deals that are carried out under the table and never appear on the tax rolls. Still, the village's heyday is long past. When the first settlers arrived there the Bouctouche River was busy with salmon, trout, bass and eel, the bay was full of oysters, clams and quahogs and the woods teeming with wild game. Today, the famous oyster beds have been depleted by over-harvesting. Long gone are the ships that used to stop in Bouctouche to load up with timber for shipwrights in Europe and New England. The mirrored $10-million plant that Mitel Corp. built in the early 1980s to make telephone switching gear sits empty on the outskirts of town, a monument to over-zealous sales forecasts. For now, the village is pinning its hopes on a "Sagouine theme park," created under the dubious assumption that it will pull in tourist dollars.

Increasingly, the village is becoming a bedroom community for commuters to higher-paying, steadier jobs in nearby Moncton, the booming centre of French-speaking New Brunswick. Most of the young have been lured away by better opportunities elsewhere. Many of those who stayed behind are happy if they can put in enough weeks in the local fish processing plants to qualify for unemployment insurance. For some, things are no better than a century ago, when the poorer Acadians in the area were left to scrape out a living working the bush camps in the winter or hibernating in grey, box-like cottages, waiting for spring to come, when they could dig clams for pennies a peck. Then, as now, the economy was largely controlled by a handful of industrious Scots merchants who began arriving in the Maritimes in the late 1700s after Wolfe vanquished Montcalm on the Plains of Abraham. Today only a few street names and some gravestones decaying in the small Presbyterian cemetery are left to commemorate those early Scots pioneers. Among them was a family named Irving.

When George Irving joined the stream of Scots into North America in 1822, he carried a name that family historians claim can be traced back to 300 A.D. and a single man named Nuath, who owned lands in the Annandale lowlands of Scotland.[3] The Irvings of Bouctouche were descended from a branch of the clan that received a charter in the country's Lower Annandale area in 1549. It is not known whether the family's New World success was prefigured by earlier accomplishments in Britain. But it is doubtful: why else would George Irving, born in Dumfries, Scotland, in 1771, immigrate with his wife, Jane, to Richibucto, New Brunswick, in 1822 if it wasn't to start life anew? From there, the couple travelled up the Richibucto River beyond Brown's Yard, which would become famous as a shipbuilding area, and on to Mill Branch, a district now known as Beersville. They were adaptable: in Beersville, they built a house and barn and cleared land for a farm on a 200-acre government grant. They were a prolific couple, who had six girls and four boys, including a son named Herbert. At the age of 18, Herbert Irving bought some land at Galloway, a settlement about halfway between Richibucto and Bouctouche. He married a woman named Catherine Dergavel and fathered two daughters and five sons. In the middle of the brood was James Dergavel Irving, who became known to his friends and later his business associates as J.D., to differentiate himself from the other Irvings in the area.

Slightly built and serious, J.D. blossomed into an unusually capable businessman, even next to the other Scots and Britons who already dominated the local economy. In 1881, at 21, he bought a small sawmill in Bouctouche. Before long he owned a farm on the outskirts of town, where he raised cattle and silver foxes and grew vegetables. Soon smoke billowed from the stack of the J.D. Irving sawmill, where 75 men toiled. Irving-owned tugboats hauled rafts of New Brunswick logs downriver to Bouctouche. When forestland was for sale he bought it. Eventually he built a grist mill that ground grain into flour and feed, and he added a sheep's-wool carding mill nearby. He built a warehouse on piles extending over the riverbank, where fishing boats would unload their lobster, oysters and smelt. Across from the family farm he opened a general store that sold tools, groceries, clothing and virtually everything else to the customers, who arrived by horse-drawn buggies in summer and sleighs in winter. "We didn' need the calendar of L'Aratouère to see Christmas comin'; we jus' had to watch 'em Arvin's windows," Antonine Maillet's famous scrubwoman reminisced.[4]

A century ago, Bouctouche was a thriving village surrounded by verdant forests, rich farmlands and productive waters and rivers. The port teemed with schooners carrying timber and pulpwood to Europe and the U.S. Before long, J.D. Irving's stranglehold over local commerce was as strong as the sway his more famous son would one day hold over an entire province. With his grave air and bushy, dark handlebar moustache, he seemed the very model of Scots sobriety. He had a long, straight nose, small button eyes and a chin split with a deep cleft. A cluster of thin, dark hair, parted precisely in the middle, topped his angular head. Irving owned the best home in town, a stately classic-revival-style residence with flat pilasters and a large centre gable with windowed balconies. When the automobile came to New Brunswick he drove one of the first, a Pierce-Arrow, along Bouctouche's muddy roads as the local children hooted and hollered. To house his beloved vehicle he converted the pigpen in his barn into a garage, which the gleaming Arrow shared nightly with the family's cows.

By all accounts he set a forthright example of Scots Presbyterianism. Along with his wife, Minnie Hutchinson Irving, he regularly attended the Presbyterian church that stood next door to their family farm and became known locally as the Irving church. It was said that he treated the lowest employee with polite formality. If he drank, it was always moderately. His only real vice, if one could call it that, was the cigars or pipe that he sometimes liked to puff after work was done, usually not until the sun set behind Bouctouche Bay. Business, it seemed, was his preoccupation. The day-to-day or-

dering of the lives of his offspring was left to his wife. Before her
early death, Minnie give J.D. a son, Herbert, and a daughter named
Jane. When he remarried, it was to Mary Elizabeth Gifford, a local
girl, also one generation out from Scotland. Together, James and
Mary Irving had two daughters, Marion and Lou Dorothy. They
also had a son, born on March 14, 1899, whom they christened Kenneth Colin.

Eighteen ninety-nine: it was the end of one age and the beginning
of another. The British Empire was on its last legs. Anarchism flour-
ished. Bismarck was dead, but the German arms build-up continued.
Henry Ford joined the new Detroit Automobile Co. as chief engineer.
The first moving pictures were getting ready to open in New York
City.

Canada was only 32 years old, and the Last Spike had been driven
into the Canadian Pacific Railway just 14 years before. In Ottawa,
Wilfrid Laurier was in power; the country was just beginning an
economic boom that would run until 1912. Prairie agriculture was
generating huge surpluses for export. Elsewhere, mineral strikes in
Ontario, British Columbia and the Klondike, the development of
hydroelectric power and the application of new techniques for making
pulp and paper meant, as historian Michael Bliss writes, "that the
rocks and rivers of the Precambrian Shield and the Rocky Mountains
became generators of wealth instead of barriers to farmers and
railway-builders."[5] The boom had even spread to the Atlantic provinces, the poor cousins of Confederation: in Nova Scotia, steel and
iron ingots were being forged in Pictou County, and Canada's largest
steel complex was being erected on Cape Breton Island. In Newfoundland, still half a century away from joining the fold, iron mines
promised industrialization. As for New Brunswick . . . well, it was
the one exception.

In the half-century after 1825, Saint John and a dozen other New
Brunswick towns built thousands of ships to sail the globe. By the
1850s and '60s, the shipbuilding and lumber industries were at their
zenith, and New Brunswick, particularly Saint John, was on the economic map of the world. It wasn't to last. By the mid-1870s iron
hulls and steam power were making square-rigged, wooden deep-

sea sailing ships obsolete. At the same time, markets for lumber products collapsed in the wake of a worldwide depression. New Brunswick was devastated. Shipyards, sawmills and factories closed one after another. Tens of thousands of New Brunswickers migrated west and into the United States.

Yet in Bouctouche in the early spring of 1899, things seemed to be pretty much as they had always been.[6] Visitors who came to town checked into the Victoria Hotel or the Seaside Hotel; both were known for their fine licensed dining rooms. Outside, horse-drawn buggies and sleighs trotted down the wide, tree-lined main street. There was still appalling poverty in the unpainted waterfront shacks. But most people made a good living from the woods and from the oysters that grew on the shallow bottom of Bouctouche Bay. The housewives who stepped along the wooden boardwalks passed fine old Victorian homes before reaching the roomy, wood-frame stores owned by merchants with names like LeBlanc, McLaughlin and, of course, Irving. They bought finely ornamented stoves from Patrick Leger's ironmonger's shop. They mailed their letters at Bernard Foley's Main Street store, which also doubled as the town post office. They bought their dairy products at the Michaud Cheese and Butter Factory. Religion ruled in Bouctouche: the French attended the Saint John the Baptist church, a gem of Gothic-revival architecture. The English, meanwhile, chose between the towering Methodist church and the tiny Anglican chapel, renowned for its early-English-Gothic style. Most, however, filed dutifully each Sunday into the Presbyterian church next door to the Irving farm, to hear dour sermons of predestination and industry.

Kenneth Irving's first recollections, fittingly enough, seem to have been about work and commerce. He was a sturdy, independent youngster, and years later he would brag that he opened his first bank account at the age of five. As early as he could remember he had a garden; his mother looked after it, but in his own mind it was his, and he peddled the produce daily, depositing the proceeds into his bank account. He knew exactly the price he could get for each item. In his 60s he could still remember his price list — cucumbers were two or three cents each, and a bundle of carrots went for four or five cents. He sold the lead that sealed up tea boxes to the local junk dealer for four cents a pound. He salvaged binder twine from the local threshers and sold it to the grist mill for eight cents a pound. "It made a lot of difference how it was cut," he once recalled. "It was worth twice as much when cut at the knot as it was if cut in the middle, for it was a nice clean cord then, 15 inches long and just the thing for tying up grain bags."[7]

In 1909, at ten, he secretly bought a used Model M Ford for $8. When his father found out that he owned a car, he ordered him to get rid of it. So he sold it to Jos LeBlanc of nearby Rexton for $11 — a 38-per-cent profit. "He wanted me to go lower, but I wouldn't drop my price," K.C. recollected.[8] While still in his teens he decided to begin raising ducks on the family farm. Before long he had built a 250-bird flock that threatened to overrun the Irving property. Soon the incessant quacking was too much for his father's nerves. So young Kenneth got an axe and invited some friends over, and together they beheaded, plucked and dressed the ducks for market and sold them for $150.[9]

The tenets of his parents' Presbyterian faith clearly coloured Kenneth Irving's business philosophy and his personal habits throughout his life. Presbyterianism descended from the teachings of Calvin, who said that the world of commerce wasn't necessarily alien to the life of the spirit, that capitalists didn't necessarily grow rich on the backs of their neighbours and that poverty wasn't necessarily a virtue. Calvinism didn't just tolerate the economic virtues, it recognized and applauded them. Hard work, prudence and thrift were the foundations of Presbyterianism. In that respect, young Ken was no different from many of the other early Scots settlers in Canada, who were lured abroad by the prospect of "getting on" and who treated money and the accumulation of it with stern respect. "Some have always wanted money for what it would buy," economist John Kenneth Galbraith wrote about his Scots ancestors. "Some have wanted it for the power it conferred. Some have sought it for the prestige it provided. The Scotch wanted it for its own sake."[10] Press baron Lord Beaverbrook, born Max Aitken, pridefully noted this characteristic in himself while growing up with his Scots father in a church manse in Newcastle, New Brunswick: "I measured myself against my contemporaries in the art of appraising values — chiefly of marbles, and in that judgement of character and opportunity that leads to a profitable 'swop'. I was a calculating youth: there was no doubt a certain measure of determination as I clinched the bargain, and my hand swept down to grab the prize. In that moment of the deal I was all Scot."[11]

Growing up in the Irving household in Bouctouche, young Kenneth learned the value of a dollar. Yet if the Kent County Scots were thrifty and acquisitive, they also had the familiar moral convictions of their predecessors. As an adult, Irving said that he grew up in a "moderately stern household."[12] Early on he promised his mother that he would stay away from liquor and avoid cigarettes. By all accounts he kept his vow. Each Sunday when his parents headed for church he was by their side. (A photograph still exists showing a 17-year-old Irving standing sulkily on the church stairs after a sermon by a visiting evangelist.) Young Kenneth was even forced to endure violin lessons in the family parlour.

As soon as he was old enough, he started working in the family store and lumber mill after school. Ken managed to complete grammar school and high school in Bouctouche. But he was no prodigy. He never acquired an interest in reading; throughout his life he often joked that he had "never read a book." At school he was known for being handy with his fists, so much so that he was once expelled for fighting and had to spend a year studying at Millerton, 60 miles from Bouctouche. More than schoolwork, he was interested in other questions — what made things happen, what made things tick. As a youngster he knew his way around a hammer and saw; he built ice boats and smelt shanties, and later other boats, which he sailed on the Bouctouche River. Fascinated with automobiles, he spent countless hours taking apart and reassembling the family car, until he was known as one of the best mechanics around.

When World War I interrupted the calm of life in Bouctouche, Irving was determined to join the army, even though he was still under age. His father wanted none of this: after Ken made several unsuccessful bids to enlist in Bouctouche, J.D. shipped him off to Dalhousie University in Halifax. There the determined teenager simply tried to sign up with one of the local Halifax regiments. Again his father intervened, and Irving found himself attending classes at Acadia University in Wolfville, Nova Scotia, as the first of a long string of family members to attend the beautiful Baptist university in the Annapolis Valley.

In 1918 he finally enlisted in the Royal Flying Corps and headed to Britain for pilot training. At Uxbridge he completed a bomb-sight and machine-gun course. Then he was transferred to Folkestone, where his Bouctouche cousin Leigh Stevenson began teaching him how to fly in a two-seater Camel training plane. Irving never completed his training. "We were on leave in London," he remembered at a reunion of World War I flyers held in 1984. "I was standing on the sidewalk, and I heard a terrific noise of people cheering. I called my chums out of the hotel, and we went up the street and heard the Lord Mayor of London announce the Armistice."[13]

So he returned to Bouctouche, safe and sound but with the restlessness that was the symptom of the ex-serviceman. Going back to university held no appeal. He worked in a local smelt fishery, then a sawmill, eventually moonlighting by selling Model T Fords for the local dealer. After a few months he grudgingly returned to the family store. But he had itchy feet: in the flying corps he had met people from faraway places — Australia, New Zealand and South Africa. He wanted to see the world.

Addie McNairn, who had also returned to Bouctouche after serving in the air force, felt the same way. In the summer of 1921 the pair packed up and headed west, ostensibly to work on the prairie grain harvest. Their real destination: Australia. "While we were waiting to find the right boat we stayed with a friend of my father's, Uncle Bob Brown," Irving said years later. "I never did find out for certain, but I have a feeling Uncle Bob might have gotten in touch with my father about this Australian thing because suddenly Addie — who was four or five years older than I was, and the unchallenged leader of the expedition — began putting it off and putting it off. After a while, it was November and Addie was still saying we'd get a better boat and a better fare if we waited just another few more days.

"And then one day he said: 'Well, here it is winter. Let's go logging in northern B.C. Then we can go to Australia in the spring.'"

"Addie," Irving said, "if I'm going logging I can go logging in New Brunswick," and he got on the next train and went home to Bouctouche.[14]

And back to the family store. One of his first jobs was collecting the store's delinquent accounts. Soon he was helping with the purchasing. But he had bigger plans than being a country merchant. Even then, he trusted his own vision and intuition. He was looking ahead. What he saw — wheezing and coughing its way down the muddy Bouctouche roads — was the automobile.

Automobiles had been slow to catch on in Canada. In 1901 most Canadians may have heard of the automobile but only one in a thousand had ever seen one. Only rich, prominent citizens like J.D. Irving could afford to own them. Motoring, many thought, was a fad that would quickly die out. All the same, ordinary Canadians gradually started to emulate the rich. In 1915 there were only 60,688 passenger cars and 533 trucks registered in Canada. By 1920 that number had climbed to 251,945 cars and 22,310 commercial vehicles. A decade later 1,061,500 automobiles and 161,562 buses, trucks and other commercial vehicles were registered to Canadian owners.[15]

In those days, most New Brunswick roads were little more than logging skidways; it wasn't until the 1940s that the roads around Bouctouche were open for the winter. The cars that moved along them weren't yet very comfortable or very fast, but they were a vast improvement on the horse and buggy. At the start of the 1920s New Brunswickers bumped along the roads in sedans, coaches and coupes built by Studebaker, Chrysler, Dodge and General Motors. For a time, they also rode in distinctively Canadian autos like the Gary-Dort, made in Chatham, Ontario, and "the Gentle Giant of Motion," manufactured by Brooks Steam Motors Ltd., of Stratford, Ontario. But mostly they drove Fords, built by Ford Motor Car Company of Canada in Windsor; half the cars on Canadian roads, in fact, were Fords. Selling Fords, it seemed, was where the money was.

At least that must have been how it looked to Kenneth Irving back in 1922 when he landed a job peddling Model Ts in Bouctouche for a dealer in nearby Richibucto named Arthur Myers. By all accounts, Irving was a superbly persuasive salesman. Before long,

Myers suggested that the relentless young man be given the agency to sell Model Ts in the southern half of Kent County. The Ford people readily agreed; in those days car companies were so desperate for agents that they leaped at any applicant. Most would-be agents had to invest capital for some kind of showroom and garage. Irving, however, had the advantage of being able to carry on his business from his father's premises. Besides, he wasn't worried. He was selling Fords, the most popular automobiles in North America.

So confident was he in the car's future that he decided to branch out into a whole new direction — the gasoline business. It made sense: the internal combustion engine had spawned a whole new service industry. Throughout the country, motorists were flocking to service stations, parts depots and body repair shops to keep their cars on the road. Irving asked Imperial Oil Co., then far and away the dominant company in the Maritime gasoline business, if he could be their Kent County sub-agent. They agreed.

Kenneth was already working hard, but he stepped up the pace another notch. Using a 350-gallon tank on the back of a truck, he serviced remote car owners. He even accepted horse-drawn buggies as trade-ins to sell more Model Ts so that he could peddle more Imperial Oil gasoline. Soon he had almost all of the gasoline and oil business in Kent County. Since he was selling both on commission, he was making big money by Bouctouche standards. It wasn't enough. The urge to expand was strong. But how? In what direction?

What happened next has passed into the realm of legend. The only living person who really knows what happened is Irving himself, and all he has ever said is that by the summer of 1924 his sudden success had started to rankle others. K.C.'s story, repeated in various versions, is that even though he was offering terms more lenient than those available directly from Imperial Oil, some of the merchants in the area thought they would be better off dealing one-on-one with the oil giant. Their concerns were understandable enough, since the younger Irving was using office and storage space on his father's premises; the local merchants, naturally, didn't like the idea of buying gasoline from a competitor. So, according to Irving, the merchants began to pressure the oil company. In a clumsy effort to maintain goodwill with their Kent County customers, Imperial suddenly revoked his agency.

Others remember the story a bit differently. Now in his 80s and living outside of Halifax, Wynton Shatford started as a sample-taker at Imperial's Dartmouth, Nova Scotia, refinery in 1925 and came to run Imperial's Maritime operations, which gave him a unique vantage from which to watch Irving grow. "The idea that we simply pulled his franchise is preposterous. He wasn't satisfied being a commission-driven sales agent restricted to a certain territory. He wanted to sell all through the countryside. We told him that if he was going to do that we would simply have to replace him. If we had wanted him out of business we wouldn't have lent him money in the form of redeemable debentures, which only had to be repaid when he was back on his feet."

Whatever the explanation, Irving's role as an Imperial agent was over; from now on he was a competitor. What's more, Imperial planned to install a new 10,000-gallon gasoline storage tank in Bouctouche to supply customers directly. K.C. had just $2,000 of capital and 30 days' credit, so he had to move quickly. [16] He ordered a railway tank car full of gasoline from Charles Noble & Co. in Tulsa, Oklahoma; he bought a rickety storage tank from a railway and raised it on concrete abutments on the outskirts of Bouctouche.

The locals told him he would be skinned alive; bucking a company with the size and clout of Imperial just because your pride is hurt was viewed as folly. Even so, his father agreed to back him. So did Tom Nowlan, a long-time family friend, who lived in one of the biggest houses in the parish. Nowlan was many things, including a rum-runner whose buccaneering exploits had made him something of a local folk hero. [17] Still, he had nothing against legitimate enterprise. He and J.D. Irving agreed to plunge $100,000 into the younger Irving's fledgling oil business — a huge amount in the mid-1920s. Later on, J.D. bought Nowlan out. But the initial loan was invaluable; in April 1924, when Kenneth was just 25, he opened the first Irving service station and garage across the street from the family general store. The K.C. Irving Oil and Gas Company was open for business.

You can almost see him there, skinny as a rake, his thin lips stretched into a broad smile, his dark hair already beginning to recede, standing proudly between the two gasoline pumps in front of the tiny operation. "It was a beautiful thing to behold, that garage," Irving said fondly years later. Perhaps he had a point. His first one was a single-storey affair with large windows that opened into a small office and repair bay. In the centre, a twin-columned canopy, decorated with a big Ford eagle insignia promising "Safety and Service," extended out towards the road. Beneath the canopy stood a series of glass-topped gas pumps. He sold Primrose gasoline — a name taken from a high-quality flour ground at the J.D. Irving grist mill — and Velco motor oil ("More Miles, More Power"). At night, as many as two dozen townsmen gathered in front of the station to talk and kibitz. When he had time, he enjoyed trading gossip with the locals. Willie Duplessis remembers watching a local drunk taunt the budding businessman one night. "I told him by God he shouldn't have to take that," Duplessis recalls. "But he just laughed and said, 'If I give some back there's no way I'll be able to sell him a car.'"

He was all business. By using railcars to bring his gasoline in from Oklahoma he had a built-in cost advantage over other dealers, who transported their product by tank truck. The Bouctouche station was busy. In the beginning, he did it all: pumping gasoline out front, doing the repairs in the small garage, then dashing into the showroom to flog Model Ts. He was always delighted to see a customer; if the station was closed, they merely had to blow their horns under his bedroom window and he would be down to serve them.

Even his hard-driving father thought he was overdoing it. "Don't you think Ken is tackling too much?" he asked Tom Nowlan. "Leave him alone," Nowlan replied. "Let Ken go."[18]

In the mid-1920s there was only one place to head for an ambitious young man dying to escape the narrow borders of Bouctouche.

2

A Visionary Gleam

*Outsiders . . . said nice things about the friendli-
ness of the people and how handsome the houses
were inside despite the grimy exteriors. The houses
were grimy because the air was grimy, and the
houses were painted only when they had to be to
keep out the rot. They were painted two shades,
green and brown — it didn't matter which, because when the grime got to them they looked
pretty much alike. Some said the place was pictur-
esque, or Dickensian, but nobody said it was
pretty.*
— Journalist Charles Lynch, describing Saint
John in the interwar years.

WHEN KENNETH Irving arrived in Saint John in the fall of 1925,
he squinted into the thick mist that, for as long as anyone could
remember, had covered the city for more than a hundred days each
year. The fog floated past wooden schooners loaded with bootleg
rum and encircled the brick foundries, warehouses and office buildings that lined the silent waterfront. It climbed craggy hills and slant-
ing streets. It swirled around brick row-houses owned by wealthy
Loyalist merchants. It clung to the wooden tenements that sheltered
the city's poor.

The fog has always been there.[1] Even, no doubt, in the spring
of 1604, when a small ship glided into the estuary of the great river
that begins 450 miles away, in what is now Maine, and breaks through
to the Atlantic in roaring rapids that tumble from a narrow limestone
gorge 100 feet above. There each day, at what would become known

as the Reversing Falls, the white water from Maine does daily combat with the Bay of Fundy, seeming to retreat when the tide comes in and then reversing itself when the ocean waters fall back again. The ship carried a French explorer and geographer named Samuel de Champlain. Beside him on deck was Pierre Du Gua, Sieur de Monts, a Huguenot whom King Henry IV of France had commissioned to "represent our person in the countries, territories and confines of La Cadie" — a region so vast that today it would include the Maritimes, most of Quebec and more than half of New England. They arrived on June 24, the day of the feast of Saint John the Baptist, so they called the river the Saint John.

The fur trade brought the early European settlers to Acadia. The key to controlling the lucrative new business was the Saint John River, by which the Maliseet and Micmac Indians moved their valuable beaver pelts from the inland forests to the white man's trading posts. In 1631, Charles de La Tour, the self-proclaimed governor of Acadia, began building a fort at the mouth of the river in recognition of the rich harvest. The outbreak of the Revolutionary War thrust the tiny settlement into the midst of the struggle between the American patriots and the British Crown. In 1778, fearful of further attacks, the British began erecting a fortress atop the knoll of ancient limestone at the head of the harbour and brought a boatload of troops from Britain to reinforce it. Five years later, 20 small craft creaking under the weight of 3,000 men, women and children from New England still loyal to the British Crown sailed into the river's mouth. On May 18, 1785, Saint John was incorporated as Canada's first city.

From the start it was a rough-and-tumble place, which once boasted 200 taverns and beer halls and was built for merchants and shipping moguls, soldiers and profiteers. And from the start, its fortunes rolled and bucked with the vagaries of foreign trade and commerce. European warfare and Britain's industrial revolution energized the Saint John economy as the 19th century dawned. By the 1830s thousands of barques and barquentines, schooners and brigantines were being crafted in local shipyards. The market for ships was wildly cyclical. But by the 1870s, an average of two ships a week rolled off Saint John slips. By then only three other ports in the world boasted more wooden ships under registration than Saint John. Not surprisingly, the city had the highest per-capita income anywhere in Canada. "Whatever Saint John is," commented a city newspaper in the mid-1800s, "it must be admitted that shipbuilding and the timber trade have done it." It was the Golden Age — or at least what would have to pass for one in the tough, grimy port where streets were still unpaved and the shiploads of Irish who arrived in the first few decades of the 19th century still huddled in grim, spirit-breaking poverty.

Then, as quickly as this strange brand of prosperity came, it departed. A worldwide depression crippled lumber exports and sharply curtailed trade. On June 20, 1877 — with the temperature hovering between 75 and 80 degrees Fahrenheit — a spark from a lumberyard landed in a hay bale. Gale-force winds fanned the flames. Nine hours later the fire had burned down to the harbour, leaving behind a gutted business section and 13,000 homeless people. Tragically, the flame that had illuminated Saint John's Golden Age had burned out. The long, cold winter began.

World War I brought prosperity back to Saint John for a while. The huge demand for New Brunswick lumber, pulp, textiles and armaments increased provincial manufacturing by 300 per cent from 1914 through 1919, all of it funnelled through Saint John. City shipbuilders picked up long-unused tools to build wooden steamers for the Allied war effort. In 1923 the Saint John drydock, the biggest in the British Empire, opened as the *Saint John Globe* newspaper boldly predicted: "A great future awaits Saint John as a national port and general distributing point for world commerce if the people of the city will only press for it unitedly, determinedly, enthusiastically."[2]

But by the mid-1920s Saint John's future looked anything but great; the munitions factories and shipyards had closed just as the war veterans filed home in search of jobs. The city's machine shops and foundries sat silent. The port was losing business to Toronto and Montreal. When North America plunged into a new recession,

more companies closed down in Saint John and the soup lines lengthened. Canadians everywhere were abandoning the rural areas for cities, but no one was heading for Saint John; its people were leaving
to search for work elsewhere.

Yet even then there was a stubborn hopefulness among those living
there. Journalist Charles Lynch wrote that they "insisted there was
beauty amid the smells and beneath the century of soot."[3] For a
businessman with an eye on advancement there were certainly opportunities. Some established firms were doing well: companies like
Crosby Molasses Co., wholesaler Willett Foods Ltd., Oland's Red
Ball Brewery and T.S. Simms & Co., which made paintbrushes. A
few enterprising outfits, such as Eastern Bakeries, even dared to open
their doors for the first time during those harsh days. A genuine
tycoon flourished, Howard Robinson, who controlled the telephone
and power companies and newspapers and lived in a big, white, pil-
lared home on the city's Mount Pleasant — the house that K.C.
would one day own, symbolizing his influence over Saint John
commerce.

The world was changing, Saint John was changing. Where there
is change, there is always opportunity. By the 1920s the city was
electrically lit and electrically powered. Banks, department stores and
mail-order houses had established branches in the city. Meanwhile,
more and more automobiles clattered through the city streets. The
first car in Saint John, in 1901, had been a steam-run model that
caused quite a sensation. "Consternation and incredulity were
aroused," reported the *Saint John Telegraph-Journal*. "When the car
was being driven through the streets, people got as far away as possible from the noisily snorting monster, which could be heard almost
a mile away. It caused horses and cattle to stampede and even struck
terror into the hearts of some of the citizens."[4]

Still, Saint Johners got used to it. By 1925 the city, like the rest
of Canada, was enjoying its first round of explosive automobile
growth. Cars were now an accepted sight on Canadian streets. Doctors used them, so did clergymen. Businessmen drove to work. Others
used the car to take the family on Sunday outings. General Motors
of Canada Ltd. exhorted people to "Support the Industry That Sup-

ports Canada." The editorialists at the *Saint John Telegraph-Journal* railed against "the daredevil driving of clattering delivery trucks by youths with lopsided caps" and drivers who "roll up behind a pedestrian without blowing the horn to enjoy the spectacle of a sudden jump."[5]

It was, all things considered, a great time to be in the auto business. K.C. Irving understood the possibilities. In the summer of 1925, M.F. Smith, Ford's regional manager, came to Bouctouche with bad news: he was closing the territory and terminating Irving's right to sell Ford cars in Westmoreland County, where he was making most of his sales. Once again, Irving maintained, he was the target of unscrupulous competitors: the Moncton Ford dealer, who had watched his sales fall off dramatically since Irving had set up shop, was complaining. Much as he protested, Irving's territory was going to be restricted to the southern half of Kent County. But when Smith returned to Bouctouche the following week, he had a compromise: was Irving interested in the Ford franchise in Saint John, one of the best and largest in the Maritimes?

In September 1925, K.C. arrived in Saint John to take over the Ford dealership at 300 Union St., formerly owned and run by a local businessman named Royden Foley. The building itself was nondescript, with a pair of gas pumps out front that had been erected by Imperial Motor Co., the Chevrolet dealership that had occupied the premises before Foley. On October 14, 1925, a full-page advertisement appeared in the *Saint John Telegraph-Journal* introducing Saint John's newest firm: Kenneth C. Irving Ford Dealer. Peering out from the grainy photo was dark-haired, jug-eared E.S. Cottingham, the sales manager, and C.T. Stanwood, the husky service superintendent manager. Between them Kenneth Irving smiled an almost imperceptible smile, looking serious and businesslike beyond his 26 years.

The local business establishment was not exactly bowled over by the young newcomer.[6] A month after arriving he went to one of the local banks to establish a line of credit for the coming year. The bank agreed, just as long as he could produce a letter from his father, stating that he would guarantee his son's debts. By then K.C. had been in business, one way or another, for five years. He had always paid his debts and was more than a little perturbed that the bank still felt they needed J.D.'s pledge of security. So a few weeks later he was happily surprised to see A.J. MacQuarrie, the manager of a local branch of the Bank of Nova Scotia, striding across the showroom floor with hand outstretched as he asked the young man, in wounded tones, "How could you do it, Kenneth?" MacQuarrie went on to say that he had been his father's friend, his friend and a family friend for years. Why, he had even visited the family home in Bouctouche, where he had gone fishing with J.D. Irving. "How could you do it," he demanded. "How could you come to Saint John and not do business with me." Irving, naturally, was overjoyed to find a friendly banker who actually wanted him as a customer. He apologized for his oversight and said that he was prepared to give the bank his business, provided MacQuarrie was prepared to arrange a certain line of credit. "I'll call you in the morning," said the banker.

In fact, he called back within the hour and said Irving had an appointment the next morning with the redoubtable Horace Enman, regional supervisor of the Bank of Nova Scotia, and a man who had more authority from Toronto head office than virtually any other banker living in the Maritimes. "[Enman] had a terrific ability to size up people," Arthur Crockett, a top Bank of Nova Scotia executive, once recalled. "He was all over the Maritimes. . . . His photograph was prominent in the offices of dozens of Maritimes businessmen."[7] The next morning, after spending a few hours in Enman's office, Irving came to the point: "Mr. Enman, we came here for a purpose, and I am wondering if you have come to any decision." Enman jumped up from behind his desk, a smile spreading across his face as he looked towards MacQuarrie, and said, "Didn't he tell you? Why, of course, you have the line of credit."

K.C. was quick to grasp a central fact about the automobile age: the big money wasn't to be made in selling cars, it was in making them run. Repair garages began popping up in the big eastern cities just after the turn of the century. But it was years before they appeared elsewhere. Even then, it was hard for a car owner to have repairs made: mechanics often had to cross several counties using train, horse and buggy to reach their destination. Fuelling up in the early days wasn't easy either. A few very wealthy automobile owners installed their own underground gasoline tanks. Most pioneer motorists had to drive to the nearest large hardware or grocery store, where gasoline was kept in a large metal barrel with a spigot. The proprietor would draw a bucket, lug it to the curb and pour it into the car through a large, chamois-covered funnel.

By the mid-1920s, full-fledged service stations were sprouting up throughout Canada. They had evolved into works of art, boasting all kinds of architectural styles and finishes in stone, stucco and brick. Usually a canopy jutted out from the station to cover the pump area. Out back was a spidery wooden ramp that the motorist drove up to enable the car to be greased. Increasingly, the emphasis was on cleanliness and service; by the 1920s the up-to-date attendant would check your tires, oil and radiator and clean your windshield in addition to pumping gasoline and selling oil. Often dressed in a natty uniform with breeches, leather boots and matching shirt, tie and cap, he dispensed gas from a towering pump topped by a graduated glass tank that showed how much you bought and how clean it was. Oil, originally sold by the jugful from barrels, now came in tall, thin bottles kept in a special stand by the gas pumps and refilled from a bulk tank inside the station.

Competition was hot in the gasoline business. By the late 1920s, price cutting and give-aways were common. The lower wholesale prices in the U.S. allowed independent Canadian operators to profitably import product at bargain prices. Even barter deals were not ruled out, including one transaction that involved the exchange of Romanian gasoline for prairie wheat. Gasoline was sold in the Maritimes as it was in the rest of Canada: the major oil companies owned their own service stations, which distributed only their in-house products. There were also countless independent dealers, garages and other outlets willing to handle the goods of any supplier who would install free pumps and tanks. Since most independent garages had more than one set of pumps and handled several different types of products, no oil company could be confident that the dealer was making any effort to push its brand over the others. Loyalty came cheaply; it didn't take much in the way of a concession to divert a dealer from one distributor to another.

Even so, mighty Imperial Oil, owned by American Oil giant Standard Oil of New Jersey, dominated the service station business in the Maritimes just as it controlled the industry in the rest of the country. Its main competitors were mid-sized Canadian-run independent companies, like Canadian Oil Companies Ltd. and McColl-Frontenac, and a few small independents who depended on low overhead to stay in business. It was tough going for the little guys; eventually most of them failed, done in by lack of capital and problems of transportation and distribution.

K.C. Irving had his own ideas on how to stay competitive. By 1927, he had Ford dealerships and service stations in four New Brunswick towns. Now, with the Bank of Nova Scotia's backing, he was ready to begin a full-scale assault on Saint John, the province's largest city. In October he appeared before Saint John Common Council to apply for permission to erect three 500-gallon gasoline pumps at a new site on Saint John's Rothesay Avenue. Months later he bought a station with a single crank-operated curbside pump from K.B. Reed, a gravel-voiced Irishman who became one of his chief lieutenants. The following year, he opened a station at the corner of Main and Portland Streets in partnership with Charles Gorman, the recently retired world speed-skating champion.

In February 1929 he incorporated Irving Oil Company, Limited, as the successor to K.C. Irving Oil and Gas. Soon afterwards, he approached the Putnam brothers, who owned a station in the city centre. "All it had was an office, a pair of pumps and a rack for the cars to drive up on. But once Mr. Irving bought it he began to modernize," recalls Ray Tanton, whom Irving hired to run the station.

Tanton, 88 and living quietly in a small house outside Saint John in 1990, remembers how his immaculately dressed boss would drive his gleaming new car into the station and greet him with a friendly "How's business, Tanton?" Irving was a hands-on owner: when there was a line-up at the pumps he didn't hesitate to doff his suit coat and start pumping gasoline in vest and shirtsleeves. Tanton also recalls how Irving seemed to know more about cars and auto parts than the boys working in the garage. No detail escaped him. "Once he was at the station and noticed a mess in the garage. He walked out front and said to me: 'Tanton, you and your boys spend so much time here that you might not notice this. But our customers do.'"

Irving operated differently than the big service station chains. From the beginning, it seems, his goal was to build a network of identical Irving Oil stations criss-crossing the Maritimes. Unlike the big operators, he usually liked to own the stations himself, installing managers to run them. He was a demanding employer, expecting his people to work as he did — six, even seven days a week. He paid comparatively well: Ray Tanton was making just $9 a week at Imperial Oil when Irving offered him $12 to run the Peel Street station. A year later Tanton's weekly paycheque soared to $25. "You don't need to have brains to succeed in this business," K.C. told Tanton early on. "You just have to have ideas and to hire the right people."

In truth, location is the key to succeeding in the service station business. The race has always been to find the best corner or intersection or the stretch of highway with the heaviest traffic. When he found an alluring location, K.C. went out and got it, even if someone had already beat him to the site. He worked quickly, recalls Imperial's Wynton Shatford: "He would ask how much the owner wanted. If Irving liked the price he would say yes — just like that. He never had to call head office. He *was* head office."

He could be extremely persuasive. Russell Fraser, whose family operated a service station on Halifax's Granville Street, was selling several varieties of gasoline when Irving — making one of his first moves outside New Brunswick — asked him to put in another pump to sell his brand in 1928. "I had just finished paying for the installation of the other pumps and told him I didn't have any more money to play around with. He told me he would help, and he really meant it, for he was soon back in overalls, ready to go to work. With a pipefitter to help him, Irving made the installation himself right under the floor of the building."[8]

He seemed to be everywhere, know everything. Johnny Wade, now retired and living in Halifax, owned a cab company with his brother in the early 1930s. One day Irving and K.B. Reed arrived at his

Halifax office. The Wades' 12-cab fleet used about 20,000 gallons
of gas a year and they had decided it would be cheaper to simply
run their own service station rather than pay someone else to fill
up. Wade was about to link up with Imperial Oil when Irving and
Reed got wind of his plans and offered him a better deal.

He was aggressive, no doubt about it. Irving rarely overpaid for
a location. If the owner didn't want to sell for his price, he would
threaten to put up a big station right across the street. Those who
thought he was bluffing learned otherwise. "When he wanted something he got it," recalls Wynton Shatford, "and he didn't care if
there was already lots of competition on a particular location."

It seemed risky. But it worked. In the fourteen-month period ending
January 31, 1930, Irving Oil made $137,576.68. In fact, K.C. had
never had an unprofitable year since entering the service station business four years before. He was already dabbling with the principle
of making yourself your own best customer, by starting a construction
company to build Irving service stations. By then the big red-white-
and-blue Irving diamond — that echoed the trademark of Imperial
Oil, which had snubbed him only six years before — adorned filling
stations in more than 20 cities and towns in New Brunswick and
Nova Scotia. His better-known products, Primrose and Hico gas-
olines and Velco and Ioka lubricating oil, were sold by nearly 700
retail distributors throughout the Maritimes.[9]

He was a growing concern, in more ways than one. K.C. had a
family now. The running of the home was left to his wife, a charming,
devoutly religious woman who also came from Scots Presbyterian
stock. K.C. met Harriet MacNairn when she worked at the Irving
family store in Bouctouche, 12 miles from her birthplace, a tiny village called Galloway. Like her husband, she was down-to-earth and
unpretentious. Together they produced a succession of sons, James
(later called J.K.), Arthur and John (Jack). Before becoming a family
man, K.C. had bunked down each night in a tiny room above one
of his service stations. Now, when he wasn't working, he returned
to his young family and his new home.

But most of the time he *was* working, hatching schemes for opening
new stations and winning market share. His desire for growth was

fed by his early successes. When the local banks became reluctant to provide more capital for expansion, he turned to the stock markets. Eastern Securities Ltd. was a small Saint John brokerage house that did a thriving little business raising capital for Maritime firms. With Eastern acting as underwriter, the newly formed Irving Oil Company, Limited, raised $375,000 in the spring of 1929 by floating an issue of preferred and common shares. "The financing now underway is expected to place the new company in a position to materially increase its storage facilities allowing them to take advantage of the lower prices which will flow from volume buying," declared the Irving prospectus. A year later he issued more preferred shares, raising another $125,000 "for the expansion of the business and to provide additional working capital to efficiently take advantage of the increasing demand for the company's products."[10]

Going public helped Irving forge a valuable business alliance. Cagey, Ottawa-born Frank Brennan was one of Eastern Securities' top brokers. "He was a lot like Irving — a gentleman, with a lot of moxie, who could be very persuasive," recalls Ronald Machum, still a working stockbroker, who was starting out in the investment business in Saint John in the early 1930s. K.C. lured Brennan away from Eastern Securities to form their own stockbrokerage outfit, Irving, Brennan and Co. Ltd. Even after Irving pulled out of the partnership Brennan remained a close ally, raising the money for a number of Irving ventures in later years.

All the same, after that first stock issue K.C. always stayed away from the equity markets whenever he needed money. Even then, control was everything to him; he plainly had mixed emotions about issuing shares and giving someone else influence over his companies. "When you go public, you have certain rules you have to go by," he once told a reporter for the *New York Times*. "Those may not make it the most convenient way of accomplishing what you set out to do. You can take a calculated risk if you only have to account to yourself."[11] Indeed, not long after the Irving common shares were issued, Brennan and his associates were scouring the countryside swapping non-voting Irving Oil preferred shares — which did not give shareholders the right to vote on matters affecting the company — for common shares. Eventually K.C. held all of the Irving common shares, although to this day it is rumoured that a few shares, now worth untold value, gather dust in Maritime strongboxes. From then on, whenever Irving had to look outside the banking community for cash he issued bonds, debentures or some other debt instrument that did nothing to diminish his control.

That first stock issue did serve its purpose. By 1930 Irving was busy erecting an 800-foot wharf along with gasoline and oil tanks at Bedford Basin near Halifax. Back in Saint John the papers were brimming with his latest plans: building three steel gasoline storage tanks, with a total capacity of 2 million gallons, on a tract of re-claimed water and mud-flats. Downtown, his men were renovating the Golden Ball Building (named after the distinctive yellow orb that dangled in front), a beige brick five-storey building originally erected in the early 1800s to hold a theatre and a tavern. Eventually it became the nerve centre of his entire business empire.

K.C. was sinking his roots deep into New Brunswick soil. In that respect he was breaking a long regional tradition. For generations ambitious men from New Brunswick and the other Maritime prov-inces had concluded that the streets paved with gold were found else-where. The list of New Brunswickers who made their mark far from home includes the names of some of the best-known politicians and businessmen ever to stride across Canada. Men like Richard Bedford Bennett, the plump Chatham-born corporate lawyer who swept into the prime minister's office in 1927. Like Andrew Bonar Law, who grew up in a church manse four or five miles above the Richibucto River before heading for London and No. 10 Downing Street. Like Louis B. Mayer, who spent a boyhood in Saint John before moving on to Hollywood, where he became the most powerful figure in the American film business. Or Maxwell Aitken, later Lord Beaverbrook, who grew up in a Presbyterian church manse in Newcastle, made millions in the merger game in Montreal and then took his knack for high finance to London. Or James Dunn, a Bathurst carpenter's son who was already in London using his boundless energy, superb connections and ruthless deal-making skills to manoeuvre his way into the centre of the international financial world when Aitken arrived.

In Irving, New Brunswick at last had an entrepreneur who was different. "Remember," Beaverbrook once told a friend, "Jimmy Dunn and I, we made our fortunes in Britain. But Kenneth stayed right here. That is truly amazing." When anyone asked why he never left Saint John, Irving would simply shrug and reply, "Saint John is my home." In truth, he had no taste for life on the bigger stage. Irving realized that there were opportunities in the small New Brunswick pond that just weren't available elsewhere. The globe-trotting escapades of Mayer, Beaverbrook, Dunn and the rest of the expatriates fascinated and titillated the world. But the Maritimes, in Irving's view, was wide open for a man with enough nerve and talent to make things happen. And if, as the 1930s dawned, he was just a small-time businessman trying to get going in tough, shabby Saint John . . . well, that seemed to suit him just fine.

3

Darkness and Daylight

Know that I am Napoleon, the great,
the magnificent tiger.
Observe how an emperor
takes possession of the ground
on which he stands, imposes his own order
on the space around him.

— *A Tiger in the Dublin Zoo*, Alden Nowlan

NINETEEN thirty-three was the blackest year of the Great Depression. As it drew to a close, K.C. Irving sat behind an oak desk in a wedge-shaped office building on the Saint John waterfront, thinking his own deep thoughts. It was a pivotal time in his life: on June 6 his father, then 73, had died. J.D. Irving's death must have been hard for his 34-year-old son. The father could not hide his disappointment eight years earlier when K.C. abandoned the Bouctouche family business for the wider horizons of Saint John. The years that followed were tough ones for the ailing father, who was forced to cut back massively on lumber production at his mill because of failing health.[1] Almost half a century later K.C. recalled that his father "knew what it was all about. He knew what hard work was . . . and how much a man would do. He knew how to fix a piece of machinery. And if he didn't know how he would learn very quickly. . . . I suppose I am a bit like him in many respects. . . . I always liked machinery and that sort of thing. I like to see wheels turn."[2]

Any grieving was done in private, far from prying eyes. In truth, there was little time for tears. K.C. had to figure out how to keep J.D. Irving Ltd., the company his father had spent a lifetime building, in business. When J.D. died, the company owned a sawmill, the family store in Bouctouche and 7,000 acres of Kent County woodlands. In his will he left his wife, Mary, 184 of 394 shares in J.D. Irving Ltd., as well as $25,000 in cash, his Bouctouche home and other woodlands. His daughters, Lou Dorothy and Marion, got 55 J.D. Irving shares apiece. Herbert, J.D.'s son by his first marriage, got 50 shares. So did K.C.[3]

But the responsibility for saving the sagging lumber company fell squarely on the younger son's shoulders. The challenge was considerable: by the early 1930s, competition for markets was fierce worldwide, and lumber prices had slumped so low that producers were forced to sell at a loss — if they sold at all; lumber production in New Brunswick had dropped sharply. Even Fraser Companies, Price Brothers and the other giants who had carved up New Brunswick's forests found the going tough. As for the small independent operators who tried to survive by operating tiny lumber mills throughout the province, many just closed up.

By 1933, J.D. Irving Ltd. seemed about to join them. When K.C. took over, the mill was turning out about 2 million feet of long lumber a year. "It was a small company — not big enough to be unwieldy," K.C. recalled, "just big enough to show me how the lumber business operated — to get my foot in the door."[4] As introductions go it was a rough one. He criss-crossed the country looking for buyers and searching for ways to market his lumber profitably. Nothing worked. Yet, unlike most other New Brunswick lumbermen, K.C. refused to sell at a loss. He held his lumber harvest for another year, then another and another after that. From 1933 to 1939 his company cut timber every year but sold only three of its harvests. In Irving's view he had no choice: if he sold at a loss, the company simply would not be in business by the time the Depression had run its course. So he waited.

The pressure must have been immense. One day during this period, Horace Enman, the man who bankrolled Irving's early ventures, called K.C.'s outstanding loans, said to be approaching $2 million.[5] In the depths of the Depression that was an almost unimaginable amount of money. But K.C. managed to come up with the funds. Where he got the money remains a mystery, but he was still in business. So was his father's lumber company. Ignoring the miserable economic conditions, K.C. bulled ahead. He cut what there was to cut, bought land, sold some and traded for other acreage. It was risky business. At least his mother, brother and sisters thought so; they wanted out. K.C. accommodated them, paying cash for all the J.D. Irving shares owned by the other family members. His way, he felt, was the only option for keeping his father's company afloat. Now, with the rest of the family out of the way, K.C. was free to make his own decisions.

He injected cash from the oil company into the limping concern and continued to pick up timberland in preparation for the turnabout. Finally, in 1939, there was hope; lumber prices started to move upwards. Six years of hanging on had paid off, and not just in long-anticipated profits. The move into lumber marked a new phase in K.C.'s business life. For the first time he was exploring outside the familiar activities of selling, fuelling and repairing automobiles. Instead of being frightened by the unfamiliar terrain, Irving was simply exhilarated. "The trouble with many businessmen is that when they have made some progress they sit back and take a rest," he once said. "We can't progress while standing still."[6] In the grim 1930s, New Brunswick was a buyer's market for a businessman with the cash and ambition to grab the opportunities.

In fact, across Canada, a new group of energetic young businessmen were coming to the forefront. For them, the Depression provided opportunities rather than obstacles. Many of Canada's largest fortunes would be amassed during these bleak days by larger-than-life buccaneers, like Edward Plunkett Taylor, then taking the first steps towards creating Argus Corp., which would come to embody the strengths and failings of Canadian capitalism. Or Garfield Weston, who had just inherited his father's Toronto bakery and biscuit plant and had raised $2 million from U.S. stock market speculators to begin a buying spree in Britain. Or smiling Roy Thomson, who was then hustling radio broadcasting licences in Northern Ontario and was on the verge of buying his first newspaper.

Even in the perpetually depressed Maritimes, where business drowned with cruel regularity throughout the decade, a new breed of entrepreneur was emerging. Former butcher boy Frank Sobey was one of them. By 1990 the Sobey empire, based in Stellarton, on Nova Scotia's northwest coast, would be worth $1.5 billion, and the family name would be stamped on supermarkets and movie theatres, drugstores and bowling alleys, hotels and insurance companies. But at the end of the Depression, Frank Sobey was still trying to add more stores to his father's tiny retail grocery store chain and to make a go of it in the fiercely competitive Maritime grocery business. Meanwhile, in Nova Scotia's verdant Annapolis Valley, industrialist and financier Roy Jodrey had plunged back into the stock markets after going bankrupt during the 1929 crash. By the time he died in 1973, the stingy, eccentric gambler had made countless millions growing apples, manufacturing pulp and paper and spinning brilliant financial deals and astute stock market investments.

Across the Bay of Fundy from Jodrey's Annapolis Valley empire, K.C. Irving was also turning adversity into advantage. The Depression had played havoc with the automobile business throughout North America. Sales collapsed and manufacturers suffered through a decade of severe excess capacity. But the cars on the road were still being driven, longer than ever, in fact. These jalopies had an enormous appetite for gas, parts and repair services. Smaller, undercapitalized service station chains were going broke left and right, but the big Irving diamond just kept popping up on more and more stations. By the end of 1934 he owned 30 service stations outright, had storage capacity for 5 million gallons of gasoline and sold his products through 3,000 retail outlets. For the year, Irving Oil had revenues of $570,410 and a profit of $174,538.[7] Its sales gains were largely at the expense of Imperial Oil, which, ironically, was finding that Irving gasoline, kerosene and fuel oils were taking a bigger and bigger share of capacity at the company's Dartmouth refinery.

He forged on. At one point, dissatisfied with the railway freight rates being charged by the Canadian National Railway, K.C. bought a tanker ship and sent it up the Saint John River to fill his Fredericton tanks. The CNR ordered him to stop. "If you persist," the railway's Maritime manager told him, "we will revise our freight rates so that you will be undercut by your competitors everywhere."[8] That was a mistake; K.C. never reacted well to threats. His response was to buy more tankers and to haul as much of his oil as possible by river and road. His relationship with the CNR, for all intents and purposes, was over. Soon Irving Oil bulk storage stations were springing up at strategic points around the Maritimes.

The railroad had learned what countless others would soon know: Irving could not be intimidated. Anyone who took him on quickly realized that he never, ever gave up. The move into the bus business was a case in point. The continent-wide slump in car sales during the mid-1930s was accompanied by a boom in bus use. In those days it was a free-for-all on the New Brunswick roads. By 1934, 60 buses were licensed to operate in the province and many more were running without licences. Since the industry was virtually unregulated, any enterprising garage owner with a sympathetic banker could buy a bus and start his own line. Trouble was that many of these newcomers knew little about running a business the size and scope of a bus line. By 1936 many of the new carriers were in trouble, mainly because of a decision by the Liberal government to pass legislation designed to ensure that the province's citizens received efficient, clean and punctual bus service. The new legislation required expenditures that many of the small operators simply couldn't afford. Their choice became increasingly clear: bankruptcy or amalgamation.

Irving, who until now had been content to sell gas, oil and automotive supplies, was there to scoop up the pieces. Some operators were too poor to afford the provincial licensing fees. Others, according to Russell Hunt and Robert Campbell, authors of *K.C. Irving: The Art of the Industrialist*, found themselves bankrupt when Irving Oil suddenly reeled in its line of credit, allowing K.C. to buy the assets at bargain-basement prices. One, discovering that 82 per cent of its annual expenses went to Irving-owned companies, simply sold out to its major creditor.[9]

Between 1934 and 1936, the number of licensed buses in the province dropped from 60 to 43, while Irving quietly snapped up nine bus companies and two trucking outfits. Almost overnight, K.C.'s newly formed S.M.T. (Eastern) Ltd. became the province's largest passenger bus and freight truck operator: in 1937, S.M.T.'s 23 buses accounted for half of those running on New Brunswick roads. The same year, the line made a before-tax profit of $160,000. S.M.T.'s buses, moreover, used 200,000 gallons of Irving fuel and lubricants, which accounted for a large part of the $544,980 in sales that Irving Oil recorded for the year.[10]

K.C. didn't stop there: soon a dozen of his employees were busily manufacturing and assembling bodies for his buses in the auto repair shop on the second and third floors of the Golden Ball Building. After all, he reasoned, why pay companies in Ontario and Quebec for bus bodies when you can make them more cheaply yourself. A pattern was emerging: slowly but surely, K.C.'s control over New Brunswick's roadways was growing. He sold cars, fuelled them and repaired them. Chances were that anyone who decided to travel by bus now climbed aboard one of K.C.'s lines. The busier the bus lines, the richer K.C. became — not just because of the fares people paid, but also because the S.M.T. buses ran only on Irving gasoline and oil, and each time a bus needed to be repaired or replaced it made work for K.C.'s repair shop. In fact, the whole thing was starting to fit neatly together. Only one gaping hole still remained in the Irving transportation grid — Saint John, K.C.'s backyard.

In those days, the Saint John bus franchise, along with the city's hydro plant and gas distribution network, was held by New Brunswick Power Co.[11] N.B. Power, in turn, was owned by Federal Light and Traction Co., which was headquartered in New York City and had a record for being the worst sort of absentee owner. By 1935 Saint John's transit system consisted of 23 miles of streetcar tracks and 34 cars, almost all of which were in poor repair. Nobody was happy with the arrangement, least of all Federal Light and Traction, which by the spring of 1935 was anxious to unload its interest in the New Brunswick utility as quickly as possible.

Everyone, including K.C. Irving, knew that the city of Saint John wanted to buy the company, keep the power assets and sell the bus franchise. In early 1936, Louis Ritchie, Irving's long-time friend and lawyer, approached Mayor James Brittain and Common Council to discuss the bus franchise. Ritchie was persuasive enough to extract a promise that the council would consider awarding the concession to S.M.T. But the mayor was about to retire. He told Ritchie to advise his client to wait until a new council was elected and until the city had received the consultant's report it had commissioned on the desirability of buying the power company. So Irving patiently waited.

Fred Manning, however, did not. The Halifax-based tycoon was everything Irving aspired to be. Starting from scratch he had built his own tightly held empire, which included an oil company, a bus line and several other interests. Crafty and aggressive, Manning was worth many times as much as the 37-year-old Irving and knew volumes more about manoeuvring his way around city and provincial governments. His Saint John lawyer was W.A. Ross, who also doubled as secretary to Saint John Common Council. Before a routine council meeting on July 27, Ross persuaded another councillor to introduce a resolution awarding a new company named Maritime Transit the franchise to run buses in Saint John for the next 40 years. When the resolution was tabled, Ross announced that he wanted to appear as Maritime Transit's lawyer. He proceeded to explain that within days of receiving the franchise, Maritime Transit could have 25 or 30 new buses running in Saint John. When asked who was behind the company, Ross refused to identify the owner other than to say that it was a "large outside concern." Even so, the resolution was passed.

Irving was naturally livid. It wasn't just a matter of business; the city, in his view, had broken its word. In a bid to have the motion rescinded, K.C. himself appeared before the council, reciting the history of his involvement and Mayor Brittain's promise and venting his indignation: "We believe the way in which this whole matter has been handled has been most unfair to ourselves . . . . We do not believe that any one taxpayer should receive more consideration than another. . . . I might also add that the actions such as the manner in which Common Council has dealt with the bus franchise certainly would discourage anyone from increasing investments or establishing new industries in Saint John."[12]

The threat worked. Council recanted on the resolution, despite threats from Manning that he would sue the city. Instead, the Nova Scotia tycoon simply ignored the council's newest decision and put his own buses on the city streets for "inspection purposes only." N.B. Power, startled to be facing a direct challenge, applied for and received an injunction to stop Manning. While they fought it out in the courts, K.C. made a bold move: hopping on an airplane to New

York, he obtained an option to buy N.B. Power from Federal Light. An agreement was finalized. Yet before it could be signed, Manning announced he had struck his own deal with N.B. Power to buy the franchise.

Though outmanoeuvred again, K.C. had no intention of giving up. In the process he displayed all the hallmarks of the Irving style — toughness, tenacity and a willingness to drag anything through the courts. It was trench warfare, pure and simple: his forces fought the deal in the courts and lobbied the council and the provincial legislature. It took more than a decade, but eventually Irving just wore the older man down. In January 1948, a costly fire in Saint John caused a crisis in the city's tattered transportation system. A battered, dejected Fred Manning told Common Council, "The main reason the system had not been improved is that every time we go to make a major move we are blocked by S.M.T. (Eastern) Ltd."[13] S.M.T., which just happened to have 17 buses in storage outside the city, was ready to come to the city's aid.

So on July 1, 1948, 12 years after the battle opened, Irving buses finally began a 13-year exclusive franchise to operate in Saint John. The meagre prize was hardly worth the time and expenses spent capturing it. Irving's victory was about more than winning a bus franchise. By facing down Manning he confirmed what many people in the Maritimes already understood — the crown was passing to another capitalist king.

The economic boom that accompanied World War II was just the thing for a country demoralized by a decade of stagnation and misery. Canadian gross national product increased from $5.6 billion in 1939 to $11.9 billion in 1945; production of war materials totalled almost $10 billion as automobile factories turned out transport and armoured fighting vehicles, aircraft plants delivered military aircraft, and shipyards repaired and refitted ships and built corvettes and cargo vessels. There were huge fortunes to be made from the war. And some of the biggest were made by New Brunswick entrepreneurs.

By then Jimmy Dunn had already grown rich and bought a knighthood in London. But his greatest coup came in 1935 when Algoma Steel Corp. of Northern Ontario fell into bankruptcy and Dunn, with $10 million of Algoma bonds, was able to take control of a company worth $75 million. Government rail contracts returned Algoma to solvency, and the war brought prosperity. When Dunn died on New Year's Day, 1956, he held 702,086 shares of Algoma Steel, worth $64.8 million on the day's market.[14]

Max Aitken, who had become Lord Beaverbrook, was also having a good war. The former bond salesman had left Canada for Britain and had entered Parliament and the peerage before he began dabbling in newspapers. "If Beaverbrook had died before May 1940, he would have been almost forgotten except as a newspaper proprietor," wrote his biographer, A.J.P. Taylor. Instead, in his 60s and hampered by asthma, he accepted the job of Britain's minister of aircraft production. The role, in Taylor's view, "was to bring him enduring fame as the saviour of his country."[15]

It also, for the first time, brought him into contact with K.C. Irving, who was making his mark back in Beaverbrook's home province. Irving had found his way of making the war pay. In fact, his decision to invest in Canada Veneers Ltd. would always stand as one of his most inspired moves. This was a company that had scraped out a meagre living since 1936 producing hardwood veneer in a former cotton mill in Saint John. By 1938 it was near bankruptcy. The directors invited K.C., already a major purchaser of plywood for his bus frames, to take control. The prospects seemed poor at the time. Even so, Irving accepted their offer. The company, after all, had one saving grace. In 1931 it had signed a contract to supply hardwood veneer to a subsidiary of the British aircraft giant Saunders Roe. After Irving assumed control, the company began experimenting with cutting aircraft veneer from spruce. The reason: British aircraft designers were studying the feasibility of using the light, strong wood to replace scarce aluminum for aircraft bodies.[16]

That's when the cloak-and-dagger stuff began.[17] By then, shrouded in secrecy in an old English mansion, De Havilland England was designing not only a revolutionary aircraft but a whole new concept of aerial warfare. It was called the Mosquito — a plywood plane in an era when aircraft were built with stressed metal skins. When senior officials in the British air ministry were first presented with Sir Geoffrey de Havilland's proposal, they ridiculed the idea and cut off funding. Undaunted, de Havilland decided to finance development of the Mosquito himself.

When the new plywood bomber took off on November 25, 1940, with the founder's son at the controls, the British air ministry brass present were impressed. It was manoeuvrable and fast, maintaining a speed of 425 miles per hour at 30,000 feet. From the moment it first flew, the Mosquito was the fastest plane in the war. By 1942 the Allies wanted the bomber, plywood or no plywood. De Havilland began plans for mass production in England, Canada and Australia.

Even before the first Mosquito flew, the British government had ordered a huge quantity of aircraft veneer from K.C.'s company.[18] A vast expansion was now needed to meet the demand. K.C. moved quickly, reorganizing management and installing new, up-to-date machinery in the plant. All the plant's other work was dropped. From then on, K.C. told his employees, they were in the aircraft veneer business. When one of the biggest veneer producers in the U.S. burned down, the Saint John company had to take up the slack. The Canada Veneers plant underwent a startling transformation: from 180 employees producing 200,000 square feet a week on two floors of the building in 1939, to over 500 employees churning out more than 4 million square feet a week by 1943.[19] "They needed everything we could pump out," recalls Art McNair, who worked for Canada Veneers during the war years. "It was going all day, every day. You could walk by the plant in the middle of the night when everything else was dark and the lights would be burning bright."

The Mosquito turned out to be a veritable gold mine for K.C. By the end of the war, a total of 6,711 Mosquitoes had been produced in Britain, Canada and Australia.[20] Canada Veneers was the world's largest supplier of aircraft veneer.[21]

Throughout the war years money was pouring into the Irving headquarters from all over. In Bouctouche, the J.D. Irving Ltd. wharfs were swarming with local workmen who laboured day and night churning out plywood landing craft sturdy enough to carry Allied soldiers to European beaches. The bus business was also booming, thanks to wartime restrictions on the use of private automobiles. In 1943, S.M.T. had revenues of $690,000 and used 223,000 gallons of Irving gasoline and nearly 28,000 gallons of lubricants. Three years later — with K.C. operating 58 buses in the province, compared with 71 vehicles among the other 26 carriers operating — S.M.T.'s revenues reached $1.4 million in New Brunswick. Its costs, as reported to the provincial Motor Carrier Board, were $1.3 million.[22] But of course almost all of that would have been spent on the 420,000 gallons of Irving gasoline and 115,000 gallons of lubricants that the line bought that year. Irving Oil, which now controlled almost one-third of the Maritime gasoline market, had a sweet after-tax profit of $413,000 during 1946.[23]

K.C. had held his own through the Depression and thrived through the war years. Now, for the first time, he had money, big money, to expand with. It was time to spread his wings a bit. And the success of Canada Veneers had got him thinking.

As a boy growing up in Bouctouche, K.C. had often heard the old lumbermen talk of driving huge tangles of shifting logs down the province's wild rivers — the Restigouche, the Miramichi, the Richibucto, the Saint John, the St. Croix and the Magaguadavic — and of the legendary lumber barons they worked for. Some attained folk-hero status, such as "Main John" Glasier, later to become Senator John D. Glasier. Tall and lean, with a projecting chin, hooked nose and gigantic shoulders, he went bald as a youth and covered his dome with a bushy brown wig, which he kept pinned in place by a black stovepipe hat. Glasier was the first man to drive logs over Grand Falls. But his mythical status stems from the time the lumbermen of Maine decided to dam the Allagash River, lowering the level of the Saint John and leaving millions of New Brunswick logs high and dry. Leading a group of henchmen into Maine, Main John attacked the local lumberjacks with fists and bullets. Then, after driving them away, he and his men went at the dam with axes, releasing a head of water that raised the water level by three feet at Grand Falls, 160 miles away.

Or at least that's how the story goes. For the mid-19th century truly was the rollicking heyday of New Brunswick lumbering. The boom in the timber trade meant just about every stream of any size had a dam and a water-driven sawmill. Men dreamed of leading big lumbering operations and building new steam mills of their own.

Eventually, of course, those halcyon days ended. Trucks replaced rivers as the main way to move logs; the lumber barons were supplanted by big business. A Scot named Archibald Fraser ushered in the new era when he began acquiring controlling interests in other companies and merged them all into Fraser Companies Ltd. in 1917. Others followed. Before long New Brunswick's Crown timberland was divided up among the province's few remaining independent timber barons and the big timber companies.

K.C. learned this in the mid-1940s, when he went looking for wood to fuel Canada Veneers' ravenous appetite and was forced to import timber and to buy at high prices from the established players — a fact that rankled him no end. He needed lumber if his mills were going to continue to make money. At the same time, flouting the accepted view, he felt the stagnant timber industry would turn around once the hostilities in Europe ended. So, flush with war profits, he started buying.

For starters, in 1943 he grabbed D'Auteuil Lumber Co., which had large timber reserves in Quebec, Maine and New Brunswick. Then he went looking for bigger game. New Brunswick and Canada Railway and Land Co., incorporated in 1899 as part of the railway building mania, had been granted 1.6 million acres of prime timberland, making it New Brunswick's largest landowner. But size alone doesn't guarantee success; when it went bankrupt 20 years later, it leased its 420 miles of track, its rolling stock and its lands to the CPR for 990 years. By 1940 the CPR wanted to sell the land, and Fraser Companies bought 700,000 acres. In mid-May 1943, K.C. picked up 225,000 acres, reportedly for an astonishingly cheap $1 an acre. Two years later, he bought the 700,000 acres that Fraser had purchased, for the same per-acre price. The deal gave K.C. a total of 1.5 million acres of prime timberland, about equivalent to all of Prince Edward Island, which made him one of the province's largest landowners.[24]

The pieces of his grand scheme were coming together. In 1944 he had moved into the newspaper business, silently buying the New Brunswick Publishing Co., publisher of the *Telegraph-Journal* and the *Evening Times-Globe*, Saint John's two dailies. (It was years before he admitted publicly to owning the papers.) Next logical step:

a mill that could turn his timber into pulp for the newspapers. The opportunity arose right beneath his long nose. Since 1899, a pulp mill had stood at the mouth of the Saint John River by the Reversing Falls. Over the years it had changed owners and gone bankrupt, and eventually it landed in the hands of Port Royal Pulp and Paper Co. Ltd., a Quebec outfit, where it prospered for a time. Even then, the mill continued to be plagued by pulp log shortages and transportation problems. In March 1946 the mill had new owners. "The Port Royal Pulp and Paper Co. Ltd. has sold to the K.C. Irving interests its mill and properties at Fairville, Fredericton and along the Saint John River," the company said in a statement. "The management is of the opinion that in the hands of Mr. Irving this enterprise will have a great future and that the employees and the community will benefit from the change in ownership."[25]

Immediately K.C. started expanding his new company. He raised $2.5 million through a bond issue and used the proceeds to buy new timberlands and to modernize the antiquated mill, which he renamed Saint John Sulphite, Limited. It was a typical Irving move: buy a failing operation, invest, add new technology and try to revitalize the property. His competitors said he was crazy. But he must have known something: as soon as World War II ended, the industry went from a state of chronic over-capacity to flat-out production as newsprint prices began climbing. Soon the mill was undergoing another $20-million expansion.

By then no business was out of K.C.'s reach. In 1946 he moved into the shipping business, starting Kent Line, Ltd. (named for his native Kent County) by buying four navy corvettes, converting them into cargo carriers at his Bouctouche dockyards and registering them offshore. Soon Kent Line's vessels were moving everything from pineapples to pulpwood along the eastern seaboard, in the Caribbean and to South America.

He hired away one of the top salesmen from a heavy equipment company, gave him a few telephones and some space in the basement of the Golden Ball Building and ordered him to start a company to sell and rent tractors, cranes and other heavy equipment. He bought W.H. Thorne and Co., Saint John's oldest and biggest retail hardware company, and began expanding it throughout the Maritimes. He bought a hotel in Moncton. He added hardware businesses in Montreal, Quebec City and Toronto. He started car dealerships in Saint John, Fredericton, Halifax and Amherst.

The oil business remained the centre of his interests. By 1952 Irving Oil owned 300 service stations, held another 90 under lease and sold its gasoline and motor oil at another 700 independently owned outlets. The company owned more than 50 bulk petroleum storage plants, along with five tankers — *Irvingdale, Nipiwan Park, Otterhound, Seekonk* and *Mollie G* — which brought the crude in from the Middle East and South America. By then he was making his first exploratory moves into the Quebec market. Irving Oil controlled 23 different companies and had assets of nearly $30 million. Including the Irving forestry companies, newspapers and bus lines, the assets under K.C.'s control would have been even greater. Altogether K.C.'s payroll topped 4,000 within New Brunswick, and there were 3,000 more employees in Quebec, Maine and Ontario.[26]

Forged within less than 30 years, it was an impressive piece of work. But during a rare interview, when a reporter asked K.C. what was next, he only smiled noncommittally. "Some days you're interested in one industry," he murmured. "Next morning, it may be something altogether different."[27] Vague as his words were, the meaning was clear: no one knew but Irving.

4

Citizen Irving

"Sir, I don't sell. I buy."
— Kenneth Colin Irving

BEFORE WORLD WAR II, K.C. Irving was just a sharp Maritimer who happened to be making a good buck in the service station business. But the startling buying spree of the 1940s and 1950s thrust him into national prominence. Suddenly journalists from across the country converged on Saint John to write breathlessly about the mysterious "tycoon of the Maritimes," the "lone wolf who battled the eastern combines," "the Maritimer who made good at home," the industrialist with the "golden touch with ailing industries." In 1948 a U.S. newspaper reported that "a Canadian financier named Kenneth Colin Irving" was considering investing $10 million to $20 million in Preston Tucker's "Car of Tomorrow" company.[1] Dan Ross, a Saint John novelist who wrote more than 300 books under dozens of pen names, even centred a romance novel titled *The Fog and the Stars* on a Saint John industrialist with a "bronzed bald head" and "hawk face." S.C. North, Ross wrote, "was a name to be regarded with awe in New Brunswick, in all of Canada, and even in the United States."

Through it all Irving remained a enigma cloaked in legend. And like all legends, his contained a certain amount of misconception, along with a deeper truth. In New Brunswick, his name inspired loyal reverence among those who worked for him, the same proud employees who seemed to willingly labour Herculean hours to help his ventures prosper. To his admirers, Irving meant successful industrial development in a province that had little of either; the Saint

John air might stink with the effluents from the Irving pulp mill, but that stink, they would say, was the smell of jobs. "New Brunswick needs Irving a great deal worse than Irving needs New Brunswick," a local Liberal MP bluntly told his colleagues in a statement of undeniable truth.[2]

Yet beyond the Fredericton legislature and outside his factories and paper mills, Irving's name was as likely to inspire apprehension as devotion. By the 1950s, to the people of Saint John, K.C. hovered in the collective imagination like a shadowy force of nature, commanding unspoken, unknown power over everything and everyone. It was said that he kept the deeds to half the businesses and most of the land in New Brunswick gathering dust in a safe in the Golden Ball Building. Many people did not even know what he looked like, or whether they themselves were on his payroll. They just knew he was there, watching over them from the big white house on Mount Pleasant that Howard Robinson used to own.

Never outgoing, K.C. had by now developed a penchant for secrecy. He hardly ever gave speeches, he sat on no corporate boards other than his own companies' and the University of New Brunswick board of governors, and he rarely appeared at public functions. His name wasn't registered in any *Who's Who*. He employed no public relations department. He seldom spoke to reporters, leaving his valued secretary Winnifred Johnson to handle the press. Normally, of course, he wasn't pushed too far on the latter point. At least not by the scribes for the *Saint John Telegraph-Journal*, who understood that stories in which he was interested or mentioned came under the closest scrutiny at the editor's desk and often would not see print.

His proclivity for remaining in the shadows was, in part, just plain "good business." Irving came of age in the 1930s, when a company, particularly a privately owned outfit like his, was beholden to no one and under no obligation to tell the public anything about what it was up to. Some, though, thought K.C.'s sphinx-like silence came from the Maritimer's deep-seated fear of being viewed as boastful or "big feeling."

It has never been easy being rich in the Maritimes. Frank Sobey slept and dined in hotels favoured by oil sheiks, rock stars and royalty in Europe and Asia, but he flew economy while in Nova Scotia just to remain one of the boys. Roy Jodrey was even cheaper: Once, friends did succeed in getting Jodrey to buy a first-class ticket so he could sit with them. His biographer, Harry Bruce, wrote, "He planted his fatness in his roomy seat, glowered at the cabin's luxury, squirmed guiltily, and grumbled to no one, 'The people of Hantsport will know about this before I even get home.'"[3]

Irving, too, eschewed the baubles of the rich. He positively refused to squander money on yachts, swimming pools, palatial mansions, exotic vacations — anything that would draw attention to him, make him appear superior to the common folk. The Irvings lived comfortably but without airs in their roomy, white wooden house with the widow's walk, which allowed K.C. to watch his tankers enter Saint John harbour. Inside, the home was tasteful but not ostentatious, with oil paintings — usually landscapes and seascapes — by local artists covering the walls. They did have a servant who doubled as cook and chauffeur, a young Scot named Ian Throckmorton, who was recruited for them by Lord Beaverbrook. But K.C. and Hattie couldn't bring themselves to address him, in the British tradition, by his last name. They called him simply "Ian."

There wasn't a pretentious bone in K.C.'s decidedly bony body; he dressed well, but not too well, favouring snap-brimmed fedoras or blue air force berets, double-breasted, pinstriped suits and tame ties that were anchored in place by a small diamond stickpin, his only outward sign of opulence. While Hattie drove their Cadillac, K.C. preferred a simple Ford, the same brand he had been selling for 25 years.

He lived austerely, keeping his childhood vow to eschew alcohol and tobacco. When kidded by friends about his monastic habits, K.C. explained that he did everything to excess and that if he acquired any vices he might not have the strength to control them. All the same, he clearly had no taste for the high life: he shook his head in bafflement at people who habituated "fancy" restaurants with linen tablecloths and crystal goblets; despite an ulcer and a touch of angina, he often skipped meals altogether, grabbing a chocolate bar on the way to his next appointment. His idea of fine eating was a meal at his favourite Chinese restaurant in Fredericton. When

McDonald's Restaurants began appearing in the Maritimes, he was quite happy to wolf down a Big Mac for lunch. On business in the outports of Newfoundland, he would have one of his underlings find a local housewife willing to prepare them ham and potatoes or some other simple meal in their home. "For him that was greater than eating in the Château Frontenac," says Charlie Van Horne, a colourful lawyer and politician who worked for Irving for a decade and went along on many of those trips. "He would kibitz with the family and kids and ask what was going on in the little village."

Hattie Irving was equally unchanged by wealth. A big, handsome woman, she was fond of entertaining the local women's bridge club and giving friends her home-made jams, jellies and pickles for Christmas. "She was no different from when she worked in the store in Bouctouche," says one of her friends. Indeed, whenever old acquaintances addressed her as "Mrs. Irving," she corrected them with a firm "I'm Hattie." When she entertained at home it was always simply. Guests usually had a glass of her cranberry cordial in the library before dinner and then sipped water throughout the meal. Big drinkers like Lord Beaverbrook had to fortify themselves with a couple of doubles before these liquor-less affairs.

Hattie was unfailingly polite to everyone. But her husband's manners were delightfully inconsistent. With those in a position to fight back — company presidents and chairmen of the board — he sometimes abandoned his politeness, pounded tables, and threw temper tantrums. But with subordinates and his casual acquaintances, he helped people on with their coats and called virtually everyone "Mister." K.C. himself was known to take the wheel on long trips while his driver snoozed in the back seat. Adrian Gilbert, one of his top Saint John lawyers, once recounted how K.C. was chauffeuring him back from his Restigouche fishing lodge in his Cadillac one night when the industrialist spotted a pair of teenagers struggling to change a tire on the side of the road. Despite the lateness of the hour, K.C pulled over, shed his coat and changed it himself.

If, as George Orwell said, everyone has the face he deserves at 50, Irving's was big and craggy, with deep-set, even, grey eyes, a long nose and a straight mouth that often twisted into a smile. His brows were dark and heavy. He was bald as an eagle, except for a monk-like ring of silver hair over his jutting ears. But his skin was un-wrinkled and his forehead unfurrowed by worry. Six feet tall, he was a trim 200-pounder with wide shoulders and slim hips. He exuded youthful energy, even when seated in his office, which, in the early 1950s, was on the second floor of the dingy, wedge-shaped waterfront building that housed Irving Oil. Though the building itself was drab, Irving's inner sanctum was luxurious, panelled in dark oak, with thick carpeting and drapes. He sat between twin glass-topped desks, swivelling around to pick up the telephones that jangled constantly or to answer the squawking office intercom announcing his next vis-itor, who might have been waiting for hours for an audience.

Then suddenly he would be off, perhaps with no more than an hour's notice, jumping in his private airplane — one of his few con-cessions to the tycoon's life — and heading to New York City, Toronto or Montreal to consummate a business deal or to the farthest reaches of the Maritimes to inspect a sawmill or service station. In 1948 alone, Irving covered about 120,000 miles in his private plane, adding thousands more by rail, car, ship and airline. A commercial traveller from Moncton once saw K.C. at the Montreal airport in the early 1950s carrying on conversations in three telephone booths at once, "like a nervous bookmaker before post time."[4] Another time, Colin Mackay, president of the University of New Brunswick, was walking down the street in Ottawa when he heard someone calling his name. Standing in a phone booth was K.C., who asked Mackay if he knew the correct way to address Yugoslavia's Marshal Tito, whom the in-dustrialist was on the way to meet.[5]

New Irving executives learned that they too had to be ready to drop everything when he called, or else find a new job. In the early 1950s one of Irving's senior officials was home after a day at the office when the industrialist phoned. Could he come along that night on a trip to northern New Brunswick? The man hadn't had his dinner and said so. "Never mind," Irving replied, "I've got it with me in the car." When they drove off a few minutes later, Irving reached into his pocket and produced dinner — a chocolate bar. The executive was soon working elsewhere.[6]

Business always came first. An oft-repeated tale tells of the day the engine on his Grumman-Millard caught fire while taking off, causing the aircraft to hit a tall spruce at the end of the runway. Gasoline poured into the fuselage, turning the plane into a mass of flames, as Irving escaped through the rear door and the pilot fled through the front hatch. Seconds later the plane exploded. Dusting himself off, K.C. examined his singed eyebrows. Then, the story goes, he returned to his office, where he put in a full day's work. Charlie Van Horne, one of Irving Oil's chief legal fixers in those days, also recalls some tense moments approaching fog-shrouded Newfoundland outports in Irving's private plane. Jagged log ends often jutted from the harbour waters. Van Horne was on board during one particularly hair-raising flight when a nervous young pilot asked the boss if he should turn the craft back. Irving's succinct response: "Dodge 'em."

His stamina was beyond belief. He could work longer and harder than anyone, going for days on end with just a few hours of sleep, snatched in the car or in the cabin of his airplane on the way to the next meeting. Once, in the early 1960s, he found himself embroiled in simultaneous negotiations with the Standard Oil Company of California (Socal) and Kimberly-Clark, the big American tissue company. The American negotiating teams took private suites in the Admiral Beatty Hotel in Saint John. "Every day," a witness to the procedure recalled, "Mr. Irving met the Standard men until 6 o'clock and every night he was back meeting the Kimberly-Clark people until 2 or 3 a.m. And then every morning, sharp at 9 a.m. he was the first in the lobby."[7] Even age didn't sap his energy: his son Arthur once recounted how he and K.C. one day talked business in Newfoundland, flew to Chicoutimi, Quebec, then to Trois-Rivières late in the evening. At 4 in the morning, K.C., then in his 70s, wanted to inspect a property he was considering buying. Arthur, who was 30 years younger and was also known for his endurance, had to concede defeat and headed wearily for bed.

He was a one-man show, with an owner's proprietorial attitude towards his businesses. A whiz with numbers — "he had a slide-rule mind," one of his old business associates says — he spent long hours keeping track of cost factors, expenses and profit ratios, ana-lysing financial statements and sales forecasts. Usually, though, he was far from the office, keeping in touch with customers, prospects, bankers and suppliers, monitoring his plants and outlets, looking for new businesses to buy and new opportunities to exploit. When one of his companies bought a piece of property, there would be K.C., pacing off the dimensions to make sure that he was getting what he paid for.

Sometimes he personally staked out opposition service stations, huddling clandestinely in a car to count the number of automobiles going through the station. He liked to think that he was still ready at any time to roll up his sleeves and pour some gas or fix a car. In the winter he snowshoed through the forests to examine his tim-berland. Once, he was standing on top of a load of logs that his men were moving down the Saint John when the shipment shifted, sending him plunging into the water.

He had a thirst to know everything, even the most minute details about how each of his businesses operated. In the early 1960s New Brunswick premier Louis Robichaud took a drive in the country with Irving. Whenever they passed a filling station on the New Brunswick roads, he knew how many gallons it had sold last month — and by then he had 1,600 stations. "If I do have a phenomenal memory it is a gift," he once said. "I've never consciously trained it. With industries that you build from scratch you just naturally know certain facts that you can use as check-points."[8]

One thing he never forgot was the importance of looking after customers. Take exceptional care of the people who buy from you, he told his employees over and over again — give them superior quality and superior service and the profits will roll in. Irving gas-oline, he liked to brag, was of higher quality than any of the com-petition's. His filling stations were cleaner, his attendants more at-tentive. The customer always got the best, even if it meant K.C. himself had to help a taxi driver push his cab to an Irving filling station. He had four telephones in his home for calls from customers — his telephone number was always listed in those years — and he always kept one of them at his elbow, even during breakfast.

A visitor was in his home one Sunday afternoon when the phone rang. The dialogue went like this:

"You Irving, the oil man?"

"Yes, sir, I am."

"Well, this is Mulrooney, of St. Patrick Street."

"Yes, Mr. Mulrooney, what can I do for you?"

"Where in the hell's my oil?"

"Haven't you received your oil, Mr. Mulrooney?"

"You're damned right I haven't."

"Well, sir, I'm very sorry to hear that, and it's a cold day too, isn't it." Irving took his address and phone number, dialled his oil-yard, called Mulrooney and told him his oil was on the way. Half an hour later he broke off a conference to call Mulrooney again and ask if it had arrived.[9]

K.C. never seemed to tire of these demonstrations of how far he would go to get and keep a customer. One Christmas Eve he and his wife were visiting a few Saint John service stations, offering season's greetings to Irving employees. The telephone was ringing when he pulled into one station. The caller's car was stuck at a church more than two miles away. Could someone please send a tow truck? A teenage attendant started to explain that the station had no truck, but Irving interrupted to find out what was going on. Then, at 70 years of age, one of the richest men ever to live in Canada paid cash to one of his own gas stations for two bags of road salt, put them in his trunk and spent Christmas Eve driving through a blizzard to help free a stranger's car.[10]

That, it seems, was his idea of fun. K.C. was a man with few interests outside work. Occasionally he dropped into Saint John's Cliff Club for a hand of poker on a Saturday night. In the early days he and Hattie saw every new movie that came to Saint John; sometimes, to relieve the pressures of work, he slipped away from his office in the middle of the afternoon to catch the matinée at a nearby theatre. Later on, when he was doing a lot of business in New York City, he attended Broadway musicals.

All the same, when it came to culture K.C. was a happy philistine. He liked to joke that the only book he ever read was *The Last Bil-*

lionaire (the life of Henry Ford), although a journalist visiting his house once saw a library that included science texts, the novels of Walter Scott and the complete Horatio Alger canon. Lord Beaverbrook, an avid art collector, once took K.C. to the Beaverbrook Art Gallery in Fredericton to view the famous miniature of Queen Elizabeth I that the press baron had recently purchased for $150,000, at that time the most ever paid for a painting of that type.

"Lord Beaverbrook," said Irving, "I recall reading somewhere that you paid $150,000 for this."

"That's right."

Irving paused and re-examined the art work. In a wistful tone he added, "Just think how much pulpwood you could have bought with that."

"Oh, Kenneth," groaned Beaverbrook, "you have no soul."

Usually when Irving had a few free days he would head for his fishing lodge, one of the best in the world, at the head of the salmon-rich Restigouche River. In the early 1960s he spent $300,000 to outbid the Fraser Companies for a ten-year lease on one of the choicest stretches of the river. Yet when he took his family or guests — big paper clients and visiting VIPs, including English lords and powerful American politicians such as Hubert Humphrey — to the main lodge on a weekend, he left the fishing to them and spent the days doing paperwork or disappeared to his nearby tree nursery to help with experiments to breed better trees.

Around people with whom he could relax, Irving was good company — funny, a first-rate yarn-spinner, and possessor of a surprisingly wry sense of humour made all the more effective by his dry, deadpan delivery. "K.C. is a Scot and all Scots can laugh at themselves," says Colin Mackay, a friend of Irving. "No matter how successful they are, regardless of how they act in public, they have their feet firmly on the ground and understand that life is a ridiculous joke." This was evident the time K.C. flew to Quebec City to meet with a high-strung Irving Oil underling who was worried because he didn't have $700,000 to pay for a tanker of gasoline already moving up the St. Lawrence River. The hand-wringing continued throughout a long, unpleasant lunch. When the check came, K.C.'s Quebec lieutenant reached for it, but Irving was quicker. "I'll pay for lunch, you just pay for the oil."[11]

Most of his close friendships have been with the men, and a few women, with whom he did business. Generally speaking, he didn't mix with the Canadian establishment in Ontario and Quebec. He enjoyed Lord Beaverbrook's company, visiting his house in Nassau and even flying to his estate in Britain to dine with Winston Churchill, a man he idolized. In 1960 he and Beaverbrook considered opening up a paper mill together and buying a big swath of timberland from the Fraser Companies. Although fond of Irving, Beaverbrook really did not know what to make of the austere Saint John industrialist. "Call me Max, Kenneth," he would say, to which Irving would invariably respond, "Certainly, Lord Beaverbrook." Once Beaverbrook, who loved his Dom Pérignon and the other trappings of the good life, tried to get down to brass tacks: "Kenneth, you don't wench, you don't smoke, you don't drink. What do you do for excitement?" Replied Irving: "I work."

What made him run so hard? No one seems to know — not even K.C. himself. Not easily given to introspection, he always seemed genuinely puzzled when asked to explain why he kept expanding his operations and buying new companies. Clearly, money wasn't the motivating factor; he has no taste for the high life and has ploughed whatever he made back into his businesses. Power, political or otherwise, doesn't interest him, other than for what it can do to help his businesses prosper. He is, say many who know him, a simple, uncomplicated man: he worked so hard simply because he never found anything he liked doing quite as much. "To him business was a game," his son Arthur likes to say. K.C. told one friend, "I can't be idle. I always have to be doing something." As he added another time, while climbing a muddy hill in Newfoundland with Charlie Van Horne and Harrison McCain, the future frozen food magnate who in those days was running a bunch of Irving service stations, "What else would I do between meals?"[12]

All the same he teems with paradox. He is a Presbyterian Scot, but one who approached business in his heyday with an almost boyish

enthusiasm rather than the grim work ethic that is bred into many
with this background. He was a free-wheeling capitalist, but one who
chose to operate from the backwater of Saint John instead of the
financial Meccas of New York, Toronto, Montreal or London. He
disdains all the outward signs of wealth, yet Lord have mercy on
anyone who tries to take any of his money away from him. Even
his most ardent supporters have a hard time defending his winner-
take-all attitude against any competitors, no matter how small and
inconsequential, with the gall to compete against him. Even the most
sycophantic Irving apologists have trouble explaining the legal suits
launched against anyone who has crossed him.

If Irving has given much money to charity — and his friends and
supporters insist he has — the public has rarely heard a word of
it. No art galleries, concert halls or museums attest to his largesse.
Once when a Saint John curling club was collecting money for a
new rink, a canvasser buttonholed K.C., hoping for a fat donation.
"Certainly," he said. "Put me down for one share [$100] — same
as everyone else."[13] The University of New Brunswick tried to whee-
dle a big contribution out of him by naming a new library on
its Fredericton campus after his first wife, Harriet. The books are
closed on whether a cent of K.C.'s money ever went into the
building.

For decades, he refused to allow United Way contributions to be
taken off employee paycheques. While giving him a lift to the Fredericton airport, a prominent New Brunswick businessman and fund-
raiser had an opportunity to try to persuade K.C. to set up a payroll
deduction plan. To buy more time to make his pitch, the businessman
just kept slowing down the car — to 30 miles per hour, 20 miles.
Eventually the car was hardly moving. But still K.C. refused. "No,
no, no," he intoned, slapping his thigh for emphasis, "all the workers
see is the line at the bottom of the pay stub."

Privately, though, he is said to have a heart. It is widely rumoured
that he was generous when it came to lending new businesses money,
so long as they weren't competing with his companies. "If the loan
had any merit they would get one," one old associate remembers.
At one point, it is rumoured, he had more mortgages and business
development loans out in the Saint John area than the Federal Busi-

ness Development Bank. K.C. also made a large contribution to the predominantly Acadian Université de Moncton.

Charlie Van Horne reports making many a clandestine run to help old friends because K.C. had heard they were sick or in need. Long after leaving Bouctouche he has kept an eye on his birthplace, donating $50,000 for a church carillon and another $70,000 for a town rink. He has a particular soft spot for the clergy, who have asked for money knowing full well they won't be turned down — even the whiskey priest from the north shore of New Brunswick who called him from Mexico City after a terrible bender and asked for help to get home. K.C. gave it, without question or comment. Indeed, in 1965 he and his wife became the first Canadians to receive the Eleanor Roosevelt Humanities Award. "Throughout his career he has quietly and discreetly supported good causes," said the citation. "Educational institutions, religious groups of all denominations, cultural projects and many individuals have benefitted from his kindness and generosity."

Not surprisingly, he was able to stir amazing loyalty among many of his workers. So what if he overworked and underpaid them, they said. He created jobs and did his best to make the Maritimes a better place to live. Besides, K.C. seemed to really care for his employees. He knew everyone by name, treated everyone with respect. He was known to fly ailing employees to the Lahey Clinic outside Boston and to quietly pay for the university education of the children of some old hands. Whenever an employee died, K.C. was always at the funeral.

Still, the warmth K.C. felt towards the working man had its limits. His clashes with organized labour over the years were legendary. He wasn't exactly against unions: "When they are well led they are excellent for labour and management both," he said. Trouble was, the way he saw things, they were rarely well led. At least that seemed to be his view of the union at his East Saint John oilyard, which went on strike in 1948. Late one day K.C. approached the picket lines outside his plant, pulled off his topcoat and yelled at the strikers, "You may be big, but I'm bigger." K.C. later said that he wasn't asking for trouble, but "it never pays to talk with your coat on." Nobody took him up on the challenge. Next day, when a non-striker balked at driving his truck past the picket lines, Irving pushed him aside, took the wheel and sped through. Two company officials followed him in cars. The strikers scattered, several of them retreating to the nearest police station, where they swore out reckless driving summonses against Irving and his two aides; the matter was later dropped.[14]

A year or so later, the union at the Irving plywood plant had no better luck negotiating with K.C., even though he was laid up in bed after falling off a ladder and breaking several ribs. For more than five hours they bargained around Irving's bedside. When asked how the patient had behaved, a union organizer later replied drily, "As well as could be expected."[15]

K.C. just wouldn't be told what to do, not by anyone. Whenever the city of Saint John tried to apply pressure on him, he muscled back. Common Council's decision to cancel his water lease in 1961 drove him to distraction, even though the lease was granted at an absurdly low price. By then he was one of the biggest champions of the Chignecto Canal, a proposed deep-water navigation canal that would run across the neck of land separating the Bay of Fundy from the Northumberland Strait. When concerns arose about how the canal would pay for itself, Irving promised to erect $100 million worth of new industry in and around Saint John after the canal was built. But with the cancellation of the water lease, the development was off. It was impossible, K.C. said, "to obtain co-operation and fair business dealing in respect to agreements with the city of Saint John. . . . You can't do business with people who only oppose and attack you."[16] The government did an abrupt about-face. K.C. got back his water rights and agreed to reconsider his plans if Chignecto went through. That, alas, never happened.

What K.C. wanted, it seemed, K.C. got — even if it meant his enterprises were granted wholesale powers far beyond what most corporations received. Almost all of the big forestry companies operating in New Brunswick were granted sweeping privileges, including tax concessions and the right to appropriate land. But only a few, including Irving Pulp & Paper Co. (formerly Saint John Sulphite) — which each day dumped several million gallons of waste-contaminated water from the Reversing Falls mill into the Saint John

River — were exempted from "nuisance suits" for polluting the water or air.[17] Even fewer enjoyed the same power that Irving Pulp retained to expropriate land for its use.[18]

Through it all, K.C.'s empire was evolving. The pattern already visible in his early disputes with Imperial Oil and the CNR — the desire for control and self-sufficiency — was fully developed by the 1960s. What he envisioned from the start was controlling all the different stages of the industrial process: producing the raw materials, transporting them, manufacturing the finished products and then marketing them. In the mid-1930s he had made the first steps towards building a vertically integrated operation: the Irving oil business had spread throughout the Maritimes; the autobody shop was proficient enough to provide regular maintenance work as well as a limited-scale bus assembly plant. Both supported the new integrated bus network. And building bus bodies was the first step into the massive profits in the hardwood veneers business.

Diversification was next: Irving's operations spread geographically, into the other Maritime provinces and Quebec, and also into new products as he branched out into the pulp and paper business. K.C. understood the importance of not being wedded to a single market or product. "Almost any New Brunswick corporation, subject to national or international competition, must if it is to survive successfully, diversify in its activities or itself become national or international in scope," he explained once. "If the latter happens, the head office will no longer remain in the Maritimes. I prefer diversification. Call it conglomerate or what you will — in New Brunswick it contributes to survival."[19]

Entering the 1950s it was time for K.C. to fill out that diversification strategy. Using imported oil, Irving Oil continued to open up new stations throughout the Maritimes and Quebec. By 1958 he had 1,500 service stations, 30 per cent of the Maritime market and a large portion of Quebec gasoline sales.[20] K.C. just kept buying. He bought land and real estate for possible station sites. When forestland came up for sale he bought it, adding to his 1.5 million acres. He bought oil tankers and cargo vessels, added more newspapers and sawmills. He opened engineering outfits, construction companies and steel fabrication companies. He bought, it seemed, anything that was for sale and lots that wasn't. And he almost never sold; instead he would swap land and property for more attractive assets. Mostly he just held on, even if an enterprise was a money-loser, because he believed that if something is worth buying, it is worth keeping.

He always trusted his intuition. The great entrepreneurs, the Fords, Reichmanns and Rockefellers, always have. "The mind of the entrepreneur works differently from the corporate executive's mind," says Gary Davis, a business professor at the University of New Brunswick. "The true entrepreneurs trust their judgement. They don't always have all the hard facts. But they have a long-term view of what is likely to happen. And they aren't scared of making mistakes."

K.C. never feared falling on his face; time after time he went where most others feared to go. There were failures: an ill-conceived foray into gold mining in the late 1930s, for one. All in all, though, Irving had an uncanny knack for buying beleaguered or bankrupt enterprises, turning them around and integrating them into the rest of the empire while, at the same time, pressing for new markets. His real genius was his ability to look ahead, to anticipate, to know where the opportunities lay. He was like a chess master planning his moves far in advance. Maybe the pay-off didn't come right away, but it came.

Pulp and paper was a prime example. In the 1940s Irving had plunged in head first at a time when forestry companies were drowning left and right. He not only bought Port Royal Pulp and Paper but, with the pulp industry in a state of chronic over-capacity, he began a $20-million expansion in 1951, which left him well positioned when the pulp and paper glut disappeared and prices began rising. In 1956 he opened a new sawmill at Lancaster, on the outskirts of Saint John. A year later he announced plans to build a $16-million kraft pulp mill nearby.

To raise the money for the new mill, he sold 35 per cent of Irving Pulp & Paper to Kimberly-Clark, the maker of Kleenex, Kotex and other tissue products. The quid pro quo was that Kimberly had agreed to build and operate an adjourning tissue mill, which, of course, would be the biggest single customer for the Irving pulp mill.

It was a sweet deal, one that K.C. was willing to go to great lengths to cement; he even personally steered through Common Council the 30-year tax and 25-year water agreements that Kimberly demanded before it would build its plant. When the mayor of nearby Lancaster indicated he was opposed to the tax bill, K.C. himself made the pitch before the provincial legislature. "Anyone who thinks this is a pushover is wrong. We need the assistance of this tax bill. . . . I don't see why we should have so much concern about the future. The future will take care of itself."[21]

With K.C. Irving it almost always did. A prime example was his decision to move into shipbuilding. Saint John Dry Dock Co. Ltd. was the biggest shipyard in the British Commonwealth — 1,150 feet long with a steel fabrication plant, an iron works, dredging operations, harbour tugs, a machine shop and a coastal ferry. During World War II it rang with activity as 1,500 workers toiled away, repairing and refitting ships and building new corvettes and cargo vessels. But the postwar slump silenced the yard's loud clatter. By the mid-1950s employment had dropped to about 300 workers, and the company, which depended upon naval refits for virtually all of its income, was just about bankrupt.

Charles Wilson, the ageing owner, had his own concerns. Worried that his sons would face huge succession duties if they inherited the shipyard, he decided to sell the yard. Somehow Irving got wind of Wilson's quandary. "They met once and couldn't agree on a price," recalls Keith Wilson, one of Charles's sons. "So they let it ride for another month and then met again. That's when the lawyers got involved." By May 1959 the yard was in Irving's hands. The price tag: $4.5 million. Within days of the deal, the dry dock announced that it had landed a $3-million construction contract.

At the time, investing in the stagnant shipbuilding industry looked like a huge gamble. But K.C.'s logic was unassailable: his private shipping fleet, after all, was growing all the time. Shipbuilding was a fresh new direction for the empire, which made it less vulnerable to the vagaries of the pulp and petroleum markets. When the yard was busy again — and he was confident that Ottawa and the province would see to that — he planned to be ready. As soon as the deal was done, K.C. commissioned two major studies, and with their recommendations in hand he began planning a massive two-stage expansion of the dry dock.

It was a decade before work actually began on the multimillion-dollar expansion. In time, the shipyard, renamed Saint John Shipbuilding and Dry Dock Co., would become the grease that lubricated the entire empire. But back in 1959, the shipyard purchase just set more people wondering what K.C. was up to. "This is a man who has at least 10,000 men on his payroll," wrote a newspaper reporter that October. "In 35 years he has built an empire worth perhaps $200,000,000 and is still — at the age of 60 — building in a region he describes as Number 1 on the charity list. He says he plans to spend $100,000,000 on expansion in New Brunswick in the next few years."[22] In fact, within just months Irving announced his biggest move yet.

From the moment he opened his first small filling station in Bouctouche, K.C. wanted to own a refinery capable of converting crude oil into the gasoline, heating oil and other products that he sold to his customers. Refineries form the key link in the oil business between producers and distributors; no company willingly relies on another at this critical stage of the business. K.C., with his thirst for control, hated having to depend upon Imperial and other big oil companies for supply. But he had no say in the matter; nobody really did in the global oil industry, which had been dominated since the 1920s by seven great companies, Esso, Shell, BP (British Petroleum), Gulf, Texaco, Mobil and Standard Oil of California.

The "Seven Sisters" bought crude all over the world and allocated it to markets according to their internal planning systems. They marketed their oil so as to obtain the highest possible prices, while paying the lowest possible prices to producers. "Their supranational enterprise was beyond the ability of national governments," wrote Anthony Sampson in *The Seven Sisters*, his definitive book on the global world of oil. "Their incomes were greater than those of most countries where they operated, their fleets of tankers had more tonnage than any navy, they owned and administered whole cities in the desert. In dealing with oil they were virtually self-sufficient, invulnerable to the laws of supply and demand, and to the vagaries of the stock markets, controlling all the functions of their business and selling oil from one subsidiary to another."[23]

As the 1950s closed the world was awash in cheap oil. The big oil companies were spending millions in the heartlands of eastern Canada and the northeastern United States to set up facilities allowing them to import crude from Venezuela and the Middle East, which was considerably cheaper than anything available in western Canada or the United States. Refineries for imported crude, tanker fleets, deep-water ports, pipelines and related facilities were the order for all the majors. Imperial Oil was building a large refinery in Dartmouth, Nova Scotia. Gulf Oil was erecting a $50-million facility in Point Tupper on Nova Scotia's Strait of Canso. Newfoundland Refining Co., a wholly owned subsidiary of Shaheen Natural Resources Co. of New York, was building a 30,000-barrel-a-day refinery in Come-By-Chance.

K.C.'s time had also come. He had, in fact, tried to build his own refinery twice before. In 1930 he had travelled to the Manhattan boardroom of Standard Oil of New Jersey, the American parent company of Imperial Oil, to discuss forming a partnership to erect one in Saint John. Hearing the price tag, though, he dropped the idea. In 1946, he thought about it again, then also backed off. A decade later, the timing seemed perfect. In early 1956 Irving approached BP with a proposal to form a partnership to build a refinery. A deal was not in the cards: BP wanted to build the refinery in Halifax, not Saint John. Moreover, BP wanted a clause giving them control of Irving Oil after K.C.'s death.

By then K.C. already had another potential partner on the hook. The worldwide oil glut had caused big headaches in San Francisco, where the tower of the Standard Oil Company of California looms over the bay like a fortress. Socal was an offspring of the break-up of John D. Rockefeller's Standard Oil empire. It was a huge outfit, but conservative, especially when it came to exploring for new crude sources abroad. Nonetheless, Socal was one of the first of the American sisters to win concessions in Bahrain and Saudi Arabia in the early 1930s. When the big U.S. sisters decided to form the Arabian-American Oil Company (Aramco) to exploit Saudi Arabia's huge petroleum reserves, Socal was left with a healthy 30-per-cent share.

But by the mid-1950s there was so much crude sloshing around that Socal couldn't find outlets for its share of the gigantic Arabian reserves.[24] Consequently it wasn't living up to its commitments to buy its 30 per cent. So in late 1955 Socal's chairman, R.G. Follis, ordered an analysis of possible new outlets in the western hemisphere for its crude. His officials came back with a surprising choice: the Canadian province of New Brunswick. The local market, his intelligence told him, was dominated by an independent Canadian company named Irving Oil, which had no facilities to handle crude and no refining capacity and which already received its supply under a contract from Socal. As well, said the Socal officials, the company dearly wanted to build its own refinery but didn't have the cash or the expertise to do it alone.

Follis had never heard of Irving Oil or the man who owned it. The Socal chairman checked around. He liked what he heard. In May 1956 Socal's officials headed for Saint John to discuss the possibility of building a new refinery in the Maritimes. The Suez Crisis interrupted negotiations. Even so, in March 1957 K.C. let slip to journalists that he was considering building a refinery in either Saint John or Halifax. When the negotiations resumed two months later, Socal was represented by Henry Judd, the oil company's treasurer, and W.H. Beekhuis, a Socal vice-president. Across the table sat K.C. and his 26-year-old son, Arthur.

It took three months to hammer out a deal. Socal agreed to buy 49 per cent of the stock of Irving Oil and to take 51 per cent of the stock of Irving Refining Ltd., the company created to build the refinery. Socal's engineers would supervise the design and construction, its scientists would provide the refining know-how, and its technicians would run the huge operation. Irving Refining agreed to buy all its crude from Socal, giving the American giant a foothold in the expanding eastern Canadian gasoline market as well as an outlet for its Arabian crude.

K.C. was no longer in control — Socal and Irving Oil each got to vote 50 per cent of the shares and had the right to appoint an equal number of directors to the board of the new company. In his view, the sacrifice was worth it. Finally he had his refinery, and a long-term supply of crude to fuel it. More than that, the refinery deal signalled a breakthrough for K.C. By 1960 he owned 55 intermeshed, intermingled companies, and the value of his holdings was placed in the $300-million range. His pulp and lumber operations were now among New Brunswick's largest. His bus lines blanketed the three Maritime provinces. His media empire encompassed four New Brunswick daily newspapers (he was also erroneously thought to own the *Halifax Chronicle-Herald* and the *Halifax Mail-Star*) as well as radio and television stations in Moncton and Saint John. His oil company ran 1,900 service station outlets and owned an estimated 150 cargo vessels. Nevertheless, with the new refinery, K.C. served notice that he was no longer a rare, regional curiosity. He was ready to walk with giants.

At precisely 1:30 p.m. on July 20, 1960, a bizarre procession began snaking its way through the streets of Saint John.[25] It was, naturally enough, a rainy day, and the grimy fog hung in the air, in places almost hiding the thousands of people lining the streets, who had been given the afternoon off to witness one of the biggest days in Saint John history. They cheered and waved, first at the convertibles carrying the VIPs, then at the long string of Irving company floats that followed: a ship's mock-up representing Saint John Shipbuilding; a colourful forest scene from J.D. Irving Ltd., complete with lumberjacks, saws and pulpwood; even a giant specimen of boiler-making by Irving's Ocean Steel and Construction Limited. The parade made its way up Loch Lomond Road towards the mass of tanks, tubes and cylinders standing in what had once been a bare 700-acre stretch of hillside. Over 20,000 tons of steel and more than 65 miles of pipe had gone into the refinery, which was the largest and, at $50 million, the most costly private industrial project in New Brunswick's history. White space-age columns stretched 100 feet into the air. To the west, six towering white tanks spelled out the letters I-R-V-I-N-G, each of them holding 6 million gallons of crude. At the heart of the vast expanse, the lights of the huge catalytic re-former or "cat cracker" flickered mysteriously, as the machine used its 1,000-degree

Fahrenheit temperatures to blast heavy oil molecules into lighter molecules of gasoline and fuel oils. Soon Irving supertankers, 50,000 tons, over 750 feet long and 100 feet wide, would arrive in the harbour to pump their cargoes of Arabian crude into the refinery through a two-mile-long umbilical cord.

On the raised ceremonial platform K.C., Hattie and their three sons sat smiling broadly in the sea of visiting dignitaries. It was a day of pomp, circumstance and carefully planned spontaneity. Edgar Hodgins, the master of ceremonies and an old Irving hand, called K.C. and his family to the centre of the platform where Louis Robichaud, the newly elected premier of New Brunswick, praised Irving's aggressive drive "and his faith that here at home there are great opportunities." Next, Lieutenant-Governor Leonard O'Brien reminded the audience that they were standing near the spot where Samuel de Champlain, 356 years before, became the first white man to set foot in Canada. "Since then, many have contributed much to progress. Yet over all the years since Champlain broke the stillness of the forest primeval nothing of this magnitude has been seen. . . . Great as it is we see more. . . . We see the clear handiwork of a gifted individual who has once again accomplished an extraordinary and very great undertaking."

When it finally came time for K.C. to speak, he was typically self-effacing: "Today, a day I have looked forward to for many years, is the result of cooperation," he said. "You provided the demand for our products — we had the idea. Now we have the refinery." Thorough as ever, he explained in detail how the huge plant operated. Then Irving stepped back as the premier-elect turned a huge valve, symbolically bringing the refinery on stream while the crowd clapped and cheered. It was a great moment — certainly for Irving, but also for the green young premier who had grown up only miles from Bouctouche. And as the two men stood there, engulfed by the noise from the cheering crowds, it must have seemed like the start of a beautiful friendship.

It was, in truth, anything but.

5

The Knight Errant's Tale

*"It is quite clear," replied Don Quixote, "that you
are not experienced in this matter of adventures.
They are giants, and if you are afraid, go away
and say your prayers, whilst I advance and engage
them in fierce and unequal battle."*
— *Don Quixote*, Cervantes

LOUIS ROBICHAUD sits waiting in his Senate office deep in the East
Block on Parliament Hill. It is still before noon in December of
1989 and a square panel of gold sunshine falls on the hardwood
floor. He is dressed casually, wearing a light blue crew-necked
sweater, navy blue pants, black loafers and steel-rimmed glasses. At
64, he is tiny — only five-foot-five — and round with wavy, snow
white hair and a pinkish complexion. Dwarfed by the cathedral ceil-
ings, Gothic windows and overstuffed furniture, he seems elfin and
grandfatherly. Up close, though, the cosy illusion crumbles: he has
a prizefighter's mug with a broad nose, small, dark eyes and a neck
that disappears before it starts.

The senator, it is said, traces his ancestors back to Françoise La
Tour, the brave and romantic heroine who held the fortress at Saint
John against her husband's enemy in 1645 when he was away seeking
military aid for the ailing Acadian French. Before he was a teen,
the chunky youngster could out-box anyone in Saint-Antoine, the
tiny Acadian village in northeastern New Brunswick where he was
born. Since 1973 the only battles he has fought have been here, among
the tired men and women who shuffle through the corridors around
the Red Chamber. It is a pleasant enough world, filled with the easy
perks and privilege of parliamentary office. Robichaud sits on his

share of committees and fact-finding missions. But those who know him say that the senator is a man most comfortable living in the past. On the walls of his office, Robichaud's life is on display in all its turbulent glory.

There, within easy reach of his desk, hangs a black-and-white photograph of him taken in front of the old stone legislature building in Fredericton where he reigned as premier during the stormiest decade in the province's modern history. Nearby is a picture of Robichaud and his old Liberal ally Pierre Trudeau, who appointed the bristly Acadian to the Senate. Beside it hangs a framed Order of Canada, the country's highest honour. On the front wall, next to the door, is a blown-up *Moncton Times-Transcript* cartoon depicting him captaining "the Good Ship New Brunswick" through troubled seas. Hanging below it is a caricature of the senator seated at a desk reading "the Memoirs of K.C. Irving" while in the background, an armoured Don Quixote-like figure tilts at a windmill bearing the tricoloured Irving Oil logo. "We built democracy in New Brunswick," he says matter-of-factly between sips of coffee, his dark eyes dancing. "I would hate to think what the province would be like if our government had never come along."

Nearly two decades after he was driven into the political purgatory of the Senate at the tender age of 48, he remains very much the scrappy backwoods politico, reliving ancient glories and levelling blasts at old enemies. Blasts at his old political nemesis Charlie Van Horne, a man he dismisses for his links to K.C. Irving and as "a menace to common sense." Blasts at the "bigoted" Michael Wardell, the high-born British socialite and confidant of Lord Beaverbrook and King Edward VIII who used the newspaper he owned, the *Fredericton Daily Gleaner*, to champion Irving's causes and to stir up anti-French racism in the province — "His actions were unforgivable." And, of course, blasts at Kenneth Irving himself, who "thought that he could own everything" and who, Robichaud insists, tried to topple the government when the premier stood in his way.

"It was common sense versus K.C. Irving and his cohorts," declares the senator, summing up his epic conflict with the industrialist. The story he tells unfolded throughout an entire decade; it was played out in full public view as well as in shadowy political backrooms and corporate boardrooms. The whole truth — if such a thing exists

— will never be known, since Irving, cast in the villain's role in the drama, has never broken his silence on the subject. But Robichaud, never short on ego, sees himself to this day in nothing less than mythic terms — a 20th-century Don Quixote daring to battle the most powerful giant ever to stride across the New Brunswick landscape. The difference, of course, is that Cervantes's famous knight errant fought giants that existed only in his troubled imagination; Robichaud's giant was quite real.

On June 23, 1960, the day after he startled New Brunswick by becoming the first Acadian elected to the premiership, Robichaud had a much different attitude towards the tycoon. A small group of supporters had gathered at Robichaud's home in Richibucto, on the province's east coast. Around 11 a.m., a deep humming sound rose above the conversation. A few heads turned to look out the front window just in time to see a float plane splashing down at the end of the otherwise calm bay. The plane slowly coasted up to the town's battered public wharf. Out stepped a tall, well-dressed, wide-shouldered man wearing a fedora. On his way to Quebec City on business, K.C. Irving had stopped to pick up Dan Riley, his real estate lawyer, and to offer his congratulations to the new premier.

The industrialist and the politician were not exactly strangers. Although a generation apart, the two grew up in towns only 10 miles away from each other. Irving may well have been in the audience in 1937 when the chunky 12-year-old Louis Robichaud pedalled his bicycle from Saint-Antoine to Bouctouche to hear Liberal premier Allison Dysart address the party faithful. Even before entering university, Louis had decided that he would follow in Dysart's footsteps. In Richibucto, where he set up a small law practice upon graduation, he paid his dues; allying himself with the right people, he won a seat in the legislature in 1952. Six years later he took a tight two-man race for the Liberal party leadership. Few people expected much from the Grits and their diminutive leader when Premier Hugh John Flemming — the man who had led the provincial Tories from the wilderness in 1952 — called an election in 1960.

Saint Louis, as he was known on the hustings, fooled them all. Tirelessly stumping across the province, he delighted New Brunswickers with his blood-and-thunder speeches, cocky confidence and

tart attacks on the Tories. The Liberals didn't have much of a platform, just Robichaud's promise to lift the $50-a-family premium tax
that Flemming had imposed to finance the province's new hospital
insurance scheme. In the end, that was enough for them to squeak
past the tired Tories.

Not everybody was surprised by the upset. K.C. Irving had been
watching the province's latest political shift with keen interest. Born
on the province's northeastern shore, he grew up in a Liberal hotbed
and always considered himself a Grit. In the 1930s he was a prominent
party bagman, criss-crossing the province with Fred Pirie, a powerful
potato exporter from Grand Falls, to raise funds for Premier Allison
Dysart, who was born in Bouctouche.[1] Yet he was no ideologue:
Irving attended Diefenbaker rallies in 1957 and 1958, and over the
years he contributed to both the Liberals and Conservatives, and
even, it is said, to the CCF once.

His interest was purely practical. "I don't think business and politics mix in New Brunswick," K.C. once said. "New Brunswick is
too small for politics." In his view, staying on hospitable terms with
the government was simply good business. After all, Ottawa and Fredericton were always some of his companies' best customers. The provincial government was one of the biggest buyers of Irving's oil and
timber; much of the woodland he developed was owned by the province; federal government contracts were the main jobs that kept the
Irving shipyards busy. Charlie Van Horne, who should know as much
as anyone about Irving's view of government, has another explanation for K.C.'s attitude towards politics: "The government has the
power to levy taxes. Irving had an absolute aversion to paying them."

Arthur Irving apparently once boasted that his father had never
lost an election in New Brunswick.[2] That may just have been the
bragging of a proud son. But certainly K.C.'s judgement in guessing
the outcomes of New Brunswick elections has been pretty well perfect. Be that as it may, his relations with governments usually followed
a familiar pattern: when a new party came in, he was at first polite
and helpful. Eventually disillusionment would set in; perhaps an Irving request would be denied. Maybe the government would make
some unexpected demands. Or perhaps they would even have the
temerity to criticize Irving business practices. Whatever the cause,

the outcome was generally the same: romances between K.C. Irving and governments were usually short-lived.

The question of how much pressure K.C. actually exerted on provincial governments has fuelled endless late-night debates among those who populate the backrooms of New Brunswick politics. One thing certain, though, is that a government seldom stayed in power for long after K.C. had ceased to smile upon it. Irving was said to have gotten along fine with John D. McNair, the stubborn, irascible Liberal who shared the industrialist's Scots ancestry and was premier from 1940 to 1952. Fine, that is, until K.C. learned that the reason an Irving bus line running from Kent Country to Moncton was doing poorly was that people living in the area had begun forming car pools. Irving, so it is said, tried to have the pools declared illegal by the provincial government. When McNair declined, the relationship became strained.[3]

McNair's Tory successor, Hugh John Flemming, another Scot, remained in Irving's favour longer than most. In the late 1950s things turned sour. Flemming, so Irving always claimed, had promised the tycoon first crack at buying a 90-acre piece of government land on Saint John's Courtenay Bay, which Irving planned to use to expand his shipyard. Things grew complicated when a consortium of foreign and Canadian forestry companies, calling itself Rothesay Paper Co., appeared on the scene and expressed interest in the same land as a site for a new pulp operation.

Flemming began scrambling to find a way to extricate the government from its commitment to the industrialist. Irving howled with anger. When the legislature approved a bill giving Rothesay the same protection from nuisance suits and expropriation that the Irving pulp mill already enjoyed, he wrote to Flemming that he was "very disappointed over the form in which the Rothesay Paper Corporation Bill was enacted."[4]

The alternative to Flemming was a fiery Acadian named Louis Robichaud. "Lord Beaverbrook and K.C. Irving were watching me on T.V. one night during the [1960] campaign," Robichaud told his biographer, Della Stanley. "Beaverbrook said, 'That is the next premier of New Brunswick.' From that moment on K.C. Irving started supporting me and the Liberal party."[5] Throughout the campaign

Irving took his usual approach of publicly allying himself with neither party. Behind the scenes, though, his allegiance — and his money — was with the Acadian.[6] To this day, some of Robichaud's enemies still claim that Irving paid off $150,000 of his outstanding debts before the election. Ned Belliveau, Robichaud's former publicity director, denies this and puts Irving's contributions to the Liberal campaign at about $35,000, still a large amount in those days. For his part, Robichaud maintains that he always left the fund-raising to others. "Nelson Rattenbury [the Liberals' chief bagman] understood that I didn't want to know who had contributed what." All the same, on that June day in 1960, the green young premier-elect knew that he had much for which to thank the Saint John industrialist.

Standing together by Robichaud's front window, the two men were a study in contrasts: the tall, teetotalling Scots Presbyterian and the short, hard-drinking French Catholic. The conversation was brief and amiable. About all Robichaud can really remember is that Irving said he was proud that another Kent County Liberal had become premier (Dysart, who was a pallbearer at J.D. Irving's funeral, being the first). After less than five minutes of polite small talk, Irving shook hands with the rest of the room. Then, with Dan Riley in tow, he boarded his plane and headed for Quebec City.

His campaign to woo the impressionable, unsophisticated premier was really just beginning. From the start, Irving, who once described the two of them as "just a couple of Kent boys trying to do something for our province," was deferential and gracious towards the younger man. When it came time for the official opening of the giant Irving refinery in Saint John, K.C. made sure that Robichaud was by his side even though it was still weeks before he would be officially installed as premier. Ned Belliveau remembers how Irving's fabled personal courtesy was on display when Robichaud travelled to Saint John, soon after taking office, for the launch of a new Irving oil tanker. K.C. was waiting to personally greet the premier and his entourage when their plane landed in the pouring rain at the Irving airport. After the aircraft had taxied to a stop, Irving drove his station wagon out onto the tarmac and hustled over to raise an umbrella over his visitors as they disembarked. Like an ageing hotel doorman, the millionaire escorted them to his car, stooping awkwardly to hold the umbrella over the tiny politician.

Robichaud, if the truth be known, was ripe for seduction. He had grown up in Kent County, well aware of the Irving legend. Charles McElman, the premier's closest adviser, once said that Robichaud "worshiped K.C. Irving as a god."[7] When Irving's shipyard needed work, Robichaud went to bat for him in Ottawa, personally calling on Prime Minister Lester Pearson and winning two important government contracts. Publicly, at least, Robichaud supported Irving's pet Chignecto Canal scheme. Before long, the two men were meeting regularly to discuss New Brunswick's industrial policy. Robichaud even came to enjoy the austere businessman's company, still chuckling years later about how Irving liked to bet that he could guess how many minutes and seconds it would take to reach their destination when they were travelling on one of his private aircraft. "K.C. was a good sport," he remembers.

Ironically, the first chill between the two boys from Kent County was caused by the very issue that had brought them together. When Premier Flemming balked at Irving's demands to keep Rothesay Paper out of Saint John, K.C. carried his fight to the floor of the Fredericton legislature, where he fought to block passage of the bill incorporating the new company. He found staunch allies among the Liberal opposition, who pummelled the government over the Rothesay question. Among Irving's biggest boosters was Louis Robichaud, then the Liberal leader, who won points with the industrialist by reading into the record an editorial from the *Fredericton Daily Gleaner* opining that the province "should not endanger a greater industry to placate a newcomer."[8]

In power, Robichaud saw the situation differently. Like every New Brunswick premier before and after, he was eager to foster new industrial development at almost any cost. The virtues of having a big new player like Rothesay in the province's pulp and paper industry were undeniable. More important, Robichaud understood that if the deal with Rothesay fell through, outside investors would give up on New Brunswick, concluding that it was Irving's private fiefdom. Anxious to resolve the dispute amicably, Robichaud summoned K.C. and Walter Forster, the Rothesay president, to Fredericton to work out a solution. After much coaxing, Forster eventually agreed to consider another piece of land on the Saint John harbour as a site for the Rothesay operation. Irving, however, made it clear that the land was not the issue. Recalls Robichaud: "The point was that he did not want Rothesay coming in." True to form when he was denied what he wanted, Irving lashed out at Forster. Eventually his harangue became too much. For a moment the two industrialists stood and squared off, apparently ready to trade punches. The diminutive premier stepped in and called a hasty adjournment to the talks.

It was up to Robichaud to reach a solution. On November 28, 1960, the contentious 90-acre site on Courtenay Bay went to Irving's shipyard, not Rothesay, for $1. At the same time, the government managed to find a nearby 110-acre site, disentangled it from a complex legal situation, sweetened the deal with guarantees of steam and water from a nearby generating plant and sold it to the foreign conglomerate. As for Irving, he said little in public to criticize the government, even after Rothesay Paper sought and received legislative authority to set up a multimillion-dollar paper mill on its new land. Still, he must have realized, perhaps for the first time, that Robichaud had his own agenda — one that had little to do with Irving's own interests.

By that time, Robichaud and Irving were meeting regularly on another matter, one that would eventually lead to the final, terrible break between the two men. Ever since a prospector had discovered iron in the hills near Bathurst in 1902, the downtrodden inhabitants of northeastern New Brunswick had dreamed of breaking their cycle of poverty. For the next 40 years, except for a brief period in 1943, the property lay dormant. Then Matthew James Boylen arrived. Florid, fat and persuasive, Jim Boylen was a mining promoter in the classic mould, a lovable rogue who made his way through life on a smile, some fast talk and big dreams. He loved the grand gesture, showering $100 bills on small-town telephone operators and giving his best friend a Cornelius Krieghoff oil painting that years later turned out to be a fake.

By 1952, with his dream of the big score rapidly slipping away, Boylen obtained an option on the Bathurst property and raised $1 million from an American syndicate led by Gilbert Kerlin, a well-connected New York lawyer. Boylen's geologists sank a series of holes, all of them disappointing. His money almost gone and his spirits at rock bottom, he was ready to give up. He probably would have, if a retired mining executive living in the area had not spread a map out on the floor one day and showed Boylen where he thought the treasure was buried. He agreed to one last effort. In December 1952 his drill bit struck one of the richest base-metal discoveries in North America: an ore body containing some 28 million tons of lead, zinc, silver and copper.

Rumours of a major find were soon circulating through northern New Brunswick. Boylen was busily staking the land in the area. His lawyer was Ed Byrne, a man who would play a major role in virtually every important event in New Brunswick over the next 20 years. Some time after Christmas, Boylen called and urged Byrne to pick up shares in New Larder, a shell company the promoter controlled. "I decided to wait and watch," Byrne recalls. "A day or so later a block of 250,000 shares changed hands. So I called my broker in Saint John and told him to buy me 250,000 shares, which were then trading for five cents apiece. It took two or three days but he finally got them. In January Boylen calls him and says tomorrow is the day."[9]

Indeed. The next day, January 23, 1953, the *Northern Miner*, the *Toronto Globe and Mail* and the other financial papers were brimming with news from Boylen's press conference announcing the find. What followed was one of the greatest trading booms in the history of the Toronto Stock Exchange. Within four days New Larder shares were selling as high as $2.60. Millions of other New Brunswick mining company shares changed hands, driving up prices in companies with colourful names like Nubar, New Norseman, Kayboycon and New Highridge, all of them controlled by Boylen. He was rich, at least on paper, and so was Byrne.

News of the find triggered a full-fledged mining boom as prospectors poured into Bathurst — sleeping in hotel lobbies when all the rooms filled up — to stake their claims. Representatives from some of the world's biggest mining concerns trooped into Ed Byrne's Bathurst office to discuss buying into the ore body. On one day alone he met with 25 different companies on Boylen's behalf. Finally Boylen decided to throw his lot in with St. Joseph's Lead Co., a New York City-based giant, which agreed to put up $9 million in capital as well as provide the managerial skills for the project. In return, St. Joe's received a controlling stake in Brunswick Mining and Smelting Corp., an amalgam of Boylen's mining interests.

But St. Joe's had huge minerals holdings in the United States and Rhodesia. As a result, the company seemed more intent on preventing Brunswick Mining's lead, zinc and silver from deflating the already soft world base-metal markets than on developing the Bathurst mine. In 1958, blaming the high cost of refining the ore and the collapse of the global base-metal markets, St. Joe's closed down the Bathurst operation altogether, putting 195 people out of work. Boylen, naturally, wanted the mine back up and running. His options, though, were limited; St. Joe's owned $2.5 million worth of Brunswick Mining shares and was owed $7.5 million by the company. On November 18, 1959, Boylen wrote to Premier Flemming that he was "working hard to have control of Brunswick Mining and Smelting restored to Canada . . . [but] as long as we owe them money they have operating control."[10] Brunswick Mining's saviour, if one emerged, would have to have deep pockets.

Throughout the 1960 election campaign, Louis Robichaud slammed the Tories for not forcing St. Joe's to keep the mine in operation; he also called for construction of a mill to convert the concentrate before it was shipped overseas. Once in power, he was determined to see his ambitions through. St. Joe's and Sogemines, the Canadian affiliate of a Belgian mining giant that now had control of Brunswick Mining, tried to appease Robichaud with a promise to build their own mill. Boylen, however, wanted no more to do with St. Joseph. He needed a liberator, one with lots of cash. So, naturally, he turned to K.C. Irving.

Irving didn't hesitate. "I asked him for $3 million," Boylen told a reporter. "He didn't blink an eyelid, and accepted."[11] Boylen wanted a mining company involved in the blossoming partnership. So he approached Erskine Carter, a Saint John lawyer, who was the president of Patino Mining Corp., a Bolivian mining group. Sogemines was also invited in. Together the group bought out St. Joseph's Lead for $10.5 million. The province agreed to guarantee the $20 million in financing necessary to build a mine, mill, smelter and chemical complex near Bathurst. It also eased Brunswick Mining's path with the usual collection of long-term tax agreements and juicy concessions, including protection from "nuisance suits" and the exclusive right to smelt lead and zinc concentrates in the province.

Control over the north shore's mineral deposits was again in New Brunswick hands. Yet not everyone was happy. Lord Beaverbrook, a friend and confidant of both Irving and Robichaud, had repeatedly warned the government of the danger of allowing the industrialist to have his fingers in too many New Brunswick pies.[12] Ed Byrne, as well, worried that the government was being overly generous to Brunswick Mining and that the loans were not well enough secured.[13] The premier, in his euphoria, ignored the sceptics.

Robichaud had big dreams, and they went far beyond simply creating jobs and bringing industry to New Brunswick. Though a political pragmatist, he was, at heart, a social reformer.

From the beginning, much of what Robichaud did as a politician was designed to redress the inequities he had seen while growing up in rural New Brunswick, where grade school was the end of formal education and health and welfare services were woefully inadequate, compared with what was available in prosperous urban centres like Fredericton and Moncton. At the root of the problems was the rotting, unworkable municipal taxation and finance system, which was the foundation for the distribution of power and money in New Brunswick. "The rich counties got richer and the poor counties got poorer," recalls Robichaud. "It was a system of inequality."

The only way to change things, as Robichaud saw it, was to rewrite the province's entire taxation and finance system. For that mammoth task he chose Ed Byrne, the canny corporate lawyer who had made a killing on the Bathurst mineral boom. Byrne agreed to head a royal commission set up in the late summer of 1960 to look into the problems. Their recommendations were startling: they wanted a complete overhaul of an "antiquated and ineffectual structure of government singularly unsuited to the needs of the times." The Liberals took almost two years to ponder the proposals. On November

16, 1965, Robichaud introduced the first of what would be 130 bills "designed to blast the province's pattern of municipal legislation into the space age in one legislative shot."[14]

Change didn't come easy; pushing through all the legislation, which became known as the Programme of Equal Opportunity, took the Liberals two exhausting years and came close to driving them out of power. What Robichaud was proposing was nothing less than a social and economic revolution; what he got was civil war, plain and simple. The loudest outcry against Equal Opportunity came, naturally enough, from those who stood to lose power and influence if the proposals became law.

K.C. Irving had strong concerns. For years he had grown rich by playing the various municipal councils off against one another, enabling him to get the best possible tax deal for his companies. Irving Pulp & Paper, J.D. Irving, Ocean Steel, Brunswick Mining and Smelting, Saint John Shipbuilding and Dry Dock and the Irving refinery all enjoyed juicy tax breaks with fixed rates, regardless of inflation and changing land values. The amounts were often absurdly low in comparison with taxes paid by private individuals. Under the original agreements, taxes for the $50-million refinery, for example, moved from $51,500 in 1960 to a projected $75,000 in 1990 — a fraction of what the usual business taxes would have been for an operation of that size. Irving Pulp & Paper paid a fixed rate of $65,000, about one-quarter of what it would normally have forked out. [15]

Now it seemed that Robichaud wanted to change those agreements. The showdown came during hearings held by the Law Amendments Committee, which was set up to give members of the public a chance to voice their opinions on the legislation. There wasn't an empty seat in the house on December 14, 1965, when Irving began to speak in cold, unwavering tones to Norbert Thériault, the ill-fated minister responsible for piloting the Equal Opportunity program through its initial stages. Although claiming the program was fine in principle, K.C. called the Assessment Act "completely unacceptable" and said that "no sane person is going to agree with the method." He added, "They should understand that some industries are liable to choke to death. Others," he hinted, "may have to pull back on expansion plans."[16]

Irving's diatribe continued for 12 brutal hours. Finally Thériault could stand it no longer. Reading from a prepared statement late in the evening, he said that there had been a misunderstanding: "There is no provision in this act whereby existing tax concession agreements can or will be broken. Nor is there any intention by the government to break any such agreements." Irving, at least in the eyes of most New Brunswickers, had faced down the Robichaud government. The battle lines were plainly drawn.

Robichaud's ordeal by fire was just beginning. The Irving newspapers delighted in the controversy, continuing to dwell on the revocation of tax concessions long after it was even an issue. Their tone was downright tame compared with that of Michael Wardell's *Fredericton Daily Gleaner*, the only non-Irving English paper in the province. Almost daily, the *Gleaner* editorial page denounced the immoral, power-crazed Liberals and their leader. "Mr. Robichaud is rattled," said the *Gleaner* editorial on January 21, 1966. "He is hitting wild and revealing the incompetence he has been at pains to conceal over the past years, when he was presenting himself as a dynamic leader and a creator of a new industrial age for New Brunswick . . . . He came to the premiership by falsehood. He has bragged and he has boasted and he has monstrously abused those who are his rightful critics."

The opposition to Equal Opportunity came from all sides — even from the pulpit, where a United Church minister accused Robichaud of accepting graft. A complete review of Robichaud's finances found no basis for the charges. But by that time the premier's private world was spinning out of control. Robichaud was drinking more regularly. A son, Jean-Claude, had just been diagnosed as having an incurable kidney disease. All the while, the attacks against Equal Opportunity grew uglier and more personal: taunting classmates harassed his four children; his wife, who was being treated for depression, was tormented by obscene telephone calls. The premier himself began receiving death threats, including one letter warning, "The KKK will get you." Eventually the Robichaud family was placed under police protection.

By the spring of 1967, the Liberals had pushed most of the sweeping reform proposals through the legislature, but at great expense.

With an election only months away, Robichaud and his party were exhausted and disheartened. Two leading caucus members had died, three others resigned. Charles McElman, Robichaud's top lieutenant, had accepted an appointment to the Senate. As if that wasn't enough, another bitter feud was brewing with K.C. Irving, this time over the mineral deposits on New Brunswick's north shore. Robichaud's grandiose plans for the Bathurst mining-smelting complex were stalled. In early 1963, Irving and Erskine Carter went to Robichaud and asked for an extension on the starting date for construction of the smelter. The project had run into technical problems, they said. Moreover, it was already clear that it was going to cost far more than the $20 million they had originally estimated.

The odd thing is that as the project sank deeper into trouble, Irving was committing his companies even further to the undertaking. A Toronto Stock Exchange statement filed in the fall of 1964 showed that K.C., by himself and through Kent Line, had quietly acquired 38 per cent of Brunswick Mining, the biggest single stake. What's more, virtually all the money being spent on the project was going to Irving companies. A glance at the October 31, 1966, accounts payable for East Coast Smelting and Chemical Co., the company building the smelter, showed that it owed $2,707,158.42 to suppliers and $7,045,314.99 to "associated companies," almost all of which were owned by Irving. Engineering Consultants Ltd., a major new Irving subsidiary, was designing and managing the construction of the smelter. Mace Ltd., another Irving outfit, was the general contractor. Naturally they hired Irving companies almost exclusively as subcontractors and suppliers. Ocean Steel and Construction was in charge of the structural steel work. Industrial Security Ltd., an Irving company, looked after security. Irving Oil supplied the oil; Thorne's Ltd. (the hardware retailer), the tools; Commercial Equipment Ltd., the cranes and bulldozers; and J.D. Irving Ltd., the wood products. Three hundred miles from Bathurst, Irving's Saint John Shipbuilding was building a 32,000-ton ore carrier to carry the concentrates overseas.[18]

K.C.'s companies had such a lock on the project that even the Liberal party faithful were left out in the cold. "At present, hard working Liberals in the area were not being taken care of as they had been led to believe they would," one of Robichaud's field men wrote in a letter to the premier in August 1964. "Unless you use Irving gas, you don't get your truck to work." Passing the report on to Irving, Robichaud commented: "There may be an answer to the problems but let me assure you that politically speaking the present situation is not too good."[19]

It was about to get far worse. When Irving asked for another extension on the smelter project in 1965, the political opposition was understandably irate. After all, the longer it took to build the smelter complex, the more money Irving made. Robichaud, however, desperately needed the smelter and the jobs it would create. In April 1966, the government guaranteed a $30-million refinancing of the project. As it turned out, even that wasn't enough. A year later Irving was back, asking the province for another $20 million. Robichaud refused. By that time the smelter was expected to cost roughly $70 million, almost four times as much as the original estimate. Brunswick Mining's losses were nearing $10 million, its working capital deficit was thought to be approaching $60 million, and Brunswick Mining shares had sunk to just a fraction of their peak price of $20.[20]

The company, for all intents and purposes, was broke. Irving blamed Robichaud for forcing construction of the project to begin prematurely. Boylen and Erskine Carter blamed Irving for running the project into the ground while his companies made millions. The premier didn't really care who was to blame. All he knew was that the government had already sunk $20 million into the project and the Irving companies were still owed another $28 million. So Robichaud called his old troubleshooter, Ed Byrne, who agreed to help. Byrne approached a number of big mining companies, including Falconbridge Mines and Consolidated Mining and Smelting, about putting money into the project. They turned him down. Ironically, so did St. Joseph's Lead, the company that had been pushed out by the Irving group. Nobody was interested.

That's where Jim Boylen's decades in the mining patch came in. In late 1966, Boylen called Alf Powis, the patrician president of Toronto-based Noranda Mines Ltd., with a proposal: why not merge Noranda and Brunswick Mining on the basis of their current share

values, then roughly $50 per Noranda share and $10 for each Brunswick Mining share? Powis was interested enough to fly a group of
Noranda officials to Bathurst to examine the operation. They returned with a favourable report about the mine but grave concerns
about the operation's huge cost overruns. When Powis asked to see
Brunswick Mining's financial statements, Boylen was reticent. Finally
he handed them over. It took Powis and the Noranda officials about
30 seconds to conclude that the company was bankrupt. "That's the
end of it," Powis bluntly replied when Boylen called the next day
to ask if they had a deal.

By now Boylen was desperate. Within weeks a banknote was coming due; the company needed to be refinanced. After much arm-
twisting he convinced Powis to travel to Fredericton one day in March
1967 to meet with a group of Brunswick Mining officials, including
himself and Erskine Carter. The group agreed on one thing: the main
problem was that the complex was entirely under Irving's control.
There was even some paranoid speculation that K.C. was deliberately
out to bankrupt the company so that he could pick up the assets
cheaply on the open market.

Finally, after many offers and counter-offers, Carter came up with
a scheme that Powis could live with. Noranda agreed to put up $50
million to pay Brunswick's debts and to lend $20 million for com-
pletion of the smelter. In return, the company would receive $49.5
million worth of bonds convertible into common shares and 100,000
preferred shares, each of which carried 100 votes per share. Noranda,
as a result, would have the equivalent of 51 per cent of the Brunswick
Mining common shares, 8 out of 15 seats on the board of directors
and management over the project. As for K.C. — he would be reduced to a lowly minority shareholder.

Just after midnight the group drove across town to visit the premier, who had just returned from an out-of-town trip. The group
outlined the proposal. Robichaud, eager to prevent the mining complex from failing, agreed to support the agreement even though he
was surrendering control of the biggest industrial enterprise ever un-
dertaken in the Atlantic provinces to an Ontario company. "It was
a case of getting the money and the expertise," recalls Robichaud.
"Noranda could provide both."

K.C. did not go quietly. At a stormy meeting attended by 63 shareholders on June 22, he argued that Robichaud and the government had pressured Brunswick Mining's directors into signing the agreement, and that Noranda was paying too little to take over the company. Indeed, Irving would claim forevermore that he was ready to make a better offer, a $63.5-million deal that would have kept the company in New Brunswick hands. The Brunswick directors, however, had made up their minds. In the end 82 per cent of the votes were cast in favour of the take-over. Noranda was in, Irving was out.[21]

It was a dicey situation. K.C. was still a large shareholder. More important, he claimed to be owed $72 million by Brunswick Mining. He wanted his money. In the fall of 1967 he filed 31 legal actions against Brunswick Mining, claiming that his companies were owed $15 million for work on the mine and smelter sites. One of the lawsuits related to a couple of ships being built to move the New Brunswick ore to Europe. Originally they were to be christened the *M.J. Boylen* and the *Louis Robichaud*. After the trouble began their names were left as the *H10-60* and *H10-70*.

K.C. was taking the whole thing personally. Busy as he was, K.C. stubbornly sat through the long, drawn-out legal proceedings. After spending one long day being grilled by J.J. Robinette, the famed Toronto trial lawyer acting for Irving, Noranda's Alf Powis happened to walk out the courtroom door at the same time as K.C. "Well, Mr. Powis," Irving said as if greeting an old friend, "we did not get much ore mined in there today, did we."[22]

The 1969 meeting began with K.C. announcing he was resigning as a Brunswick director. "I'm getting off because I do not agree with the way Brunswick Mining is being operated and I do not agree with the treatment people of this province are being subjected to." Shareholder after shareholder rose to demand that Brunswick pay its debts to the Irving companies. Arthur, K.C.'s son, called for the provincial government to nationalize the mine — an absurd suggestion, considering his views on the role of government in business. The shipyard workers, back for another visit, demanded a provincial royal commission to investigate the company's conduct. Tempers flared. Adjournment after adjournment was called so that the feuding parties could negotiate in private.[23]

It was wild stuff, more suited to the union hall than to the corporate boardroom. And it continued right through the 1970s and early 1980s. K.C.'s capacity for remembering a slight was infinite. At each Brunswick Mining annual meeting, Irving or his representatives would show up and harangue the Noranda directors over their management of the company. It was tedious and embarrassing; over the years, Noranda officials regularly approached K.C.'s three sons, offering to buy the family's shares, which still amount to about 20 per cent of the company. Their reply has always been the same: "Not while Dad is alive."

Certainly Irving never forgave Noranda, but his greatest wrath was reserved for Louis Robichaud, who had frustrated him once too often. A hint of what was ahead occurred during a Brunswick Mining directors' meeting in 1966, when Irving was warned that Robichaud would never consent to a particular proposal he had made. "In that case," K.C. countered, "perhaps we should get a new premier."[24] For that purpose, the austere businessman chose an unlikely tool — the flamboyant, fantastical Charles Van Horne.

To find Charlie Van Horne these days you have to look in the Calgary telephone book for a company known as Hospitality Management Consultants (HMC), which, its advertisement says, has been "serving hospitality businesses since 1964." HMC is found in the northwest end of Calgary, which is a lonely place on a bitterly cold Saturday afternoon in December. The office, in a low-rise building on a scrubby, deserted street, turns out to be a tiny, one-bedroom apartment that doubles as home for the former member of Parliament, former New Brunswick cabinet minister and former leader of the provincial Progressive Conservative party. There, from a large wooden desk next to his bed, he also conducts his other business sideline, which is selling gleaming Western-style hunting knives.

In his prime, he was a robust, imposing figure, nicknamed "Hurricane Van Horne" for his energy and whirlwind organizational abilities. Before politics he served in the RCMP and the wartime army, studied law by correspondence course and spent nearly a decade learning the art of business in the employ of K.C. Irving. These days Van Horne looks somewhat less mythic. Five heart attacks have robbed his body of its once-imposing girth, leaving him, at 68, painfully shrunken and frail. He walks slowly, as if trying to move his spare frame uphill.

With his white cowboy hat, skinny string ties, sparse moustache and Western-style leisure suits, he looks more like a tired pensioner on a bus tour than the charismatic wild man of New Brunswick politics he once was. In his heyday Van Horne was a hustler and populist whom the *Toronto Globe and Mail* once called "as close to a reincarnation of the late Huey Long of Louisiana as is likely to be inflicted on any province in Canada."[25] Full of bluster, he was a classic ward-heeler who entered the House of Commons in 1955 in the wake of accusations that on election day he had been seen offering a constituent a drink from "a small bottle." "Knowing my constituents," replied the unrepentant Van Horne, "I would have lost the election had I insulted any one of them by offering a drink of liquor from any kind of *small* bottle."[26] Seventeen years later, he left politics under the same shadow. He was forced to resign as New Brunswick's minister of tourism after the RCMP uncovered evidence that the most lucrative government tourism contracts were going to big-time Tory campaign contributors.

By his own admission, he would do anything to get a vote. When he had just started his political career, that meant canoeing alone down the Miramichi River to canvass voters in the villages and isolated cabins along the river's banks. Later, when he had some financial backing, he travelled the province by bus, giving away snappy white stetsons to anyone who crossed his path. These days his trademark white stetson and a roomful of photographs, plaques and other memorabilia are all that remains of Van Horne's bizarre political career — that and the bombast and rough charm that made him one of the most colourful figures ever to enliven the Canadian political scene.

Amazing stories roll off Van Horne's tongue. How he investigated Quebec separatists during World War II. How, after leaving the House of Commons in 1961, he sold Honda motorcycles to Utah Mormons, using bikini-clad girls riding trail bikes and wearing signs emblazoned with "My Honey Wears a Honda." How he helped run Ronald Reagan's campaign for governor of California in 1965. "I can't complain," he says, dark eyes flashing. "I have always done what I wanted. I have always had fun."

Yet the bravado fades when Van Horne is asked about the generally accepted notion that K.C. Irving brought him back to New Brunswick in 1966 to topple Louis Robichaud. Van Horne had spent more than a decade doing legal work, acquiring new properties and acting as a general fixer for Irving. The relationship continued while Van Horne was in the House of Commons; Irving continued to ask his opinion on business deals he was considering. "I returned because I had not gotten all the things I wanted done while in federal politics," Van Horne insists over cognac in his Calgary apartment, "not because Irving beckoned."

All the same, a few days before he announced his bid for the Tory leadership in 1966, an ad appeared in Wardell's *Gleaner* that quoted an unnamed New Brunswick industrialist describing Van Horne as "probably the best project organizer in Canada." When Van Horne was nominated for the Conservative leadership, K.C. Irving stood among the crowd on hand. Irving, so the story went, had paid off all Van Horne's outstanding debts so that he could return to New Brunswick and remain a member of the provincial bar association.

When asked if he was really Irving's puppet, Van Horne shakes his head. He says that this whole mistaken notion arose because, just before returning to New Brunswick, he had borrowed $50,000 "from some Americans who knew nothing about Irving" to cover some debts from an earlier campaign. When it comes to how much Irving actually contributed to the campaign that Van Horne and the Tories mounted against Robichaud's Liberals in 1967, his memory suddenly fades. "I think one Irving company contributed $15,000 but I can't be sure," he says. And when he says that, his weathered face wears an almost beatific innocence.

As the 1967 New Brunswick election campaign unfolded, it became clear that the Tory party was hitching its hopes on selling the personality of its charismatic leader. Sporting the slogan "Charles Cares," Van Horne bounded along the campaign trail with Don Messer and his Islanders in tow, waving his white stetson, tossing off wild promises and assuring New Brunswickers of "the complete and absolute suppression of the Robichaud dictatorship." Robichaud's old enemy, Wardell of the *Gleaner*, wrote gleefully, "[Robichaud] toyed with the opposition for years. He will toy no longer with a bold, two-fisted slugger pummelling him and his policies."[27]

Bold and two-fisted he was. Virtually ignoring the Equal Opportunity controversy, Van Horne unveiled his 113-point "Blueprint for a New Tomorrow," a document that promised everything from Fundy tidal power and a canal across the Isthmus of Chignecto — two of K.C. Irving's pet projects — to $30 million in pensions for widows, handicapped people and seniors. When it came to campaign invective, few could sink as low as Van Horne, who ridiculed Robichaud's drinking by stating, "These half-breeds shouldn't take liquor. . . . Louis can't take a drink, he has too much Indian in him." The premier, he said mockingly, was "a David of the Bible — a poor barefoot millionaire boy from Waterloo Row in Fredericton, fighting a mythical Goliath he calls the establishment."[28]

Even so, his early chances looked good. As an October 1967 *Toronto Star Weekly* profile of Van Horne said: "Charlie Van Horne is bold, bombastic, charming, cruel of tongue and full of hustle — a throwback to the days when politics were the same . . . .Four times, he's been successfully sued over bad debts, and neither his house, nor any of his three cars is registered in his own name . . . . Right now it looks as if he might be the next premier of New Brunswick . . . Holy Smokes!"[29]

That might have been true had Van Horne's insults and clumsy attempts to outbid the Liberals not played right into Robichaud's hands. Laboriously unrolling an eight-foot roll of newspaper clippings entitled "Conservative Platform," Robichaud mocked his opponents and raised doubts as to the credibility of Van Horne's grandiose plans. In public the Liberals stressed "responsible" government, in private they depicted Van Horne as an opportunist and puppet of K.C. Irving. Near the end of the campaign, Robichaud finally took aim at his real enemy. "If there is a man who wants to run this province, let him present himself to the people and be elected to office," he told a predominantly Acadian crowd in Bouctouche, Irving's home town, a week before the election. "This man who had his home not far from here, this man wants to run the province. Well, if he wants to run the province let him, like me, present himself before the people and seek election. That's democracy."[30]

"How does it feel to beat $500 million," asked the anonymous telegram Robichaud received on October 24, 1967, the day after the Liberals won a six-seat majority over Van Horne's Conservatives.[31] Within hours of the results, the Conservative leader had jumped in a camper van and headed across the U.S. border. He didn't get far, just to the Lahey medical clinic that K.C. Irving regularly visited outside Boston, where he checked in at K.C.'s expense to have his chest pain looked at. Robichaud, in truth, wasn't in much better shape. Pushing through the massive Equal Opportunity legislation and fighting the Van Horne–Irving axis had left him battered, exhausted and concerned about his family's and his own future. The Liberals were left directionless and dogged by internal dissension. Forced to raise taxes to rebuild a badly depleted provincial treasury, the government saw its popularity sag. Meanwhile, Robichaud's old enemies continued to dog him — including K.C. Irving, who showed up himself at the legislature in March 1969 to protest routine changes to the provincial Companies Act that would weaken the powers of minority shareholders and, he charged, remove him from the board of Brunswick Mining, which he was then suing.

When Robichaud called a snap election for October 26, 1970, he hoped the party could stir itself into action one last time. Richard Hatfield, the new Tory leader, chose the dullest of campaign themes: "We Need a Change." K.C. Irving, naturally, was in his corner.[32] Despite losing the popular vote, the Tories took 31 seats to the Liberals' 27. Within months, Robichaud had resigned his seat. He was through with politics. Instead, in 1973, broken and tired at the age of 48, he accepted Pierre Trudeau's invitation to enter the Senate.

Twenty years after accepting his just reward, Louis Robichaud squirms in the leather chair in his Senate office as he thinks back on his stormy political career and assesses his accomplishments and defeats. "I did everything I set out to do," he concludes. "I had no ambition to attain anything beyond the premiership of New Brunswick. I had had it with politics by the time I left." As for his old nemesis: "I think the last time I saw him was in Saint John. . . . Yes, that's right, at the opening of the Summer Games in 1985. Arthur, his son, said hi, and Brian Mulroney came over and gave me a big hug. But Kenneth Irving — he just pretended he didn't see me."

6

The Fourth Estate

Who controls the past controls the future. Who controls the present controls the past.
— *Nineteen Eighty-Four*, George Orwell

TUESDAY, MARCH 11, 1969, was a wet, blustery day in Ottawa, the kind of day that left the bureaucrats bustling along Parliament Hill soaked to the bone and swearing to write the foreign service exams at the earliest possible opportunity. The thermostat, no doubt, had been cranked higher in the crimson upper chamber where the venerable members of the Senate of Canada conducted their traditional business, which consisted mainly of neutering legislation that conflicted with the interests of the business community. If any of the ancient legislators were dozing in the heat, their eyes snapped open when Charles McElman, the Honourable Senator from New Brunswick, rose to his feet and began speaking. Dour, dark-haired and wearing his characteristic thick-rimmed glasses, McElman had entered the upper house three years earlier after spending more than a decade in the backrooms of the New Brunswick Liberal party. Since moving to the Senate, the shrewd Maritimer had quietly kept his own counsel. Today McElman broke his silence.

The occasion was an earlier motion by Senator Keith Davey — the bear-like former radio ad-man, Canadian Football League commissioner and Liberal party organizer — to launch a special Senate probe examining the ownership and control of Canada's media. McElman dropped a bombshell on the proceedings. "Sources that should have authentic information" had informed him that K.C. Irving had secretly bought the *Fredericton Daily Gleaner* six months earlier. This meant that the industrialist now owned all five of New

Brunswick's English-language daily newspapers, as well as one of the province's two private television stations and one out of only two radio stations in Saint John. His voice rising, McElman said the situation was simply intolerable. There have been many situations in New Brunswick "that cried out for media coverage because of involvement of public interest, but they received little or no attention from the Irving group because of the danger of involving an Irving interest other than the mass media." He urged the government to begin an immediate investigation into Irving's media holdings. "And if the evidence shows an improper monopoly, then I should hope that the law will be applied to remedy the situation."[1]

McElman's revelations were startling for all New Brunswickers, and even more so for employees at the *Gleaner*, who had no inkling that they were being paid by the province's most powerful businessman. *Gleaner* executives immediately began searching for the source of the leak, but came away empty-handed. The news had originated with Michael Wardell, the *Gleaner*'s former owner and still its publisher, who had spilled the information when he ran into a friend of McElman's on a trip to the United Kingdom.

Two days after the senator's speech, *Gleaner* readers opened up their papers to a front-page headline — "Control of the Daily Gleaner" — above two stories, "Wardell Remains Publisher" and "Irving Issues Statement." Both treated the deal as nothing more than a minor financial reorganization. "Mr. Irving some months ago became a major shareholder in the company which controls the Daily Gleaner," wrote Wardell. "For the good of the province and in the interests of the staff of the Gleaner, to retain control within the province as well as to safeguard my own interests, I invited Mr. Irving to acquire this interest in the company. I still have a substantial shareholding and I continue to exercise control of policy and full direction of the newspaper, with the help of a fine and efficient staff."[2]

K.C. also struggled to downplay the deal: "There is nothing secret about it. . . . In fact all the details of my involvement are included in a brief being submitted this week to the Canadian Radio and Television Commission in Ottawa."[3] Irving said that he could only presume that somehow McElman knew the information was being made available that week to the commission. "It is no secret that

Senator McElman is using his position in Ottawa to carry out a personal campaign to reflect on me and the news media in New Brunswick." Irving went on to deny that there was anything sinister about his latest media investment.

> I have not been involved in any way at any time in either the editorial or business operations of any of the newspapers, in the radio or television station . . . . Senator McElman has implied that there is something wrong with New Brunswickers owning and building businesses in New Brunswick. I don't agree with him. I have spent my whole life working in New Brunswick and I don't think New Brunswickers have to turn any enterprise over to outsiders. Does Senator McElman also believe that Canada would be better served if the news media were foreign owned and controlled? I have had many opportunities to sell the newspaper properties over the years, but it has been my view that they should be operated by New Brunswickers, not by some company with a head office in Toronto or some foreign country.

That was that; case closed as far as K.C. was concerned. A few years before he might have been right. After all, for decades New Brunswickers had suspected that the Irving-owned newspapers — the *Moncton Daily Times, Moncton Transcript, Saint John Telegraph-Journal* and *Saint John Evening Times-Globe* — gave their owner rather special treatment. Many people had no problem with that. Irving deserves good press, his adherents argued, and why shouldn't he have it? But the critics have always viewed things somewhat differently. Where were the stories about the effluents flowing from the Irving refinery and the poisoned air from the Irving pulp mill? Why during strikes involving Irving companies did the union side of the story never make it into K.C.'s papers? Why did the Irving papers' editorials mirror so closely the industrialist's own views on a whole range of subjects?

To this day no newspaper owned by a capitalist — and in Canada, which isn't? — is immune to this sort of criticism. How many stories, for instance, do the Thomson newspapers break about Ken Thomson's business interests, or do the Southam papers run about their owners' non-newspaper activities? In 1970 these two chains between them accounted for more than 32 per cent of English-language newspaper circulation. Irving's newspapers, by comparison, had less than 3 per cent of Canadian newspaper readers at that point. So why single out the New Brunswick papers? The difference was that in most Canadian cities and provinces, readers could buy another paper, one not owned by a single owner. In New Brunswick, finding an alternative point of view was difficult enough when Wardell, K.C.'s greatest booster, had owned the *Gleaner*. Now it had become downright impossible: if people wanted to read a daily English-language paper, they had to buy an Irving paper.

If Irving's papers were unlikely to give his affairs heavy scrutiny, who was? Certainly not his radio station, CHSJ, or its sister television station, which was the first privately owned TV station in the Maritimes when it went on the air on March 29, 1954; in 1970 it was Saint John's only station. As for probing reporters working for other employers, there simply weren't any. Occasionally a reporter from Toronto or Montreal made a pilgrimage to Saint John to write about the Irving empire. Otherwise K.C.'s media were virtually without competition. New Brunswick was the missing link in CBC Television's English-language network — the only province without a station owned and operated by the corporation. Over the years the CBC had made sporadic attempts to buy CHSJ. In 1970 they even applied for a licence for a new television station in New Brunswick before the Canadian Radio-Television Commission. The CRTC refused, saying the New Brunswick market, already served by CHSJ and a Moncton CTV affiliate, was not big enough for another competitor.

No doubt Charles McElman's critics were right when they said that he was the mouthpiece of the New Brunswick Liberal party's hostility to Irving. But the senator had a simple rationale for revealing K.C.'s *Gleaner* purchase when and where he did: he thought the only way to spark some coverage of the media monopoly in New Brunswick was to grab the attention of the central Canadian papers and the Canadian Press, the national wire service that sends its stories to member papers throughout the country, including the Maritimes.

McElman's proddings hit a nerve in Ottawa. In fact, it had been obvious that the federal government was starting to look askance at Irving's communications monopoly two years earlier, when the CRTC had refused his application for a Saint John cable-TV licence. Now the pressures really began to build.

No one ever really believed that K.C. personally meddled in the day-to-day affairs of his papers. Unlike many of the great press barons, he clearly wasn't interested in having a personal platform; he took great pains to point out that "editorial policy" was something he didn't really understand. K.C. always contended that he ran his newspapers just like his other businesses, to make money. Newspapers, after all, fit nicely into the empire, providing a market for Irving paper and an advertising outlet to promote his other businesses. K.C. actually seemed to view himself as the saviour, rather than the enemy, of the New Brunswick press. His critics might claim that he bought virtually all the province's media outlets because it was the easiest way to quiet independent commentary and analysis of his business operations, but K.C. waved the patriotic flag, claiming that he bought newspapers simply to prevent them from falling into the hands of outsiders.

In fact, Irving has always had a healthy respect for the power of the press, ever since he bought his first paper in the mid-1930s to give him a propaganda outlet in his battle with Fred Manning over the Saint John bus franchise. Before K.C. got hold of it, the *Maritime Broadcaster* used to run radio listings and was owned by a local auto-parts dealer. In the late 1930s the paper announced it was changing its name to the *Saint John Citizen* and henceforth would be published daily. At first, even the small reporting staff didn't know who the new owner was. "It quickly became clear that we had an editorial axe to grind. All of the Irving interests were sacred cows," recalls Charles Lynch, who started out as a $7-a-week reporter at the *Citizen* in 1935 and then went on to an illustrious journalistic career.

As a business, the *Citizen* was an immediate success: circulation grew, and soon it was sold all over the province.[4] Fred Manning, in retaliation, started his own paper, more like a pamphlet really, called the *Free Press*. So in 1936 Saint John had two new papers to challenge the established *Telegraph-Journal*. Competition was fierce among the three dailies; Lynch recalls that during King Edward's abdication at least a dozen special editions hit the Saint John streets in a single day. The Saint John newspaper war didn't last. Once the bus line battle with Manning ended, Irving sold the *Citizen* to the *Telegraph-Journal*, which closed it.

K.C.'s dabbling in the media, though, was just beginning. For one thing, he had already forged intriguing links with the *Halifax Herald* (later merged with the *Chronicle*), owned by Senator William Dennis. Gordon Daley, Dennis's corporate lawyer, surfaced in Saint John in 1936 as publisher of the *Citizen*. Soon afterwards the newspaper's typeface and masthead began to closely resemble the *Halifax Herald*'s. Rumours that Irving was part owner of the Halifax newspapers continued to circulate well into the 1970s, particularly after Daley's son, Lawrence, a senior member of the board of directors of the Halifax papers, became one of Irving's main legal advisers and president of his broadcasting interests.[5]

But the big move into newspapers came in 1944 when he bought the New Brunswick Publishing Co., which published both the *Saint John Telegraph-Journal* and the *Saint John Evening Times-Globe*. Four years later, when he took control of the Moncton Publishing Co., which published the *Moncton Daily Times* and the *Moncton Transcript* (later merged), he was on the way to building his own tiny but influential newspaper chain.

K.C. and his sons were rarely glimpsed at the newspaper offices. Then again, their personal presence wasn't really required. No one rose within the ranks of the New Brunswick papers without sharing their owner's basic values and philosophy. The newspaper executives didn't have to be told what K.C. wanted; they just instinctively understood. They kept vigilant watch over the shoulders of the reporters, rewrite men and editorial writers to ensure that nothing that they thought would disturb their owner darkened the pages of their papers.

When Tom Drummie was at the helm of the Saint John dailies, the fact that the Irving interests ranked over everyone else's was baldly stated in the newsroom. A former ad salesman, Drummie was an irrepressible snob who once berated a reporter for writing that a prominent businessman had died of a heart attack "while on the way to work." Screamed Drummie at the astonished reporter, "People like him don't go to work. They go to the office!" K.C., of course, received even kinder treatment. It was Drummie who dictated that any time Irving Oil was involved in an oil spill or some other accident, it would be identified only as "a local oil company." And it was Drummie who made sure that K.C.'s photograph never appeared in the pages of the Saint John papers.

Even Ralph Costello, his successor as publisher, had to admit that the Saint John papers were a sorry lot under Drummie's stewardship. "They didn't really know what a newspaper was. And — much worse — sometimes they didn't care," Costello recalled upon his own retirement in 1987. "Those were the days when advertisers, the establishment, the owners had a lot of influence."[6]

Things clearly improved when Costello took the publisher's office. A squat, pugnacious Irishman who grew up poor and worked his way up from a teenage sports reporter, Costello immediately began brightening up the paper's layout and writing. He shared many of Irving's traits: his distrust of unions, for one, and his sense of loyalty and noblesse oblige towards employees. Costello's professionalism, many said, was above reproach. Poet Alden Nowlan, a former *Telegraph-Journal* employee, could not remember a single case during his years at the papers when a news story detrimental to the Irving interests was deliberately suppressed. "Those who make the charge would be satisfied by nothing short of the Irvings mounting an editorial campaign against themselves — and that strikes me as being a little unrealistic, even on the part of the liberal intelligentsia," he wrote.[7] Geoffrey Crowe, a long-time *Telegraph-Journal* employee, now retired in Saint John, also denies the Irvings got a free ride under Costello. "You could criticize anything that related to Irving, even the smell of the pulp mill. The Irvings were never treated any differently."

Others, though, recall events otherwise. Costello was a newspaperman, no one disputed that. But first and foremost, he was an Irving man. Under his tenure as publisher, the pressure to guard the Irving interests became more subtle than flagrant, but it was still there. Frank Withers, who was city editor of the *Telegraph-Journal* in the early 1960s before leaving to run weekly newspapers throughout the province, recalls a story involving an Irving tug that went aground while trying to make it through the Reversing Falls. "There was a young captain running her, and he let me aboard to look around. It was a good story and I decided to run with it. The next day I was called in and told I shouldn't have. Apparently it was bad for the insurance rates for the Irving tug company."

Another journalist who ran afoul of Irving newspaper management was Jon Everett, city editor of the *Saint John Evening Times-Globe* from 1974 to 1976. Everett decided to run a feature about a shanty town that served as home to many of the tradesmen working on an expansion of the Saint John refinery. The piece was killed because, Everett was told, it might "inflame" the tradesmen. He found himself in hot water again when a strike vote was taken at the refinery. The paper had already run a string of labour stories involving big Saint John industries; in the same period, they were printing reports on police car chases in which shots had been fired. None of the chase stories had been sensationalized. But on the same day that a strike vote at the refinery occurred, Peter Stanton, a policeman in Rothesay, New Brunswick, happened to be testifying about shooting at the tires of a car speeding towards him in a parking lot. "I played the strike vote as the top story," Everett later wrote. " 'Wrong choice,' I was told."[8] The next morning, the *Telegraph-Journal* blew up the Stanton story, effectively overshadowing any follow-through about the refinery vote. As for the hapless policeman, he lost his job soon afterwards.

Sometimes the biases were downright ludicrous. How else could one describe the events in January 1971, when a fire and explosion ripped apart the crew's quarters aboard the *Irvingstream* oil tanker in Saint John harbour. The *Telegraph-Journal* editorialized that the cause of the disaster was that the federal government did not provide enough fire-boats, even though its own news story reported that the fire chief had ruled out fire-boats as an issue in the mishap.

Reporters at the Moncton papers seemed to have more leeway, perhaps because they were less likely to cover "Irving" stories. "They were run by people who tried to anticipate what the owners wanted," recalled one former executive. "But we were never ever told to tone down a story or to ignore one altogether." The Moncton newsrooms were even unionized, something that never happened in Saint John, or at the *Gleaner*, where unions were unable to make head-way.[9]

What about the *Gleaner*? Frank Withers, who worked there in the late 1960s, recalls that editors at the Fredericton paper kept an even closer watch on Irving stories than the editors in Saint John. When he joined the *Gleaner*, log drives down New Brunswick rivers had been discontinued because of the damage they caused to the rivers. The Irvings, however, had special dispensation to complete their final drive down the Nashwaak River. Withers handed in a story that said the Irving drive had not been completed by the pre-agreed deadline. But the editors at the *Gleaner* sat on the story, even after fishermen began complaining that the Irving logs were blocking the river. Eventually they ran it, by now far out of date. Confused and angry, Withers confronted his editors. "There was a big blow-out," he recalls. "I was fired." Hours after being axed, he ran into Wardell on the street. When Withers complained about his treatment, Wardell replied only that he was "out of the picture" and was leaving for Britain. A few days later Withers and the rest of New Brunswick learned that Irving had bought the paper.

To be fair, though, things were strange at the *Fredericton Daily Gleaner* long before K.C. became owner. Michael Wardell, the previous proprietor, was one of the great characters of Canadian journalism, a man whose life resembled something hatched in the imagination of Rudyard Kipling.[10] Born in Wales of well-to-do English parents, Wardell was as British as dark stout and Sunday-afternoon cricket. He grew up around Britain's rich and famous, was educated at Eton and the Royal Military College at Sandhurst, then joined the 10th Hussars and was badly wounded at the Battle of Ypres. In 1925 he took off his uniform and rejoined civilian life.

Back in the civilian world he joined Lord Beaverbrook's newspaper organization and began a quick ascent through the ranks. Tall and erect, Wardell sported a black eye patch after losing his left eye; a black thorn from a hanging branch had pierced it as his horse hurdled a fence in a fox hunt. It was not true, as Lord Beaverbrook maintained, that a jealous husband had gouged Wardell's eye out.

(Beaverbrook once introduced Wardell by saying that he was the co-respondent in 11 divorces, to which Wardell replied, "Only eight, Lord Beaverbrook.")

He cut an impressive figure in British society. Thrice married — his last wife was a Hungarian countess — he once dated Tallulah Bankhead, who later wrote in her autobiography: "Michael was one of the great beaux of London. With a menacing black patch over one eye, he looked like a swashbuckler from the Spanish Main and behaved in the same fashion." He was a man to be reckoned with; friend and confidant of the Prince of Wales, he acted as a go-between during the Prince's courtship of Wallis Simpson. But his most important friendship was with Beaverbrook, the low-born Canadian publisher. Wardell was an employee, running the *London Evening Standard*, but also a constant companion. At one point Beaverbrook considered making Wardell chairman of all his newspapers, but then reconsidered. Wardell rejoined the army at the outbreak of World War II, reaching the rank of brigadier by the time hostilities ended, even though Beaverbrook always referred to him as "Captain."

A civilian once again, Wardell decided to visit New Brunswick, the quiet little Canadian province that Beaverbrook spoke so much about. On a fishing trip on the Miramichi River in 1950, he spent a long, boozy afternoon with a member of the Crockett family, which owned the *Fredericton Daily Gleaner*. By the end of the day Wardell had agreed to buy the paper, which he did through University Press of New Brunswick, a company he formed. "I can't tell you why," he later said. "It's an emotional thing. It's not a story of logic and a planned decision at all. I didn't originally intend to stay."

No one, in fact, was ever quite sure why he left the glamour of postwar London to run a small daily in the colonies. There were rumours that Beaverbrook bankrolled the purchase. A.J.P. Taylor, the press baron's biographer, hinted that running the *Gleaner* left Wardell conveniently placed to look after Beaverbrook's interests in New Brunswick. A bizarre theory that circulated among reporters at the *Gleaner* was that Wardell was dispatched to Fredericton to set up a reserve operation in case Beaverbrook's British papers were disabled by the nuclear war that then seemed to be threatening. British journalist Malcolm Muggeridge once speculated that Beaverbrook had sent Wardell to New Brunswick as some sort of prank, to see how he would contend with life among the colonials.

Wardell was certainly an exotic bird in sleepy, class-conscious Fredericton. He brought in highly paid, experienced reporters from all around the globe to work there. He experimented with printing several editions of the paper to be dispatched by a fleet of trucks throughout the region. "He tried to bring Fleet Street to Fredericton," says New Brunswick broadcaster Paddy Gregg, who worked for Wardell in the early 1960s. Socially, he moved among Fredericton's WASP upper crust, sitting on a number of community boards and even organizing a local riding club. His reputation was surely enhanced when Queen Elizabeth was visiting the Fredericton racetrack in the 1950s. The story goes that Her Majesty was scanning the crowd when she noticed a militarily erect man wearing a black eye patch. "My God," she was heard to say, "is that Mike?"

As much as Wardell stood out in Fredericton, he clearly understood one fact about life there: the importance of making an ally of K.C. Irving. The *Gleaner* and Wardell championed a number of Irving's pet causes, fought a nasty battle against Robichaud's Equal Opportunity program and backed Charlie Van Horne in his ill-fated 1967 campaign. Whenever possible the brigadier wrote glowingly about Irving and his accomplishments, both in the *Gleaner* and in the *Atlantic Advocate*, a monthly magazine he also published.

K.C., in turn, seemed to like Wardell, whom he repeatedly praised as "a great champion of New Brunswick" and a "man of vision." It is hard to know how genuine K.C.'s feelings were. When Wardell decided to sell University Press of New Brunswick in 1968 in preparation for retiring to his castle in Wales, he naturally turned to the industrialist. The Toronto-based Southam chain had already offered to buy the *Gleaner*, but without the money-losing printing plant and the *Atlantic Advocate* magazine. Then a group of local Liberals who were weary of Wardell's venomous attacks on their party made an offer. That was the last thing K.C. wanted; whatever his reasons — and this question was at the centre of the storm that followed — he agreed in May 1968 to take the *Gleaner*, the *Atlantic Advocate* and the accompanying printing plant off Wardell's hands.

Irving never liked giving out information about his business manoeuvres. This time he outdid himself: even his highest officials apparently didn't know about the deal. When he appeared before the CRTC a few months later, Lawrence Daley, president of Irving's New Brunswick Broadcasting Ltd., which operated CHSJ-TV and CHSJ Radio, testified that Irving "was not involved in the operation of either the Fredericton Gleaner or Halifax newspapers." Irving had by then owned the *Gleaner* for four months. When Senator McElman drew this discrepancy to Daley's attention, he expressed surprise and said, "Well, if that is so, I certainly was not aware of it at the time."[11]

McElman's 1969 outcry in the Senate wasn't, as K.C. hoped, the end of his headaches. No sooner had the senator finished his speech than he marched over to the Combines Investigation Branch of the Department of Consumer and Corporate Affairs to swear out a complaint against the Irving papers for operating a monopoly. A week later the upper house approved a motion to set up a special committee "to consider and report upon the ownership and control of the major means of mass public communications in Canada." The purpose of the study, Keith Davey said, was to determine whether the mass media in Canada in 1969 were contemporary and relevant. That, however, was just the prelude to the main act. "There is no question in my mind," Richard Hatfield, the former Tory premier of New Brunswick, said in an interview shortly before his death in 1991, "that the only reason for setting up the committee was to break up the Irving newspaper chain." At the time, Irving was said to be shocked by the federal government's attitude towards him. "He thinks it is a plot to get him. But if he had people around him who did any reading, they would have told him this sort of thing was inevitable," a provincial politician told a magazine writer in 1969. "It's symptomatic of their operation. They're great on figures, but awfully light on philosophy."[12]

The Davey Committee hearings kicked off on December 9, 1969. All the while, Charles McElman, one of 15 senators on the committee, was working methodically away on his own agenda. Time after time he rephrased the same hypothetical question to each witness: suppose there was a region where the one man who owned the only newspapers also owned television and radio stations, he would say. Perhaps he also owned woods, pulp mills, oil refineries, shipping lines and bus lines. Perhaps he was even the biggest single employer in the area. In that situation, he would ask, could the newspapers do a good job of reporting? Without naming names McElman was making his point. So much so that Dalton Camp, the Conservative power-broker from New Brunswick, told the committee, "As a Maritimer I have been interested in the Committee's close examination of media in New Brunswick. For a time, I suspected that the Committee might not have any other purpose."[13]

It all became crystal clear on the afternoon of Tuesday, December 16, when K.C. Irving took his seat beside Keith Davey, the businessman's spare, erect frame a sharp contrast to the senator's bulk. For the first time since the hearings began, the room crackled with anticipation: within moments Irving was about to make not only his first public statement about his newspaper proprietorship but also his first public appearance on the national stage. The drama of the moment seemed to unnerve even Senator Davey, who introduced the witness as Kenneth Charles Irving, and had to be corrected by the witness, who said his middle name was Colin.

Dressed in a dark, pinstriped suit and speaking in a level voice, Irving wasted no time before attacking Louis Robichaud for trying to destroy Michael Wardell. Then he aimed his sights at McElman, reading into the record a letter he had written to the senator a year earlier: "Dear Senator McElman: Your plan is quite clear and your intentions obvious. [Signed] K.C. Irving." The industrialist went on to tell the committee that McElman had been overheard months ago telling someone that the licence for Irving's CHSJ-TV in Saint John would be revoked by Christmas. "I hope the senator will have the good grace to acknowledge his statement," said Irving. McElman, who had been noticeably quiet while Irving spoke, called the charge "patently false."[14]

Then things got really interesting. Senator Harper Prowse raised the question of motivation. Why did Irving buy newspapers? Radio stations? TV stations? Why did he buy anything, for that matter? "Why do I buy newspapers," Irving mused as he groped for an answer. "It is kind of hard to tell you that. Why do I buy a ship or something else? Well, opportunities in New Brunswick are quite limited. We have our own problems. . . . We have to build up our own resources to have money to do things. That necessarily is the basis for policies we have adopted." It might look peculiar that he takes no money out of his media holdings, "but it's the only way I know to get along in New Brunswick and the only way to retain control of some part of your activity."[15]

When Davey asked to what extent Irving might be concerned about concentrated ownership in the news media, he said he'd be concerned if the one person who owned all the newspapers in Canada lived in Toronto. But ownership of all the newspapers in Canada by somebody in New Brunswick would be "wonderful." Pausing for a moment, Irving said earnestly that he intended that last remark to be a facetious comment — "Excuse me." Pressed about community participation in newspaper ownership, he admitted that might be possible in New Brunswick. But "if you lived in New Brunswick and wanted to do certain things there you might have very good reasons why that wouldn't be desirable." Irving declined to specify what those reasons might be. Instead he said that he had "very good reasons" for doing business his way and that "if I change it I'd have to see what the outcome would be. Why change something that works all right? Leave it alone." He said he had amassed his holdings to create activity, not necessarily to make money. "With new activity," he explained, "it's all grist to the mill."[16]

Ralph Costello, Irving's stocky media lieutenant, was equally truculent. "This week I feel like an accused," he said, beginning his testimony. Costello said that "our newspapers" had been the butt of thinly veiled accusations by inference or the use of hypothetical questions that had been "about as hypothetical as a sledgehammer on the head. . . . In New Brunswick we have difficulty in publishing newspapers — and holding the public confidence — not because of any interference or direction from the owner but mostly because of questioning and criticism by people such as Senator McElman. . . . If an Honourable Senator suggests that a newspaper is giving a story a wide berth because of its owner's interests — or that labour might not be given a fair deal in a dispute — and if the senator makes the statement often enough, like the relentless drip-drip of the Chinese water treatment, then some people are going to believe him."[17]

Taking the stand, Wardell let loose with his own attack on McElman, who, he claimed, had been trying to break him since the early 1960s, because the publisher consorted with former prime minister John Diefenbaker. "I protest the bias of Senator McElman," said the brigadier in his clipped English. McElman, he said, had "defamed us" by asking the Combines Investigation Branch to investigate the English press in New Brunswick. "I'm damned well on trial here," he snapped. "I've been treated as if I were a member of the Mafia." When Senator Harper Prowse asked him whether he tried to second-guess Irving, he retorted: "Are you suggesting, sir, that I am influenced by him? I am not, and he has never tried to influence me."[18]

The senators, though, were not persuaded. Sixteen months later the verdict was in. The first volume of the Davey Committee's report, *The Uncertain Mirror*, did not focus on New Brunswick per se; it looked at the ownership situation across Canada. Still, the committee left no doubt about its opinion of the New Brunswick situation. "New Brunswick, of course, is the outstanding example of conglomerate ownership," they concluded, calling the situation "about as flagrant an example of abusing the public interest as you're likely to find in Canada."[19] The New Brunswick situation had turned the Maritimes into "a journalistic disaster area."[20] The report went on to vividly describe the type of bad newspapers that characterized such an area:

The kind that prints news releases intact, that seldom extends its journalistic enterprise beyond coverage of the local trout festival, that hasn't annoyed anyone important in years. Their city rooms are refuges for the frustrated and disillusioned, and their editorial pages a daily testimony to the notion that Chamber-of-Commerce boosterism is an adequate substitute for community service. It is our sad impression that a great many, if not most Canadian newspapers fall into this classification. Interestingly enough, among them are some of the most profitable newspapers in the country. A number of these newspapers are owned by K.C. Irving.

Concentration of ownership such as was found in New Brunswick, they said, "could also — but not necessarily — lead to a situation where the news (which we must start thinking of as a public resource, like electricity) is controlled and manipulated by a small group of individuals and corporations whose view of What's Fit to Print may closely coincide with What's Good for General Motors, or What's Good for Business, or What's Good for My Friends Down at the Club. There is some evidence, in fact, which suggests that we are in that boat already."

It was scathing stuff. Yet even that apparently didn't go far enough for McElman. When the report was tabled, he launched a scorching two-hour attack on Irving and Wardell, which set off bitter verbal crossfire in the normally sedate Senate chamber.[21] Wardell, he said, used the *Gleaner* "in attempts to stir up racial disunity, hatred, prejudice, malice, bigotry and distrust within New Brunswick. . . . Through his dedication in that newspaper to divisive filth he resurrected old prejudices that had long been subdued." As a concerned New Brunswicker, McElman said he wished "God speed and good riddance" to Wardell now that he was preparing to leave Canada after selling "that yellow journal."

At that point David Walker, a Conservative senator from Toronto, rose on a point of order and exhorted McElman to stop his "slanderous statements about Brigadier Wardell and, so far as that goes, about Mr. Irving." Angered, McElman relaunched his attack as M. M. Hollett, a Conservative Newfoundland senator, moved for adjournment. The motion lost. "This has been a filthy afternoon listening to you," Walker told McElman. In any other place, he said, the New Brunswick senator "would be guilty of the grossest kind of slander." But McElman was back at it when the Senate resumed sitting the following day, telling his colleagues that his motive was to "free the press of New Brunswick," a province where the English-language papers are controlled by a corporation with the "principles of an alley cat, . . . the power of the lion, the appetite of the vulture, the grace of the elephant, the instincts of the barracuda."[22]

The Irving papers lobbed a few volleys of their own. Said Wardell in a statement in the *Gleaner*: "The truth is that [racial bigotry and distrust] are the very evils that I fought against over the years in the Daily Gleaner. The printed copies of the Daily Gleaner stand as testament to me and as contradiction of the senator." The *Saint John Evening Times-Globe*'s editorial said that it could hardly improve on the reaction of fellow senators to McElman's attack: " 'Filthy afternoon' — what a condemnation for a fellow senator." Added the *Moncton Daily Times*: "Senator McElman sounds the alarm time and again about the dangers inherent in powerful conglomerates gaining ownership and control of the newsmedia. One cannot deny that dangers exist . . . for that matter everyone is a potential murderer . . . but there is a vast difference between what was and is happening and what Senator McElman says could happen."[23]

What of the proprietor himself? A few days after McElman's tirade Irving did say something — sort of. When the *Telegraph-Journal* finally asked him to comment on the senator's charges, he said he might be able to make an appropriate reply if it weren't for the Bible. Irving referred the reporter to Matthew 5:22, which begins: "But I say unto you, whosoever is angry with his brother without a cause shall be in danger of the judgement. . . . But whosoever shall say, Thou fool, shall be in danger of hell fire." He added that it was impossible for him to take the senator seriously. "I'm just wondering who let him out," he said.[24]

It went off with the precision of a military manoeuvre. On an April morning in 1971, squads of RCMP officers and investigators with the federal Combines Investigation Branch marched into the offices of the *Saint John Telegraph-Journal*, the *Saint John Times-Globe*, the *Moncton Daily Times*, the *Moncton Transcript* and the *Fredericton Daily Gleaner* just as other agents arrived on the doorsteps of the homes of K.C. Irving, Michael Wardell and Ralph Costello. Clutching search warrants, they were hunting for evidence that the Irving family ran its three newspaper companies as a monopoly. They peered into desks, rifled through files and pored over records, looking for anything related to the sale of the *Gleaner* and to the way the Irvings exercised control over the Moncton papers. When they finally left, the investigators carted away some 3,800 private documents from the newspaper offices and homes. Irving's lawyers tried to quash the search warrants; a judge ruled the warrants to search the corporate offices were in order, but threw out the ones that had allowed access to the private homes.

For nine months, the investigators studied the documents. On December 8, the federal government charged K.C. Irving Ltd. (K.C.'s holding company) and the three newspaper companies with operating a newspaper monopoly and contravening the Combines Investigation Act, the first time newspapers in Canada had been charged with breaking competition law. It was a gamble; Canada's laws on mergers and monopolies have always been pathetically weak. During the 1960s, the Crown lost every major anti-combines case to come before the Supreme Court of Canada. Historically, whenever the government in power tried to give the anti-combines legislation some teeth, it met such strong opposition from the business community that the proposals were invariably dropped. As it stood, the Combines Investigation Act did not make monopolies illegal. The Crown had to prove that they were actually and intentionally detrimental to the public. Demonstrating this beyond a reasonable doubt was extremely difficult.

Plainly they would get no help from the main defendant himself. Five weeks after the charges were laid, the Saint John newspapers received a terse, three-sentence statement from the Bahamas: "I am no longer residing in New Brunswick. My sons, J.K. Irving, A.L. Irving and J.E. Irving, are carrying on the various businesses. As far as anything else goes, I do not choose to discuss the matter further. [Signed] K.C. Irving."[25]

He had left in the dead of night. His home telephone number had been changed to a private listing; he had not been seen in public since the Brunswick Mining meeting the previous month, when he reiterated his old charges of mismanagement against Noranda. When reached by telephone in the Bahamas, Irving would only say, "I left last year," and he refused to give any reason for his departure. Some blamed the newspaper prosecution, others the succession duties that Premier Richard Hatfield planned to introduce in the spring 1972 sitting of the legislature. Whatever the reason, K.C. Irving was gone, and the suddenness and secrecy of his move unsettled even his foes. "This doesn't mean he has abandoned New Brunswick," said Senator

McElman. "His interests are so immense he couldn't do that. . . . My differences with the man were in respect to his control of the media. I don't agree with all his approaches, but he has done tremendous things for New Brunswick."[26]

The *Kings County Record* in the dairy town of Sussex was one of the first newspapers to comment editorially on K.C.'s exodus. "The darkest day in the history of the province," it said. But it was left to Irving's own *Saint John Telegraph-Journal* to say farewell: "Is New Brunswick richer or poorer, not in a financial sense but in every other way, because he has taken his leave? Is New Brunswick richer or poorer? Does the sun shine? Is there water in the ocean? Is it dark at night? There are some questions which do not need answers. There are some questions for which everyone knows the answer."[27]

Irving had gone to Nassau, the site of two companies he had recently incorporated to handle the importing of Saudi Arabian crude for his Saint John refinery. His businesses, in theory at least, were now in the hands of his three sons, J.K., 41, Arthur, 39, and Jack, 38. Regardless of whether the newspaper charges drove the patriarch from his homeland, his absence certainly made the family's next move easier: on June 16, Jack Irving issued a statement announcing that he had bought the companies that published the Moncton and Fredericton papers. J.K. and Arthur Irving, meanwhile, each bought 40 per cent of the *Saint John Telegraph-Journal*, the morning paper, and the *Saint John Evening Times-Globe*, the evening paper, from K.C. Irving Ltd., which held on to the remaining 20 per cent.

The Irvings couldn't possibly have thought that the thinly disguised ploy would persuade Ottawa to drop its charges. Still, splitting up the newspaper interests might at least make the Crown's monopoly charges a bit muddier. As it turned out, they needed all the help they could get.

The trial of *R. v. K.C. Irving Ltd., Moncton Publishing Co., New Brunswick Publishing Co. and University Press of New Brunswick Ltd.* convened at 10 a.m. on October 17, 1972, in the Supreme Court of New Brunswick in Fredericton. When the special federal prosecutors and Irving's team of defence lawyers, led by the fabled Toronto litigator J.J. Robinette, entered the courtroom that fall morning, they found they were playing to a courthouse packed with onlookers, eager to see the province's most powerful family thrust into the public spotlight. When the proceedings ended 17 days later, 30 witnesses had appeared, the testimony ran to 1,673 typewritten pages and the exhibits submitted by the lawyers for both sides totalled more than 11,000 pages.

The prosecution's case, from the very beginning, was crystal clear. They were bent on demonstrating that the Irving papers failed to criticize the shortcomings of K.C.'s business interests. They wanted to prove that all of the papers operated under the control of Ralph Costello, the Saint John publisher. The Irving press, they contended, tried to put its only daily competition, Moncton's French-language *L'Évangeline*, out of business. The Crown's lawyers even hinted that some of Irving's newspapers were kept going at a loss with the express purpose of blocking the entrance of competing publications.

All this might have been easier to prove if the man who was really on trial had shown up to testify. K.C., now no longer a Canadian citizen nor technically running the empire he had built, was under no compulsion to appear. Instead, Crown prosecutor William Hoyt had to settle for a lengthy testimony he took from K.C. in the Bahamas the previous June as part of the preliminary hearing. Nothing surprising there: in the industrialist's view, the charges were simply an attempt by "some politicians" — Charles McElman was the only one named — to make him "their whipping boy." Irving once again denied any suggestion of central control or interference in the papers' operations. He repeated his claim that he had bought the *Gleaner* to keep it from being sold outside New Brunswick or falling into the hands of the Liberal party. For the umpteenth time, he said that his business got no preferential treatment in his papers. "I think they bend over backward to put me in black ink just to keep their skirts clean."[28]

With Irving refusing to step inside the New Brunswick courts, the brunt of the prosecution's attack fell on Ralph Costello, who sat in the witness chair for five of the 13 days of prosecution questioning. In a speech at his retirement party in 1987, Costello singled out the newspaper combines case and the Davey Committee hearings as the two high points of his career. That may be an odd admission for a man who spent more than 40 years in the news business, but there's no denying that Costello was at his resolute best under the bright light of the Crown's interrogation.

All the same, he proved to be the source of the most damaging piece of evidence against the Irvings' case. Among the 42 documents that the federal combines officers seized during their raid of Costello's home was a small reporter's notebook, filled with the publisher's handwriting. There was one passage in particular that the prosecution wanted to bring to the court's attention: "The ownership of all English-language newspapers cannot be defended," said the notes, identified and read in court by Costello himself. "Dedicated respected newspaper editors and publishers will not agree that it is in the best interest of the province or people." According to Costello, the notes were arguments written before a meeting with K.C. and J.J. Robinette, to discuss the Irving group's testimony before the Senate hearings. Said Costello: "I served as devil's advocate perhaps. . . . Mr. Irving advanced his arguments as to why he thought the *Gleaner* should be retained."[29]

The prosecution leaned heavily on expert witnesses from within the newspaper game. Claude Ryan, editor of Montreal's *Le Devoir*, said that from the moment Irving owned "all the newspapers in New Brunswick," his ownership became detrimental to the public interest. St. Clair Balfour, president of Southam Press Ltd., which had twice offered to buy the *Fredericton Daily Gleaner*, added that it was a policy within his company to confine itself strictly to communications companies as well as a single media outlet in a single city.

The defence countered by trotting out its own expert witnesses, among them John Dauphinee, general manager of the Canadian Press, who said that he thought no newspaper or news agency could slant the news and get away with it for long because of competition from the other media. Jess Markham, a Harvard University economics professor, testified that, according to his analysis, "the citizens of New Brunswick in all counties have available a very large and diverse number of information media. Not one of them could constitute a monopoly." Also advancing the defendant's case was a surprise witness — Dalton Camp, the former national president of the Progressive Conservative party, who told the courts that the province's Irving-owned daily papers had improved more in the previous decade than any comparable group of Canadian newspapers. Noted Camp: "There was criticism from press critics when the Irving papers expressed no editorial opinions. Once the Irving papers began to express an opinion against the government it became a monopoly."[30]

When the verdict finally came down, on January 24, 1974, Judge Albany Robichaud found K.C. Irving Ltd. and all three publishing companies guilty of forming a monopoly. In his 129-page judgement, Robichaud said he was convinced that the five Irving newspapers have complete editorial autonomy "and that the owners have never cast over their columns any editorial shadow whatsoever." K.C. Irving was "a great New Brunswicker and an impartial citizen of our province." Nevertheless, K.C. Irving Ltd. had acquired the right to control the five papers, even if he saw fit not to exercise it. ("The potential was always there to be exercised at any time and the likelihood that such control could be exercised was always present.") The judge held that, although it had to be established that the arrangement was to the public's "detriment," "once a complete monopoly has been established . . . detriment, in law, resulted."

On April 2, Robichaud passed down his sentence: K.C. Irving Ltd., New Brunswick Publishing, Moncton Publishing and University Press of New Brunswick were fined $150,000 between them. The more important ruling came later in the month, when Robichaud ordered the Irving group to sell its Moncton newspapers.

Irving detractors crowed with delight. The press immediately hailed Robichaud's judgement as a landmark decision. But an appeal, of course, was inevitable. When he appeared in the New Brunswick Court of Appeal, Crown prosecutor William Hoyt repeated his claim that Irving's editorial monopoly threatened democracy in the province. The argument from Robinette, Irving's lawyer, was equally straightforward: trial judge Albany Robichaud had found no public harm caused by Irving's ownership of five newspapers, although the potential was there. The lower court decision, he argued, was mistaken.

The appeal court bought Robinette's argument. On June 4, the court overturned Albany Robichaud's decision. It ruled that the judge erred in disregarding his own finding of fact — that the Irvings al-

lowed their newspapers editorial autonomy — and "becoming involved in the realm of theory." The appeal court judge admitted
that Irving had created a complete monopoly "in the dictionary meaning of the word" when he took control of the *Fredericton Daily
Gleaner*. But he disagreed with Robichaud's finding that "once a
complete monopoly has been established . . . detriment in law
resulted."

It was a profound decision, and it stuck when the Crown appealed
before the Supreme Court of Canada. The reversal was a bitter blow
to the country's combines investigators, and not just because it left
the Irving monopoly intact. The appeal court's ruling meant that
detriment caused by a monopoly had to be found as a fact, not as
a matter of law. Moreover, detriment had to be specifically proven,
and proven, apparently, in terms of economic harm. As Tom Kent's
Royal Commission on Newspapers observed in 1981: "It is
. . . through the courts' interpretation of the phrase 'to the detriment
or against the interest of the public' that the Combines Investigation
Act has lost all vitality. The decision in *Irving* was merely the administration of last rites."[31]

Ottawa's attempt to show the Irvings who was boss hadn't just
failed, it was a total, abysmal disaster. The Irvings, with their high-
priced legal help, had not just beaten the charges, they had also
gutted the government's combines legislation. During the 1970s, the
Crown lost every major anti-combines case to come before the Supreme Court of Canada. It seems somehow fitting that the family
that had turned an entire province into a virtual monopoly would
be the one to incapacitate Canada's combines police.

Not that K.C. and his sons were necessarily interested in striking
a blow for free enterprise. The newspaper decision simply confirmed
what K.C. had always felt in his heart was true: no one, not the
federal government, not the courts, had the right to take away what
he had earned. Indeed, by 1974 K.C. Irving was at a stage in his
life where the question of how to keep his empire intact preoccupied
him. He need not have worried.

7

The Changing of the Guard

*"It was a harrowing experience and utterly
exhausting. . . . Irving really put on a performance
and said that he would not be boxed in by us and
if he wanted to run an oil business wherever he
chose he would do so. For emphasis he hurled his
briefcase to the floor."*
— W.H. Beekhuis, a Standard Oil of California
vice-president, describing negotiations with K.C.
Irving in 1969.

THE VICTORY over Ottawa must have tasted bittersweet to the ageing
king, living in self-imposed exile hundreds of miles from the fiefdom
that he had ruled for all those years. K.C. Irving turned 75 in the
midst of these troubles, but with his lifelong restlessness he could
find no peace. Neither he nor Hattie liked life in Nassau, the sun-
dappled Bahamian tax haven to which they had fled after leaving
Saint John in late 1971. Within months they moved to Bermuda,
another popular asylum for the tax-averse rich, which boasts the
highest per-capita income in the world on its 21 square miles. With
their few servants in tow, they eventually settled in a small home
behind the 600-room Southampton Princess Hotel. "It was a mis-
erable little place, a cottage really," recalls Ed Byrne, who had moved
to the island a few years earlier. "It didn't even have heat, which
can be a problem during the Bermuda winters." The location was
the redeeming feature: the front bordered on the Princess golf course,
and the back offered a breathtaking view of the blue waters of the
Great Sound. So K.C. razed the cottage, erected a rambling white
stucco $2.5-million mansion and retreated behind its closed doors.

By now his need for privacy had taken on new proportions. Occasionally someone caught a glimpse of the Irvings on the beach. Normally, though, they seemed to leave their grounds in Bermuda only rarely. They avoided the island's active cocktail and dinner party circuit. Even the other wealthy Canadians who had retired to Bermuda were surprised to learn that the shadowy tycoon and his wife had taken up residence there. In the early years of exile the couple continued to make secret trips to see their family. When a reporter from one of the Irving newspapers finally tracked K.C. down in Saint John in the spring of 1973 and asked the city's most famous citizen if he ever anticipated moving back to New Brunswick, he replied, "I have no such plans."

No one who visited the Irvings' new home ever heard K.C. bemoan the treatment he had received back in New Brunswick. Still, he had become a man without a country. After a lifetime spent making wheels turn, he found little allure in Bermuda's restful beauty. Hattie missed her friends and family back in Saint John. By then, New Brunswick, along with most other provinces, had dropped its plans to introduce succession duties. But, as one of his tax advisers recalls, "the province had made him panic." K.C. wasn't willing to gamble that New Brunswick would not change its tax laws, and he certainly was not about to see his life's work taken away from his family just to pay taxes.

K.C. now was well into his seventh decade, but he looked and acted as ageless as ever. Another man might have been shaken by his critics — by the fact that after 50 years of work and sacrifice, after half a century of bringing jobs and enterprise to his home province, he had been driven out by unfriendly governments in Fredericton and Ottawa. K.C. had no time for self-pity. Everyone knew that while his sons directed the day-to-day affairs of the empire, the old man still held the real power. Now, having laid the groundwork for the future, he wanted to guide the empire into maturity. With a personal fortune reliably placed in the range of $50 to $60 million, K.C. was wealthy, but nowhere near as rich as most people thought. Even that figure was deceptive since he resolutely ploughed the profits back into his businesses. He really had no other choice: the shipyard, paper mill and refinery investments had yet to pay off, and the rest of the empire remained vulnerable to cash-flow problems caused by everything from sluggish demand for pulp and paper and gasoline to the fluctuating economy. As K.C. set out to put his financial house in order, he knew that sooner or later those expensive earlier investments would ripen. Yet even he couldn't have predicted the strange events, far beyond his control, that were to transform his empire into one of the world's richest.

From the beginning, the 1957 deal with Socal had caused K.C. headaches. The partnership itself was not a problem: K.C. and his clan still had 51 per cent of Irving Oil and 49 per cent of Irving Refining Ltd. Opening the Saint John refinery in 1960 had given Irving Oil a built-in supply of crude for his burgeoning service station chain. Irving Oil's sales, indeed, skyrocketed from 6.9 million barrels of gasoline, heating fuel and other refined products in 1959 to 12.5 million two years later. The problem was the price Irving Oil was paying for its crude. K.C. laid out his predicament in a letter to R.G. Follis, Standard Oil's chairman, dated September 4, 1962:

When we entered into our original contracts we agreed that the prices charged the Oil Company by the Refinery and the Refinery by your company should be computed by a formula based on competitive world prices. In drawing up the contracts your people felt that some misunderstanding might develop if these expressions were used so they suggested that the pricing formulas be based on posted prices. At that time posted prices were true selling prices. . . . Unfortunately this condition no longer exists. Posted prices are now artificially maintained at the same time that sales are being regularly made at a percentage of these so called posted prices. . . . By using a price formula based on these artificial standards, Irving Oil has been overcharged approximately $13,776,000 in the past eighteen months. We are now placed in the position where the harder we work to develop sales for the oil company and refinery, the greater is our loss. . . . We are at a point where my personal obligations to not only Irving Oil and Irving Refining but to my family make it necessary that I press immediately for a realistic pricing formula instead of an artificial standard which no longer represents true pricing conditions. . . . If the present trend continues we will bankrupt Irving Oil and Irving Refining and I estimate the personal loss of my family to be close to $15,000/ day.[1]

K.C. wasn't the only oilman lamenting his lot in the early 1960s. The other refiners active in eastern Canada — Imperial, Gulf, Shell and Texaco — also used imported crude to fuel their refineries. As Canadian subsidiaries of huge multinational oil companies, they too were locked in to buy crude for transfer prices that were higher than world market rates. The situation did not develop by chance. The foreign oil giants not only ensured that their Canadian subsidiaries paid comparatively high rates for the offshore crude, they also worked together to "harmonize" prices — a practice that allowed the companies to overcharge Canadian gasoline consumers by billions and to drain similar amounts of taxable dollars from Canadian oil firms.

Irving Oil, of course, wasn't technically a Socal subsidiary. Because of the earlier crude supply contract it had signed with the U.S. outfit, it might just as well have been. When K.C. sat down in 1962 and compared his costs with the price he was paying for Socal crude from the Middle East, he found that he was overpaying about 3.2 cents per gallon, or about $1.12 per barrel.[2] His company was feeling the drain: during the 12 months ending January 31, 1962, Irving Oil's net income fell 32 per cent from the previous year, to $1,422,364. In the next 12 months, profits fell another 11 per cent. The next year Irving Oil made a paltry $163,224, less than it made back in the very beginning when K.C.'s empire consisted of just a couple of stations.[3]

Socal, an equal partner with K.C. in Irving Oil and Irving Refining, plainly did not want to see the enterprise go bankrupt. In 1964, and again a year later, it cut the price it charged Irving for its Saudi crude. Irving Oil's profitability sprang back. But K.C. dearly wanted to avoid finding himself in a similar price squeeze again. There was a way out: the original contract with Socal included a clause that gave either side the right to renegotiate prices after 10 years. By 1969, K.C. had plenty of bargaining leverage for reopening the pact: the global glut in oil was pushing crude prices further downwards. More important, the Irving Oil relationship had grown in significance for Socal, which once again was failing to buy all the crude it was obligated to take as a member of Aramco, the partnership of American oil companies in the Middle East. The king of Saudi Arabia was pressuring Socal to increase its purchases. Conveniently, the Saint John refinery was now preparing to expand by another 50,000 barrels per day within the next two years, providing a new market for the Socal crude.

Negotiations for the new contract began in the spring of 1969.[4] Carrying the Socal standard were W.H. Beekhuis, a senior vice-president, and H.D. Armstrong, the company treasurer. Across the table, usually accompanied by his son, Arthur, sat K.C., who was determined to pour all his tenacity and negotiating savvy into this deal. The American oilmen were prepared for a tough round of haggling, but even they were taken back by the vehemence of K.C.'s response when he arrived in Brussels with J.K. and Arthur and hurled his briefcase in anger after receiving Socal's first offer.

K.C. had an unalterable agenda: as always, he wanted to lock in a secure supply of crude for his refinery and service stations. Naturally he wanted to buy the crude at the lowest possible price. However, he was also determined to strike a deal that would allow Irving Oil to share in the huge profits Socal was earning for producing the Persian Gulf crude and transporting it to Saint John. These were considerable: as John Blair stated in his authoritative book, *The Control of Oil*, in 1969, it cost about 15 cents to produce a barrel of Middle Eastern oil and about 60 cents to move it by tanker from the Persian Gulf to North America. With North American buyers paying roughly $2 a barrel, that meant a hefty profit.[5]

Socal, while willing to share these vast profits, had its own concerns. For one thing, it didn't want to sell crude into Canada at lower prices than some of its other subsidiaries and customers were paying in the United States. There were also tax considerations. If Socal simply passed on the transportation profits to Irving Oil, those profits would be subject to Canadian tax law. From Socal's point of view that was unacceptable. As if things weren't complicated enough, the oil markets were in turmoil. In 1970 Libya unilaterally raised taxes, and therefore prices, for crude for the first time. Later in the year, the Organization of Petroleum Exporting Countries (OPEC) met in Venezuela and agreed to negotiate with the oil companies on behalf of all the producing nations and to demand increased prices and increased taxes starting in early 1971.

As he appraised the situation Otto Miller, the new Socal chairman, knew only one thing: it would be idiotic for his company to enter into any long-term crude supply agreements until the price situation had stabilized. Even so, he did not want Reuben Savage, the vice-president who had taken over the negotiations with the Irvings, to know that Socal had no intention of striking a deal while the price uncertainties existed. As Miller later recalled: "It was a very important venture to us and I was fearful that if we told Mr. Irving that we were not going to negotiate any further at this particular time he might have just walked away from our company. . . . Mr. Savage had a very difficult job. . . . To negotiate with Mr. Irving is quite an undertaking. . . . If I told him this, it would just make it much more difficult for Mr. Savage."[6]

That would have been unlikely. Not only had K.C. rejected Socal's first contract proposal in September 1969, he also dismissed the amendments Socal proposed a month later, even though they raised the possibility of a substantial cut in the crude price. The main sticking point for K.C. remained the fact that none of the Socal proposals provided his family with its cut of production and transportation profits. At one point they had even discussed whether Irving Oil might take a position in Aramco, the American oil consortium in the Middle East, but K.C. wasn't interested.

Then, finally, a breakthrough: in April 1971, after the big oil companies had reached price and tax agreements with the Middle Eastern governments, Otto Miller felt comfortable enough to conclude negotiations with the Irvings. Miller's position was unchanged; he wouldn't sell crude into Canada at a price below the market level, because he would not subject the production and transportation profits — which, in his words, "had nothing whatsoever to do with Canada" — to Canadian taxes. So Miller instructed the head of Socal's tax department to, as he put it, "find a way to come up with some scheme, procedure that would permit us to import crude oil into Canada at competitive market prices and also to share a part of our producing and transportation profits with Mr. Irving outside of Canada."[7]

Socal's tax expert presented his solution in a memorandum, dated April 29, 1971. A week later Reuben Savage flew to Saint John to discuss the matter with K.C. and Arthur. The plan was for Irving Refining and Irving Oil to form a non-Canadian subsidiary. The offshore ancillary would purchase the crude from Socal at "delivered cost," which was the cost of producing the oil in the Persian Gulf, plus the transportation cost. Then it would deliver the crude to Irving Refining at the competitive market price. The trading company's profit, therefore, would be the difference between the lower price that it paid to Socal for the crude and the higher price at which it sold the oil to the Irving refinery. The offshore company would then pass on the profit to Irving in the form of dividends, which were tax-free under the laws of the day. As an added bonus, Socal agreed that if K.C. built oil tankers in Canada, it would use them to move the crude from the Middle East to Saint John.

The concept was nothing revolutionary. By the mid-1960s tax authorities in Canada and the United States were starting to question the inflated transfer prices that the domestic subsidiaries of the big oil companies were paying for their offshore crude. Big Oil had to find a new way to fatten its tax-free profits. The solution, in many cases, was creating a nice, handy offshore trading company, which would purchase foreign crude at the lowest possible price and then resell it to the Canadian subsidiary at the highest possible price, leaving a tax-free profit with the offshore subsidiary that would eventually return to Canada by means of tax-free dividends.

K.C., then, was just following the pack. He and his sons spent two months straightening out the details. There was a final meeting in the New York office of K.C.'s lawyer. Then, on July 28, 1971, Irving Refining and Irving Oil each acquired half the shares of Bomag International Ltd., a shell company incorporated in Bermuda, for $2,500. Twelve days later the crude supply contract was signed.

On paper the deal looked simple enough: Bomag purchased its crude from Socal for $2.10 to $2.24 per barrel. Bomag, in turn, would sell the crude to Irving Oil at $2.90 per barrel. Bomag's "profit" on the deal therefore would be 66 to 80 cents per barrel — the difference between what it paid Socal and the price it charged Irving Oil. Bomag, like other offshore trading outfits, wasn't really much of a company. It had a president — a retired Socal employee — and a board of directors as well as a three-room office in Hamilton that housed some filing cabinets, a telex, a telephone and a secretary. Neither the president nor the secretary had much to do other than read the *Bermuda Royal Gazette*. According to the sales agreements: "Title to crude oil shall pass to (the buyer) at ship's permanent hose connections at the loading port."[8] Translation: ownership of the oil went from Socal to Bomag and from Bomag to Irving Oil in the flickering of an eye. The tanker, as it had always done, simply left the Persian Gulf and headed for Saint John with its cargo of crude.

The oil world was in chaos when Irving and Socal signed their deal. Arabian crude was mired in the range of $2 (US) a barrel, and well-known economists were actually predicting "dollar oil" within the decade. How quickly things changed. On October 6, 1973, Egypt and Syria invaded Israel, setting off the Yom Kippur War. OPEC, for the first time, decided to establish its own price for crude. By the new year, the price had rocketed to $11.65.

The world oil crisis had begun. As he had been during World War II, K.C. Irving was again ready to turn crisis into huge profits. Every couple of weeks a Socal tanker arrived in Saint John to unload its cargo of Saudi crude at the refinery. Meanwhile, millions of dollars were flowing in and out of an account with First National City Bank in New York City. The account was registered to Irving California Oil Co. (IrvCal), Bomag's successor company. Some of the money was earmarked to cover IrvCal's administrative expenses. Some was placed in Eurodollar time deposits. Most of it, however, went to Irving Oil in the form of tax-free dividends.

In fact, during the five years after IrvCal was created a total of 141 oil shipments, worth $1.2 billion, passed through IrvCal's books. Since IrvCal did little more than send telexes back and forth to Saint John and Socal's San Francisco headquarters, it spent only $273,869 in administrative expenses.[9] During the period 1971–1975, the shell company accumulated $142,026,637 (US) in offshore profits for its efforts, $137,100,000 of which it returned to Irving Oil in the form of tax-free dividends. [10]

Irving Oil's overall profits, of course, grew exponentially. In the 12 months ending January 31, 1971, before the supply contract was signed, it made $4.7 million. During the following 11 months profits doubled, even though the contract was in place for only five months. The next year Irving Oil made $17 million. But the real money started pouring in after 1973, when crude prices were reaching for the sky: for the 12 months from May 31, 1973, until May 31, 1974, Irving Oil made $50 million. During the next seven months (ending December 31, 1974), profits soared to $56 million. Through 1975, it made another $50 million. [11] The large profits were made all the sweeter because Irving Oil paid virtually no income tax during this period. The offshore dividends, which made up almost all of the company's profits, were non-taxable.

As usual K.C. put the profits back into the company. In the early 1970s he spent $50 million to double the refinery's capacity and another $15 million on a dock to handle Socal's new supertankers. Later most of the profits siphoned off in Bermuda went towards a $200-million refinery expansion announced in 1973; it was the most expensive project the Irvings had ever undertaken. They had arrived. With a $450-million line of credit in Canada, Irving Oil had no trouble coming up with the additional funding for the expansion. They also borrowed from the international banking community, through the Export-Import Bank of the United States — which lends to companies involved in large-scale import and export trade with the United States — and London's prestigious Morgan Grenfell Bank. Some money was raised on the Eurodollar market, which exists for American dollars held outside the United States.

Still, it was a gamble. Even the European contractors who worked on the refinery privately mocked the folly of expanding in the face of a worldwide oil glut. Once again K.C. was looking ahead. When complete in 1977, K.C.'s was far and away Canada's largest refinery, capable of boiling 250,000 barrels of crude daily into gasoline, heating oil and other products. Some of the refinery's increased production was earmarked for the New Brunswick Electric Power Commission as part of a 12-year contract to supply $200 million worth of bunker oil. The Irvings were also busily finding other innovative ways to keep their refinery busy. One example: swapping product with other companies so that Imperial, Gulf and Shell received their New Brunswick oil from the Saint John facility, while Irving stations depended upon the other companies for product in Quebec and Nova Scotia.

Ultimately, though, the big reason for expanding at such a prodigious rate was that K.C. and his sons saw an opportunity to increase exports into the northeastern U.S., where not a single refinery was located. At first it paid off: in 1977 Irving Oil exported $37.5 million worth of refined products into the U.S., compared with just over $2 million the year before. Then the shifts in the world oil markets turned against them. The problem was a global glut in refining capacity for residual oil — used mainly for industrial heating — which did not look like it would disappear for years to come. In 1978, Irving shipments into the U.S. fell to $11.1 million. [12]

At home there were also problems. Like Irving, other refiners had expanded heavily in the years following the OPEC crisis. When the Canadian market for refined products contracted, oil companies found themselves with too much refinery capacity and too little demand for their wares. Anxious to keep these immensely expensive installations running at any price, refiners spewed oil products onto the market, causing slashed prices and minuscule profits. The problem was greatest east of Ontario, where most of Canada's refineries were located, and where capacity outstripped demand by roughly 70 per cent in 1977. Two years later, the Irving refinery was running at less than half-speed. Profits plummeted. Everyone agreed that the outlook was grim.

And just when it looked worst of all, along came another oil crisis. Just the thing to improve an oil company's lot.

In the spring of 1979, the oil market was overheating. Within weeks the spot oil price, a sensitive indicator of world supply and demand, had doubled to almost $40 (US) a barrel. The cause of the turmoil lay in Iran, where the collapse of the shah's regime in late 1978 had unleashed a series of events that were shaking the world. Increased production by Saudi Arabia and other producers soon made up for the disruption in Iranian supply. But the Arabs could do little to change the perceptions of importers that a supply shortage was looming.

Tankerloads of oil changed hands at a feverish rate as South Africa, Israel and other panic-stricken countries that had been boycotted by the Arabs scrambled to increase their oil stocks by buying on the spot market. Spot market oil, which accounts for about 10 per cent of world production, is the crude and refined products that aren't under contract to the major firms. Most of the action in New York, London, Geneva, Rotterdam and the other financial centres, where shirtsleeved brokers trade supertankers full of crude on the strength of a telephone call, telex or fax, comes from sales between companies that strictly produce, refine or distribute. But the fully integrated oil companies that do all three use the spot market, too, almost always as buyers, to pick up refined products needed to balance inventories. In 1979 the major oil companies were also in on the action, paying huge mark-ups for their crude and, in the process, adding millions of dollars to the value of these cargoes a few nautical miles out of port.

The 1979 spot market panic was a gold mine for companies with oil to sell at these skyrocketing prices. K.C., for the first time in his life, became a speculator: from the moment spot prices began climbing in early 1979, Irving Oil was wheeling and dealing itself to huge profits. The company continued to buy tankerloads of crude from Socal at contract prices. But many of the ships never reached Saint John. Instead, the cargoes were sold on the spot market for prices many times higher than Irving could get in Canada.[13]

The returns on refined crude were even greater — mainly because the run-up in refined product prices was far above the increase in the price of crude. The Irving refinery had lots of extra room to crank up production to take advantage of the price discrepancy; fulfilling the needs of its own service station network only required roughly 80,000 barrels of the refinery's 250,000 barrel-a-day capacity. All along, K.C. knew that having loads of excess production capacity would one day pay off. Now, suddenly, the refinery was receiving calls from all over the world from customers eager to buy gasoline and other refined products. The buyers had to use Irving vessels, if available, to make the delivery.

Some days tankers were lined up five deep in the waters of the Bay of Fundy, waiting to fill up with Irving products. Then the vessels would begin their journeys across the high seas to deliver their cargoes to buyers in Scandinavia, the Netherlands, Italy, Turkey, Israel, Hong Kong, Indonesia, South Africa, Zaire, Liberia, Senegal, Brazil and Bermuda. Less than 30 per cent of Irving Oil exports were now going to the United States. Starting from nowhere, Irving Oil had become one of the world's great oil traders. [14]

The returns, naturally, were massive. During 1979 Irving Oil exported $793 million in refined petroleum products — only $291 million to the U.S. — and registered a profit of $291 million. In 1980 Irving exports hit $835 million ($200 million to the U.S.), and the company made another $207 million in profits. [15] Putting the whole situation into perspective was Irving Oil's failure, due to an inadvertent office error, to report to Canada Customs the $800 million in export sales that it had made during 18 months in 1978 and 1979. With the correction made, Canada's trade surplus for 1979 was 33 per cent higher than originally announced. [16]

With all the profits pouring in, even the Irvings themselves could laugh at the mistake. For K.C.'s boys, this was their first taste of sweet independence. But the huge profits they were making brought them to public attention for the first time. For that, they were ill prepared.

Ottawa's interest in the Irving empire had not waned when K.C. lit out for Bermuda. No sooner had the courts overturned the newspaper monopoly conviction than the Irvings again found themselves under the government microscope. The vehicle was the Royal Commission on Corporate Concentration, launched after Quebec financier Paul Desmarais tried in 1975 to take over Argus Corp. Commission head Robert Bryce and his staff set off across the country to study the families that were accumulating more and more control over Canadian assets. Usually commission researchers were received if not cordially, then at least civilly. But not always; K.C.'s three sons would have nothing to do with them. The commission came close to suing the family for failing to comply with its demands for basic financial information, calling its run-in with the Irvings "a vivid illustration of the deficiencies in the law, which should be remedied."[17]

Finally Bryce himself showed up in Saint John and managed to obtain a brief audience. "I was amazed by how quickly they lost their tempers. They knew that we were preparing a study on them in particular, and this troubled them," recalls Bryce, now retired and living in Ottawa. "They resented the Upper Canadians coming down to pry into their affairs. I guess they had so many tentacles in New Brunswick that they didn't like to see them exposed and written about."

The Irvings can't have been too upset by the result of the commission's probings. Overall, it concluded that corporate concentration was a necessity in a country the size and nature of Canada. Given no access to the Irving empire, Bryce's staff chose not to probe too deeply; there was so much concern about being sued for libel that the researcher who prepared the case study on the family was never identified. The report concluded that the family was, on balance, a positive force for the province and the region, and it urged "an objective and realistic perspective on the company's development, its net contributions to the province and the region, and an understanding of the real difficulties of living with an acceptable alternative."[18]

However, the commission offered some advice to K.C. and his clan: "For the Irving companies, the time may well have arrived for a basic reassessment of their approach to corporate secrecy and disclosure, if only for the reason that it is better to anticipate voluntarily a situation than to have to submit unwillingly. For in the long run, what may have appeared as adversaries in the past could well be the allies sought out in the future."[19]

The Bryce Commission was just the beginning. In October 1978 Revenue Canada notified Irving Oil that it had disallowed the $142 million in tax deductions the company had claimed from 1971 through 1975 for the cost of buying crude oil from IrvCal. The ruling wasn't surprising: four years before, Ottawa had disallowed similar claims by Imperial Oil, forcing the oil giant to pay $18 million in back taxes. Other reassessments followed. Each time the oil companies quietly paid up. However, $142 million was a different matter altogether, and the Irving family's hatred of the taxman was so deep-seated as to be pathological. So they decided to appeal the reassessment, triggering the biggest tax case in Canadian history, one that would take 13 years to wind its way through the courts.

Suddenly it seemed Irving Oil was getting it from all sides. In 1973, federal combines investigators had scoured its headquarters, along with the offices of Gulf, Shell, Texaco, Esso and seven other oil companies. The investigators left carrying some 200,000 pages of documentation, which they hoped contained evidence that the oil companies had conspired together to fix prices. Robert Bertrand, director of the Bureau of Competition Policy, and his staff failed to find a "smoking gun," a tape recording or an agreement in writing that would send oil executives to jail. But they found enough to conclude that Canadians were out of pocket by about $12 billion (in 1980 dollars) because of overcharging by the major oil companies between 1958 and 1973.

Bertrand's 1981 report, entitled *The State of Competition in the Canadian Petroleum Industry*, was really about lack of competition.[20] Bertrand alleged price-fixing at every stage of the business: importing, pipelines, refining, marketing. The bulk of the condemnation was levelled at the Big Four — Imperial Oil, Shell Canada, Texaco Canada and Gulf Canada — which used Canada as a "laboratory" for price-fixing techniques.

Irving Oil did not emerge unscathed. The study showed in detail how Irving and the other Canadian branch-plant subsidiaries bought imported crude and petroleum products from their parents at inflated prices and under agreements that didn't reflect changing world price conditions. Bertrand also noted that the crude swap deals involving Irving Oil and the other big refiners reduced the incentives each might otherwise have had for independent action. The report concluded that the refining companies also reduced competition by selecting which firms received refined products and at what price.

A month after the Bertrand report hit the streets, the Irvings were under fire from yet another federal inquiry, the Royal Commission on Newspapers, launched to investigate the simultaneous closings of the *Winnipeg Tribune* and the *Ottawa Journal*. The family's growing sense of persecution at the hands of the federal government was evident during the testy, often bitter exchanges with the commission members. "Why have you singled us out, why are you picking on us? Maybe because we've got a tail to kick, we're fair game for you," Arthur Irving asked after the commission's legal counsel questioned the brothers about their business interests.

Although commission chairman Tom Kent repeated several times during their testimony that the inquiry was not "out to catch the Irvings," they remained deeply suspicious. "The government appointed this body with motives we're uncertain of. We believe in free enterprise and it hurts like hell to think there could be government controls and regulations to control newspapers," added Arthur, during one lengthy outburst. "I hope the government won't get into socialism — we're terrified of government interference." Arthur went on to give the most passionate explanation of the family's attitude to newspaper proprietorship. "We like the Saint John paper and that's the only one I'm involved with. I own 40 per cent and I intend to keep it forever. . . . It is our privilege to own it, and nobody in this God-given room is going to take it away from us."[21]

To be fair, the Irving brothers had good reason for being cranky. By then the country was beginning a painful recession, and their empire would not escape the hard times. In 1983, troubled by the slump in the province's forestry sector, J.D. Irving Ltd. cancelled its annual planting of 11 million pine and spruce seedlings, the first time that had happened since 1958. The Saint John newsprint mill they had bought two years earlier for $145 million was in and out of shut-down. The shipyard faced an empty order book for the first time in a decade, once it delivered the $150-million semi-submersible drilling rig it was building. The slump in New Brunswick construction had hit a whole range of Irving operations in structural steel fabrication, precast concrete, heavy-equipment rentals and prefabricated house building. They closed the morning edition of the Moncton papers, merging the two into the *Moncton Times-Transcript*. Even their minority position in Brunswick Mining and Smelting was suffering, because of low base-metal prices.

One troubled sector overshadowed all others. Falling consumer demand for petroleum products was squeezing Canadian refiners.

At the same time, the U.S. government had once again brought in legislation to cut imports, slowing the flow of Canadian products into New England to a trickle. In 1982 Irving Oil's exports to the United States had fallen to a paltry $33 million, compared with $484 million during the previous year.[22] In 1983 they cut back on the refinery's capacity. Still, the refinery was running at just half-speed, far below its break-even level. Refineries, in fact, were closing at a dizzying rate across the country; during the next three years six shut down in Montreal alone. Some people thought Irving Oil's might follow.

It was a waiting game. Better fortunes for the family depended upon a strong revival in export markets, for both forest and refined oil products. Any sort of a turnaround was months, perhaps years off. Most other organizations simply battened down the hatches and prepared to weather the recession as best they could. Not the Irvings. Instead of pulling back when things get tough, they continued expanding and scouting for new opportunities. Again, it paid off. For during the dark days of 1983 they cemented a deal that changed the complexion of the entire empire.

The 1970s oil and gas boom had pumped new life into the Irving shipyard. Oil giants from around the world were tripping over one another to find yards capable of quickly turning out tankers and icebreakers for offshore oil exploration. Early in the decade Saint John Shipbuilding had beat out 22 other contenders for a contract to build half a dozen oil tankers for the U.K. energy giant Shell Oil. The yard produced two tankers for Exxon, an icebreaker for Dome Petroleum of Calgary and a semi-submersible drilling rig for Husky–Bow Valley, a Calgary consortium. And, of course, the Irving oil empire required its own ships. "We were so busy in the 1970s," says Andrew McArthur, president of the shipyard until 1985, "that we couldn't have built a tin box if you had come and asked us."[23]

Even so, by the end of the decade, J.K. Irving, K.C.'s oldest son, had started thinking about diversifying the interests of the yard, which had grown overwhelmingly dependent on the energy business. By coincidence, their old enemy the Liberal government was then finally turning its attention to modernizing Canada's ageing navy.

Early in 1977, Vice-Admiral Robert Falls unveiled the government's preliminary plans to a gathering of naval brass in Ottawa's Château Laurier hotel. The navy, he said, would order no fewer than 20 new naval frigates, with the first deliveries scheduled for the mid-1980s and the last of them to be commissioned by the early 1990s.

The orderly progression of new ships was meant to replace the Canadian destroyers built in the late 1950s and early 1960s, which were still patrolling the Atlantic and the Pacific. However, the federal cabinet was not convinced that the navy really needed 20 new ships. In December 1977, Defence Minister Barney Danson revealed the results of a cabinet compromise: the navy would order only six new frigates, with a total cost of $1.5 billion, measured in 1977 dollars. Navy and industry alike were mollified by the understanding that the government eventually planned to order three more batches of six ships each. Whatever the ultimate size of the project, one thing was clear: a competition to build the first six was under way. Moreover, it was quite likely that whoever won the first round would have a better-than-even shot at winning all subsequent orders.

Within months, Saint John Shipbuilding had formed a partnership with Marine Industries Ltd. (MIL), the owner of a Sorel, Quebec, shipyard, and Sperry Rand, a U.S. weapons expert. MIL was the lead company in the group, because it had helped build four Tribal-class destroyers delivered to the navy in 1972 and 1973. Sperry's role was also key, since electronics and weapons systems would make up the majority of the project's costs. Since it had never built a warship before, Saint John was relegated to a mere subcontractor's role.

By August 1978, five separate alliances had been formed to bid for the lucrative contract. Already it was clear that there were three front-runners: Pratt & Whitney Canada, with Montreal-based German & Milne and John J. McMullen Associates; Montreal's Canadian Vickers, teamed with the Quebec-based Davie Shipbuilding Ltd., Litton Systems Canada of Toronto and Burrard Dry Dock of Vancouver; and the MIL–Sperry–Saint John group. Each group was supposed to submit preliminary proposals to the government. Then a team of military experts would evaluate the designs and pass their assessment on to the federal cabinet, which would choose two finalists and give each $20 million and 18 months to prepare detailed construction estimates.

Fine in theory, but the contest did not work out quite so neatly. Late in 1978 MIL pulled out of its partnership with Saint John and Sperry; Sperry now took the lead role. More delays followed as the Trudeau government fell to Joe Clark's Tories in May 1979, then resurrected itself nine months later. During that period, the frigate contenders were busy refining their bids and trying to gauge just who was the front-runner in the eyes of the navy evaluators.

Here the role of Canadian Vickers became important. The critical development was a decision in late 1978 by the British parent company to sell its stake in Vickers, making it 100 per cent Canadian-owned. At the time, the Vickers consortium was under the leadership of Litton Systems Canada, a subsidiary of the U.S. military giant. By 1980 Vickers management realized that its group was running third behind Sperry–Saint John and the Pratt & Whitney group. So Vickers decided to play off the Trudeau government's new-found nationalism.

Vickers executives asked Defence Minister Gilles Lamontagne if the government would accept a new bid from their group. Only this time Vickers, not Litton, would be at the helm. It was an easy sell: cabinet was so taken with the idea of putting a Canadian firm in charge of the project that it suggested that all contenders for the frigate contract rearrange their affairs accordingly. Within weeks Saint John, the neophyte warship builder, had emerged as the leader of its consortium, while Sperry, at least on paper, was demoted to subcontractor. As well, Pratt & Whitney Canada, a wholly owned subsidiary of United Technologies, created its own Canadian-owned holding company, Scan Marine, which would manage the project if its team won.

In December 1980, Vickers learned its efforts had failed. The Saint John and Scan Marine groups had been picked as finalists. Eight months later, after the navy had narrowed down exactly what it wanted in the new frigates, the government gave each of the contenders its $20 million and sent them off to prepare their best bids. Almost from day one, Saint John's proposals were considered the most promising, in spite of the yard's lack of warship experience. The Saint John–Sperry team planned to build the six frigates in a straightforward, conventional manner, with a strict hierarchy outlining exactly who was in control at each stage of development. The Scan Marine bid, by contrast, involved a shell management company, which by itself was unconventional enough to make the navy brass nervous. Moreover, the Scan bid was also coming in significantly more expensive than the Saint John proposal.

By the time key cabinet members completed their preliminary evaluation of the bids, it was already clear that Saint John had won the battle to manage the project. Now began the contest for the political spoils. The navy and Saint John agreed that the cheapest, most effective way of managing the project was to build all six ships in one yard. Yet it was equally apparent that things were not going to happen exactly that way. Federal cabinet, for starters, had asked each of the finalists to prepare separate cost estimates based on three possible scenarios: a project involving six ships built in the home yard; one in which only four would be built at home; and a third in which only two would come out of the home yard. Clearly the project was going to be split. Cabinet simply wanted to know how much extra it would cost.

By September 1982, Saint John Shipbuilding president Andrew McArthur could read the writing on the wall as well as anyone. The Trudeau government had nine cabinet members from the area around Longueuil, Quebec, which was the headquarters for Scan Marine. If Saint John wanted the contract, it would have to provide plenty of ways to subcontract to Quebec and other regions of the country. Marc Lalonde, then finance minister, was the key player. Exercising his considerable powers as the cabinet member in charge of Quebec patronage, he ensured that at least three ships would be built by Quebec yards, in this case the ones owned by Vickers and MIL. (A third Quebec shipyard, Davie, wasn't entirely left out of the picture; cabinet agreed it would be guaranteed the shipyard portion of a separate military contract involving the modernization of four Tribal-class destroyers.)

So in 1983, when J.K. Irving signed the $3.8-billion contract, his moment of triumph was marred by the knowledge that Lalonde and the Quebec politicians had forced his family to subcontract three of the six ships to Quebec yards and the weapons integration work to Montreal firms. The real prize, however, was still to come. By then J.K. was well aware that the navy was planning to order a second batch of six frigates. This time the Irvings, who had argued since 1982 that they could have done the whole job more economically on their own, wanted the whole thing. So did the MIL yard, which was prepared to fight for the right to run the second half of the 12-ship contract, relegating Saint John to a secondary role. Both sides had powerful allies. The Defence Department argued that the Irving yard should get the contract because it made little sense to select a new company to build the second project when the design was supposed to be the same on all 12 ships. MIL's bid was backed by the Industry, Science and Technology Department, which felt a bidding war would force Saint John or MIL to create new high-technology ventures linked to the project. A not insignificant factor in MIL's favour was the succession of federal industry ministers with a Quebec power base.

In the end, it all came down to dollars and cents. The federal cabinet bought the navy's argument that a single project manager was the best approach. They were also impressed with the Defence Department's estimate that using a single shipyard would save tax-payers roughly $200 million. Splitting the contract was simply not in the cards.

It was just a week before Christmas 1987 when the 3,500 workers gathered in the football-field-sized warehouse at the Saint John ship-yard.[24] J.K., Arthur and Jack Irving stood on a platform at the front of the building, surrounded by a swarm of visiting navy and government officials. The crowd erupted when Perrin Beatty, the youth-ful defence minister, announced that Saint John Shipbuilding had won the management contract for a second series of six frigates. The question was how many of the ships would be built at the yard. Rumour was that two of the six were destined for MIL. It was left to the federal minister of state for forestry and mines, Gerald Mer-rithew, a man who had championed the Irving cause as a local MLA and later the area's MP, to provide the answer.

Merrithew began reading the list of ships to be built at the Saint John yard. "HMCS *Montreal*, HMCS *St. John's*, HMCS *Winnipeg*, HMCS *Charlottetown*. . . . " Here he paused for effect, and some in the anxious crowd began shouting "Go Gerry!" and "Keep going." Then, ending months of speculation, he added a fifth name, "HMCS *Ottawa*," bringing such a roar from the crowd that it drowned out the name of the HMCS *Fredericton*, the final frigate.

Atop the makeshift platform, J.K., the usually reserved chairman and chief executive of Saint John Shipbuilding, ran from person to person, shaking hands and embracing the visiting dignitaries. Then he stepped to the microphone. "We have come this far together, and now, for the first time, we can see years of work and stability ahead," he said, his words echoing off the inside walls. "We are in a position to build a future not only for the men who now work at the shipyard, but for their children, and perhaps, their children's children." In truth, he could just as well have been talking about his own family. The shipyard's long-promised moment of fulfilment meant that the Irving empire was no longer at the mercy of the cyclical economy and fluctuating commodity prices. And no one was happier than the patriarch of the clan, who, only months before his 89th birthday, had finally seen his vision fulfilled, albeit from faraway Bermuda.

8

Gassy, Grease and Oily

"We like to own things too."
— Arthur Irving

THEY HAVE SPENT their lives in his shadow. And even as J.K., Arthur and Jack Irving enter their 60s they still run the empire with one vision — K.C.'s. Well into his 80s the patriarch insisted on being involved in every aspect of the empire. No matter how much their father's faculties diminish, the three sons still keep him involved in any important decisions. Even today, their loyalty to him remains absolute. The Irving brothers never finished university, have never lived outside of the Maritimes and have never worked for anyone other than their father. Individuality was not something K.C. prized; he wanted to raise three boys who could shoulder his legacy and carry on the work he had started. In that goal he succeeded. During their boyhoods, through college and into manhood his sons have led similar lives. You can see his influence in everything about them — their cult of secrecy, their passion for work, their sober and serious private lives, their faith in family management and vigilance. Often they sound eerily like their enigmatic father, sprinkling their talk with the same antiquated phrases and figures of speech that flowed from his thin lips. "We had the world's best teacher," J.K. says. "Our father has always been able to look at things and do what was required to run them correctly for the long run. He got a lot of things moving, and we are having fun running them."

Fun indeed. Not one of the three Irving boys is quite the man their dad was in his time; perhaps none of them could have built the multibillion-dollar organization by himself. Underneath, K.C.'s sons are three different men with distinct temperaments, styles and abilities. Yet whatever their differences, they always put up a common front. As a group they are formidable — unrelenting in their pursuit of growth and their drive to keep their army of companies at the top. "Their greatest strength," says one high-ranking employee, "is their frightening single-mindedness." No wonder: like their father before them, they have embraced commerce as the ultimate good. For them, as for K.C., the family empire offers not just immense riches and power but a source of fulfilment and meaning in life.

Father-and-son relationships in this family, as in other dynasties, have never been simple. It is said that the boys accepted their destiny with a sense of resignation; life has not been easy beneath K.C.'s shadow. In many ways they have changed little from the three youngsters who grew up in the big white house on the hill, raising chickens in the backyard and peddling the eggs to neighbours to try to impress their demanding dad. The only difference now is that they at last seem comfortable with their place — a place created in part by inheritance and in part by design.

The Irving brothers stride straight out of the 1930s, their father's era. Old-fashioned capitalists with old-fashioned instincts, they run the empire with the paternalism of landed gentry and an unswerving conviction in the rightness of their actions. To a large degree their vast wealth reflects their persistence in holding on to the properties that K.C. built as they grew more valuable. Nevertheless, like many heirs to great wealth, they have felt compelled to undertake extraordinary challenges. Their touch has guided the empire in new directions. Trapped in cyclical industries and wedded to limited markets, they have shifted gears, adding new businesses, redirecting and modernizing old ones and spreading their network farther into the other Maritime provinces and Quebec and deeper into the United States.

As if to emphasize their new-found independence, they ended the 1980s by decisively dispatching their father's old partners. They bought out Kimberly-Clark's 35-per-cent stake in Irving Pulp and Paper. They snapped up the tissue plant that the American outfit had opened next to their pulp operation. Then the *coup de grâce*: they bought out Socal's interest in the refinery and Irving Oil. Once their people knew how to run the refinery, there was no need for them to continue the cumbersome relationship. So in January 1989, in a typically terse two-paragraph press release, the Irvings announced that they had acquired the 51-per-cent interest owned by the oil giant. The price tag for Socal's stake was estimated to be over $1 billion, and Socal booked a loss of $100 million (US) on the transaction. The symbolism of the event was unmistakable: the flagship had been repatriated. A new era seemed to be dawning, one in which the Irving companies no longer had to depend upon strategic alliances to battle the big boys.

But not so, say the sons of K.C. Irving, who still seem to think of themselves as mere saplings among the redwoods. The Irvings, to quote J.K. himself, "just run a small family-owned Maritime business," or to quote Arthur, "are small companies trying to compete with the big boys." This, of course, is simply nonsense: taken individually their companies may be small by international, even national standards. But the total picture — 25,000 employees, 300 or so companies, a personal worth estimated to be as much as $7-billion — points to staggering wealth. Indeed, the indisputable truth is that J.K., Jack and Arthur today wield their power over the New Brunswick economy in a way that K.C. only dreamed of when he sold his first Model T on the dusty main road of Bouctouche.

Even as youngsters they hugged the background. K.C., like his father before him, left the parenting to his wife while he busied himself in building an empire. Clearly he spent enough time with his sons to pass along his entrepreneurial bent; as soon as they were old enough, the boys were out after school peddling magazine subscriptions. Still, Hattie Irving brought up her sons to be just like everyone else. As youngsters, attending grade school alongside the sons and daughters of stevedores and day labourers, they were shy and never had extra money in their pockets. Later, all three headed for Rothesay Collegiate School (RCS), the private boys' school outside Saint John favoured by the New Brunswick gentry. At RCS they fit right in.

Jim, nicknamed "Oily," was a dashing rugby forward and managed the hockey team. Even then he was serious — playing a drum in the cadet corps, where he attained the rank of corporal, and displaying an early knack for business by setting up a mock corporation known as the "Irving Eel Company," where "his dexterity in handling dividend-hungry shareholders had more than a flash of brilliance."[1] Arthur, known as "Grease," was the most popular one in the family; good-looking and full of energy, he was a deadly rugby tackler, star forward on the hockey team and an avid member of the scout troop. As for Jack, the quietest brother ("Gassy"), he made his mark as a chess champion, a guard on the basketball team and captain of the rugby team, for which he anchored the scrum. According to the school yearbook, his ambition was "playing football." Jack's destiny: "$25 million."

The brothers didn't act like the heirs to immeasurable riches; at RCS they were known for keeping a close watch on their money. Ian Doig, a Calgary oil analyst who attended RCS in the 1940s (nickname "Beaver"), recalls that it was common practice for students to borrow a few pennies from one another to make up the difference in the price of a chocolate bar or some other snack from the school tuck shop. If you borrowed from the Irving boys, according to Doig, they always meticulously noted that you owed them one or two cents. He remembers being on the school basketball team when they travelled to Fredericton for the provincial finals. Because the train let them off a few miles outside of town, they had to take a cab to the gymnasium. Short on change, Doig borrowed a quarter from Jack Irving. "That was in 1948," recalls Doig. "Two years later I was walking down Barrington Street in Halifax and ran into Jack. He wanted to know if I had the quarter I owed him."

Even then the brothers had an eye for a business opportunity. One morning after a fierce rainstorm, the RCS students ran out of their residences to hunt for chestnuts shaken down from the huge trees on the school lawn. The chestnuts served as ammunition for conkers, a favourite game of Canadian youngsters, which is played by running shoelaces through two chestnuts and then taking turns with an opponent in trying to smash each other's conkers into pieces. Finding only a few chestnuts scattered on the lawn, they were puzzled — until they left church and were greeted by Arthur and Jack with heaping trays of nuts for sale.[2]

Next stop for the trio was Acadia University, the tiny, idyllic Baptist school in Wolfville, Nova Scotia, which K.C. attended during his brief university days. At Acadia they were good athletes and capable carousers, particularly Arthur, who shared a residence with five others, including a young man named Richard Hatfield, from Hartland, New Brunswick. Hatfield would later go on to have his own impact on their home province. Arthur ran with a group of rowdy Cape Bretoners and was first out on nocturnal raids of the women's residences and the nearby henhouses and apple orchards. Once, they terrified the matron at their residence by leaving a skinned deer carcass hanging from the ceiling in the basement. Arthur, like his brothers, failed to distinguish himself academically.

At Acadia there were only vague hints that the Irving boys lived a different life from everyone else: the short-wave radio that Jim kept in residence to communicate with his father; the family airplane that flew them back to Saint John for the holidays. Acadia, in a way, was a vacation before their real work began. The brothers simply weren't built for university. Jim was the first to leave: "I quit school on a Friday," he recalls, "and Monday morning I was 250 miles north of Saint John, helping move Irving logs down the Saint John River." Arthur dropped out a couple of years later. Jack, knowing full well where he was destined, soon dutifully followed his brothers back to New Brunswick. Never again would they leave. Time for the real education to begin.

Growing up rich does not guarantee success. Many wealthy children lack the spark that drives others. Parents may neglect to teach their heirs how to maintain the family fortune. Those certain to inherit may grow lazy and squander their legacy. Others feel too intimidated by a forebear's accomplishments to attempt to make their own mark. Some fall victim to the hangers-on and con men drawn to their wealth.[3]

K.C.'s boys never had a chance to fail. In their father's book the only place to start learning the nuances of business was by his side, and that is where they began, watching him seduce new customers, bang together new deals and put the finishing touches on his empire. Today the three Irving boys operate in distinct spheres of influence: Irving Oil and its dozens of subsidiaries are strictly Arthur's territory; Jack, the youngest and least public, looks after some of the family's newspapers, Thorne's hardware and their slew of construction companies. The empire's woodlands operations, as well as the huge shipyard and all the other companies that spin out of it, are the purview of J.K., the acknowledged leader of the group.

To the public, though, the three of them have coalesced into a single personality. The brothers have done little to dispel that perception. Their offices are within spitting distance — Arthur and Jack in the Golden Ball Building, still as grimy and yellowed as when K.C. ran things, and J.K. a parking lot away in the newer but still utilitarian Irving Building. Until J.K. decided to move outside the city in 1991, the trio lived in well-appointed, understated homes, within blocks of one another. They work and socialize together, rarely talk publicly about their businesses and don't really mix with others. They dress alike. They even sound alike, constantly talking about "our family" or "we," never "I."

On the job, they can seem almost interchangeable. Anyone who knows the brothers knows that, like their father, they work 12, 14, 16 hours a day for days on end, grab lunch on the run and rarely take vacations. They have inherited K.C.'s mania for secrecy, and armed guards patrol their homes when Irving companies are on strike. The brothers even refused to cooperate with a writer they themselves had hired to compile a family biography when he asked for a list of their companies. They are obsessed with cutting costs: J.K. and a handful of his top executives once found themselves on their knees at 3 a.m. digging up Irving paving stones by hand so they wouldn't be ruined by a backhoe scoop. When the three brothers once flew by private jet into New York's La Guardia Airport, they spent 20 minutes waiting for a cab because J.K. was unwilling to spend the $24 it cost to take them to their business appointments. (The stubborn wait paid off: J.K. was finally able to beat a driver down to $19 for the trip.)

Most of all, they remain fixated with being in control, a goal that becomes harder to attain the larger the empire grows. Still, they persist. Unwilling to delegate authority, the brothers are old-fashioned autocrats who make all the decisions themselves and demand to know every detail about their operations: why a plant isn't operating smoothly; why a service station is momentarily running a bit below capacity. Each month, all 300 or so of their companies send profit and loss statements to the head offices so that the brothers will know where they stand. If there's a new product being designed, the Irving boys don't just want to know about it, they want to see it, hold it, run it through their fingers. Since they like to see things for themselves, they keep a fleet of aircraft — five jets, two turboprops and a helicopter — on stand-by to fly them wherever they need to go. They don't travel in the same aircraft for the same reason that government officials from small South American countries don't fly *en masse* — "You never know when a plane is going to go down," growls Arthur. "Somebody has to be here to pay the bills." So they fly separately, or simply drive, whatever it takes to constantly keep on top of their operations.

Yet no matter how hard they work, or how much they accomplish, they are forever doomed to be *K.C.'s boys*; when people look at the three Irving brothers what they see is their father all over again, sober and unrelenting, but without the old man's polish and undeniable personal charm. And that is true, although only to a point. Burrow beneath the veneer, past the obvious similarities, and you'll eventually find three vastly different individuals who have spent their days struggling to conform to a life for which they were always destined.

Like the four-wheel-drive vehicles he is so fond of, J.K. Irving is wide, powerful and efficient. He has an intimidating presence: severe steel-rimmed glasses, pale complexion and a hairline that has receded almost to the back of his skull. J.K., who was born in 1929, masks his considerable intelligence with a rough-hewn manner and an impatience that can be withering. "At heart, he's still a lumberjack," one of his old hands says. Not surprising, considering that he spent his early working years running the family's northern lumber camps, sleeping each spring in tents in the woods as he and his men shepherded the wave of Irving timber to its destination.

He was shrewd back then, recalls Frank Jean, a Fredericton stockbroker who was in the hardware business in northern New Brunswick in the early 1950s. "Jim would come to buy two nails from us and end up selling us three from Thorne's hardware." Others remember him as a born timber boss who earned a reputation for toughness by running roughshod over hardened lumbermen twice his age. "He was constantly bawling out the guys, which was something that K.C. would never have done," says one older former Irving employee. Once, while overseeing a logging operation from a low-flying Beaver aircraft, he noticed a man lounging on the sidelines. So J.K. leaned out the window and started bellowing at him through his loud-hailer to get to work. It was several days before he learned that he had been shouting orders at a farmer standing on his own land.[4]

In his early years he was something of a plodder, running the businesses with a firm but uninspired hand. Strange, then, that he would evolve into the trio's leader, a man who now seems to be at the peak of his life. He is the steadying influence: he keeps Arthur in check, carries the ball during the touchiest business negotiations and acts as the front man for the empire's surprising new public relations push. But he remains the most guarded of these secretive brothers. Unless he is angered, words don't flow from J.K. as much as they are stubbornly extracted. Ask if he ever had any ambitions beyond business and he replies, "Oh, it would have been nice to be an artist or maybe a writer. But one does what one does best." Ask what motivates him and he rejoins, "We do what we do because we enjoy it." Why does he enjoy it: "I like the competition. I enjoy working with the family and passing things on to the family."

Business, family and duty: these are the themes of J.K.'s life. The empire is liberally sprinkled with his offspring. Jim Jr., his oldest boy, looks after the family's forestry operations, while Robert manages Cavendish Farms Ltd., their frozen food company, and some of the trucking lines. For a time his oldest daughter, Mary Jean, was a pivotal figure in their bid to overtake the McCain family, New Brunswick's second most powerful clan, in the frozen food business. Judith, his youngest child, ran a photo operation that once had the contract to take all the photographs for the frigate construction program. His wife, Jean, has a hand in the business too, operating a flower shop downstairs from J.K.'s office.

There's nothing flashy about his world. Whenever possible he has his breakfast bacon and eggs with Jim Jr. at a diner a few blocks from their offices. For advice he leans heavily on his wife, a prominent member of a local fundamentalist church. For decades they lived within blocks of his brothers and their families. In 1991 J.K. and Jean moved to Rothesay, the bedroom community for Saint John's élite, to be near Jim Jr. and Judith. There they live in a huge, *Dallas*-style bungalow, surrounded by a high wall to protect them from prying eyes.

Like his father's before him, J.K.'s life lacks balance. His family constantly urges him to take time off to tramp around in the woods, fish or just lie around at Irvingmere, the lavish family summer home — complete with private airstrip and heated outdoor pool — outside of Bouctouche, less than a mile from the house where K.C. returns for his regular visits to his birthplace. He rarely listens. When he does steal some free time, he likes to study strategy, whether in Canadian politics, which he follows closely, or in war movies, which he watches for the same reason. Although not a collector, he also enjoys paintings, particularly landscapes, and has a fondness for old maps and other antiquities.

He inherited his father's puritanical streak, eschewing booze and tobacco and driving a four-wheel-drive Ford. His only known affectation is the wide-brimmed fedora he sometimes sports while barrelling through town behind the wheel of his car, talking on his car phone with his trusted secretary, Diane Godfrey. And perhaps that is how he sees himself: adventurous, a touch roguish — J.K. Irving, the intrepid industrialist, on a quest for more profits and more business opportunities and the greater glory of the Irving empire.

For J.K., more than either of his brothers, is a man of the present, a man bent on moving the 19th-century empire at least partially into the 20th century before the dawn of the year 2000. He calls himself an environmentalist and backs up his talk with action, serving on the Premier's Round Table on the Environment and Economic Development, appearing before Common Council to explain the family's attempts to fight pollution and cooperating, within limits, with the provincial environment department. He is also said to be responsible for the Irvings' new-found taste for public philanthropy — for the $700,000 donated for a new heart wing on the Saint John Regional Hospital, and for the $666,000 that the family gave towards the restoration of an old Saint John theatre. It was J.K., with Jean's influence, who broke the family's long-time rule about not allowing charity donations to be taken off company paycheques. He even grants the rare interview to his newspapers and makes the occasional speech on subjects like free trade or other themes in which the family has a vested interest.

Could J.K. actually be mellowing? "He realizes the value of public relations when it comes to getting what they want," concludes a business associate. Some have even suggested that J.K. is interested in "enhancing his family's good name." But even his critics grudgingly admit that it is too facile to dismiss his interest in the environment and philanthropy as merely a bid for good publicity. After all, this is the same man who sent his security guards to find the thief who hot-wired his car and then quietly gave the culprit a job within the Irving organization because he claimed to have turned to crime to feed his family. Not the sort of benevolence one is accustomed to hearing associated with the Irving name. But, then again, just the sort of quiet gesture that K.C. himself seemed so fond of.

Arthur Irving is so tightly wound, you fear he is going to explode. Words may need to be coaxed from J.K., but they fly in machine-gun bursts from his younger brother. Pacing restlessly around his office, he seethes nervous energy — sitting down, standing up, leaving the room to make a telephone call, then striding back in a few minutes later. Born in 1931, he has the energy of someone half his age. Though he bears the bald Irving dome, he remains lean, rugged and just under six feet tall, with quick, clear eyes and the taunt, sharp features of an ageing Marlboro man.

It is as if all this tension bottled up within rejuvenates rather than ages him. For he cuts a youthful figure, looking not unlike how he must have done nearly 40 years ago when he was just starting out in the family business and exuded all the effortless grace of an F. Scott Fitzgerald hero. He was good company back then. "Arthur was always smiling and laughing in those days," says one early friend. "You couldn't have asked for a better person to spend time with." Indeed, he remains the splashy one with the charisma in the family. The one with the green BMW, the wife 25 years younger and K.C.'s white-pillared home on the top of Mount Pleasant. A real "man's man," he jogs, takes his sons canoeing in the Northwest Territories, fishes for salmon at the Miramichi family lodge and shoots ducks; he is past president of Ducks Unlimited, an organization dedicated to preserving wetlands. The most overtly political of the trio, he socializes within a limited circle of friends that includes a handful of past and present New Brunswick politicians and extends to Toronto lawyer Edgar Sexton and his wife, *Toronto Globe and Mail* society columnist Rosemary Sexton.

Yet Arthur Irving is far from happy-go-lucky today. A businessman as powerful as he is will naturally step on a few toes. When angered, however, Arthur has been known to cow subordinates, lose his temper during business negotiations and loudly berate critics, no matter whether during government royal commissions or cocktail parties. One admiring ex-employee, who worked closely with him, says Arthur "will tear a strip off the president of the refinery the same way he does a mail boy." In fact, when he walks into the room, you can almost hear his underlings click their heels together like lowly NCOs in the presence of a five-star general.

His short fuse is famous. New Brunswick lawyer Ed Byrne, dining at K.C.'s Bermuda home one evening, was railed at by Arthur throughout the meal for his role in the Brunswick Mining saga, by then almost a decade past. A government official involved in the Atlantic Canada Opportunity Agency, set up by the Mulroney government to provide venture capital financing for Maritime businesses, recalls visiting his office; Arthur asked him whether he saw the prime minister. When he replied that he did, Arthur said, "Well, you tell him that he is a fucking liar."[5] Mulroney's crime: promising while on the election trail to privatize Petro-Canada, and then failing to live up to his words.

There was a time when Arthur was described as "the easygoing brother," the one who was "known to sit at his father's side in business conferences for hours without saying a word."[6] What hardened him? Some people around Saint John say his 1980 divorce from his first wife was partially responsible. Joan Carlisle was an Audrey Hepburn look-alike from Sackville who, it was said, met Arthur at french fry millionaire Wallace McCain's wedding. They made a striking, popular couple and soon were a regular fixture in Saint John's smart young crowd, hitting house parties and dances and weekending in the country with friends. They had four children, named Kenneth, Arthur, Jennifer and Emily. The break-up, when it came, was bitter. Joan's lawyer told the *Wall Street Journal* that Arthur claimed that some of the household paintings belonged to Irving Oil, even though they had hung in the Irving house for up to 25 years. The story is that K.C. eventually intervened and told Arthur to settle the spat, which he did, providing Joan with a $1-million trust fund and $500,000 in cash, believed to be the largest settlement in New Brunswick history.[7] (She later married and divorced another industrialist, Norman Keevil, founder of the Vancouver mining colossus Teck Corp.)

Rumours — and these were nothing more — had it that the unpleasant divorce and all the attendant publicity cost Arthur his favoured-son status with his father. Later, he remarried, to Sandra Ring, the daughter of a middle-class Baptist Saint John family who worked in the traffic ticket division of Saint John city hall. Although his new wife was nearly 25 years younger, they soon began another family with the birth of a daughter, Sarah, in 1988. But, says one old friend of Arthur's, "the divorce tore him up inside. He has soured a bit on life."

One thing hasn't diminished through all of this: his drive to win. Arthur Irving's ambition to come out on top is all-consuming and more than a little frightening to watch. When he stares you straight in the eye and says that the Irving companies have "the best people and the best products around" and that "we will go wherever things take us," he almost dares you to disagree. Tireless, he is said to rise at 5:30 a.m. and often does not return home until midnight. Throughout the long day the intensity never lets up. He is constantly spinning ideas ("I have more ideas before breakfast than you guys have all day," he once told a roomful of employees in exasperation). Arthur, like his father, is not scared of getting his hands dirty. When a poorly parked automobile was backing up traffic at the grand opening of one Irving station, Arthur, then in his late 50s, rolled up his shirtsleeves and joined the gang of Irving employees who picked up the car and moved it.

His enthusiasm can be contagious. When he meets employees face to face he sounds like some sort of latter-day Vince Lombardi as he exhorts them on to greater effort in the Irving name. Screw up, though, and you have him to reckon with. Nobody, not the highest-ranking company president or the lowest labourer, escapes his criticism. The same goes for his sons, whom he used to treat more harshly than most employees, and even his brother Jack, whom he has been known to chew out publicly, in front of underlings.

He makes no apologies for how he acts. As far as he's concerned the end, winning, justifies the means. "Look, it's like playing hockey. If you are going to be a good hockey player you have to be aggressive, right? Well, it is the same in business. We are small and we are competing with some of the world's biggest oil companies. To stay in that ring you have to be a little aggressive. Otherwise you are not going to be in there."

Clichés, maybe. But in the straightforward world that Arthur Irving inhabits, there is no room for compromise, or for doubt.

Jack Irving is forever destined to be the younger brother, the one hovering tentatively in the background. He has spent his life walking in the footsteps of his older, tougher, more forceful siblings — at Rothesay, then Acadia, and finally within the empire itself. It is a role that suits him: with his metal-rimmed glasses and balding pate, he looks strikingly like his brother Jim, only smaller, gentler and softer around the edges. His round, elfin face is quick to smile. There's a shy, uncertain quality about him, particularly when you see him in action around J.K. and Arthur. "He is terrified of his brothers," says an employee. "He constantly defers to them." When the brothers make their rounds, J.K. and Arthur do all the talking; every now and then Jack breaks in with an obligatory question for an employee or plays the cheerleader, blurting out some maxim about "providing top-quality products and the best service in the industry." Usually, though, he just stands there, listening quietly.

He's the one nobody seems to have a handle on. Around Saint John they say that J.K. is the leader and Arthur is the toughest of the lot. Jack — well, if they say anything at all, it is usually that he is the nice guy in the family . . . nice but sort of irrelevant. Nothing could be farther from the truth, says one of his good friends, an old-time Saint Johner who protests that Jack is "merely misunderstood." People who know him well say that he is the Irving brother with the most well-rounded existence, "the one closest to a fully developed human being."

Born in 1932, he has the reputation of being the kindest and most considerate of the trio. As for being the lightweight in the family — that seems to stem more from sheer force of personality than from intellect. "He gives the impression of not being able to answer questions," a friend says. "But he is not stupid. He has a very curious nature." A former employee says that Jack's grasp of the construction industry and the other companies he handles is truly impressive. And, as docile as he seems when his high-powered brothers are around, in private Jack Irving's wrath can make employees cringe.

In some respects, he doesn't quite fit the Irving mould. Jack's interests are eclectic: he has an impressive collection of antique handguns and rifles, which he keeps under lock and key in his Mount Pleasant home. He's the reader in the family, the one most interested in the arts. He's a good dancer who, according to one Saint John woman, "can really jitterbug." He takes an interest in world politics, although his view on some events is thought to be somewhat muddled; like many capitalists, he tends to see a communist down every path.

Jack's family also seems to realize there is more to life than the domain of the Irving empire. His wife, Suzanne, sits on the board of governors of the University of New Brunswick. Daughter Anne, the oldest child, is studying at the University of Toronto. One son, John Jr., did a few years in the oil company before leaving to do an MBA at Harvard; he then returned to Irving Oil. The other, Colin, is showing signs of being the first rebel in the clan: instead of submissively moving right into the family business after university, he taught skiing in Vermont, and when last heard of was working as a producer at an Ontario radio station.

That Jack keeps the lowest profile of this decidedly low-profile group of brothers is understandable. One Friday evening in 1982, he was coming home with his wife and 11-year-old Anne when a young man shoved a .45-calibre revolver in his face and ordered the three of them into the house. Inside he tied up Suzanne and Anne. Then he forced Jack into a car and drove to a nearby van, where he bound, gagged and blindfolded him, covering his body with an old blanket. For the next 10 hours the kidnapper drove the van through the Saint John streets, stopping at regular intervals to negotiate from phone booths for the $600,000 ransom he demanded. All the time, more than 40 police and a squad of RCMP officers were scouring the city. Eventually they tracked the van to a parking lot, rushed the vehicle and overpowered the kidnapper.

Some say Jack retreated further into the shadows after the abduction. Others, though, say that perhaps there's more than meekness behind his desire to take a back seat to his brothers. After all, Jack, more than any of his siblings, seems to have found a middle ground between life as he wants it to be and his obligations to the family and the family business. There are those who argue that this attitude makes him the smartest of the lot.

9

The Irving Way

*Know the enemy, know yourself; your victory will
never be endangered. Know the ground, know the
weather; your victory will then be total.*
— *The Art of War*, Sun Tzu

ONE MORNING in January 1989 the three Irving brothers gathered,
as they often do, in Arthur Irving's spacious mahogany-panelled office at the top of the Golden Ball Building. To the right hung a
large world map, dotted with tanker-shaped magnets marking the
locations of the Irving Oil fleet. Nearby, a studded drill bit sat on
a low desk. From the back wall, an oil portrait of K.C. Irving loomed
symbolically over the room. Dressed in conservative business suits
and paisley ties, the three billionaires sat serious and unsmiling.

After months of requests, the Irving brothers had agreed to a meeting — largely, it seemed, because they knew my father and uncle
from university. My first question was a lob, designed to defuse the
obvious tension. "Perhaps I could start by asking if there are any
misconceptions about your family or your businesses which you feel
you want to clear up."

They looked at one another, then back at me. Then Arthur Irving,
lean and athletic like his father, said, "We feel no reason to explain
anything." Silence settled over the room. Finally Arthur swivelled
his head towards J.K., 20 pounds heavier and three years older, and
broke the lull.

"I don't even know what I'm doing here," he said. "You got me
into this. I'll do whatever you want."

"Let's just go have a look around," said J.K., ever the conciliator.
"How about that?"

No one said yes, but no one said no either. So J.K., Arthur and Jack stood and headed towards the door. What followed over the next two days was more a guided tour than a conventional interview. Travelling by car, van and airplane, they covered hundreds of miles and showed me most of the major components of their empire — the shipyard, the oil refinery, their fleet of oil supertankers and the army of service stations. We visited the Irving woodlands and the pulp, newsprint and lumber mills. We walked through their home furnishings and convenience stores and lunched at their restaurants.

Through it all, the brothers remained exceedingly polite, but guarded. They talked freely about the generalities of their operations. When the questions became too prying for their liking, they simply declined to answer. Their reluctance to surrender too much information was not surprising: the Irvings remain as secretive today as in K.C.'s time. At the same time, though, perhaps there was also a certain logic in J.K.'s decision to explain the Irving Way not through words but by demonstrating it in action.

"We are hands-on operators — always have been, always will be," J.K. cheerfully admits as he manoeuvres his car with short, quick jerks of the steering wheel across the wet, potholed Saint John streets. "If we had to sit in the office all day, we would die." As the three of them barrel across town that winter morning, there seems little chance of that happening. Not necessarily because they relish trying to keep tabs personally on the day-to-day operations of 300 companies. But because running things hands-on was how their old man did things, and this, therefore, is how *they* do things.

Despite its immense size and complexity, stress cracks have yet to appear at the top of the Irving empire. If not symbiotic, they are certainly in sync; the brothers stay well within their areas of control, always keeping one another informed about what they are up to. Big decisions are made together and in consultation with K.C. As J.K. points out, there are no committees running the family enterprises: "As long as the four of us are together we can have our shareholders' meetings right here, right now. We can make quick decisions we wouldn't be able to make if we were a public company. That's one of our great advantages."

One of many. Viewed against the rest of the industrialized world, the Irving organization seems frozen in time; that, indeed, is part of their secret. Alfred Chandler, the influential American business historian, argues that the main reason so many big U.S. concerns were foundering by the end of the 1980s was that they had become prisoners of their own success.[1] As they grew from industry-dominant firms into multinationals and conglomerates, their managers got into businesses they knew little about, overloaded themselves, lost touch with the foot-soldiers and, above all, found themselves under relentless pressure to maximize profits and dividends.

The Irvings have never lost their bearings or their unique corporate culture. They have resisted growing bloated and bureaucratic. They have stayed in businesses they understand and have maintained their long-term perspective. They have kept the empire grounded in the concrete, not the conceptual; all in all their businesses are gritty and blue-collar, and as far from the glamorous world of high tech and high finance as their own drab Saint John office buildings are from the gleaming glass towers of Bay Street. Most of all, they have kept the glint on their entrepreneurial edge, constantly pushing for new markets and greater chunks of existing ones. "Are we old-fashioned?" Jack Irving asks rhetorically. "Well, there's nothing wrong with being old-fashioned."

Through it all, they have stayed true to K.C.'s vision, and perhaps it is the 3,000 Irving service stations — with their clean lines, white façades and long canopies overhanging the pumps — that epitomize the empire's evolution, the way it has clung to basics, honed and refined them and used them to steamroll the competition. "It's amazing," says one prominent Saint John businessman, not an Irving fan, who nonetheless marvels at the efficiency of their service station operations. "I'll stop and go in for gas. Maybe I'll have a snack in the restaurant. Then I'll go into the store and buy some groceries. Get some money out of the banking machine. Rent a movie. Before you know it, you're $50 in the hole."

Evaluated purely in terms of gasoline sold, the Irving stations are far from industry leaders. Evidence presented during a 1983 federal government inquiry into the petroleum industry showed that Irving stations badly trailed the competition from 1973 to 1981 in the quantities sold by stations in such critical markets as St. John's, Halifax, Dartmouth and even Saint John.[2] Still, by sheer force of numbers they have an iron grip on the Maritime market. Each year Irving Oil sells $600 million worth of gasoline and heating oil in New Brunswick, which accounts for nearly 45 per cent of the provincial market. In Nova Scotia, by comparison, their 27-per-cent market share brings in roughly $275 million in annual sales.

The Irving stations are money-spinning machines. They range from mom-and-pop operations with a single pump to Irving truck stops with a half-dozen multi-pump islands, restaurants and convenience stores with restrooms and showers for the truckers. The biggest ones are worth $1.5 million and employ 25 or 30 uniformed employees who run the pumps, tinker with engines in the garage, wait on tables in the restaurant and run the convenience store cash registers. Annual sales are regularly in the range of $12 to $15 million.

The vast majority of the stations are leased from Irving Oil, for either a percentage of gasoline sales or a flat rate. The person who manages the whole complex can take home $100,000 a year. But, as one former superintendent explains, they earn it. "It is a day and night job, whatever it takes to get the work done. Arthur knows the sales volume for each station, whether it is up or whether it is down. If it is down, they want to know why. And if nothing can be done about it quickly, you'll be gone. They always want to push to increase the volumes. They are never satisfied."

That fact becomes abundantly clear the more time one spends watching the Irving brothers operate — for example, at the sprawling Saint John shipyard, which, along with oil and forestry, has developed into the third support underpinning the empire. In early 1989, some 3,500 workers toiled at the yard, building frigates under the $6-billion contract for the Canadian navy. As J.K. picks his way through the yard's controlled chaos, he tells me with undisguised pride that the yard was almost bankrupt when his dad bought it 30 years earlier, and that his family has since built it into Canada's only real naval shipyard, capable of building four huge frigates simultaneously.

Asked how the navy frigate project was progressing, J.K. adjusts his hardhat and replies that it is a "great success" and is bringing hundreds of millions of dollars and thousands of jobs to the New Brunswick economy. Actually, by the time of our tour the frigate program was mired in difficulty. Everyone involved had underestimated the sheer magnitude and complexity of the job. HMCS *Halifax*, the prototype being built at the Saint John yard, was slipping farther behind schedule. So were the three ships being built by MIL, the Montreal-based subcontractor. The level of the Irving family's concern was underscored by the $1.7-billion lawsuit the Irving yard launched against MIL in late 1990, claiming it had "failed to provide the necessary financial and management resources to its shipyards," thus jeopardizing the success of the whole project.[4]

In their hearts, not even the eternally optimistic Irvings expected to make money on the first vessel. The pay-off, if it comes, will be in the second batch of frigates, when the Saint John yard knows how to do the job well enough to cut costs, enabling them to increase their profit margins. By then, they expect to have the technology and expertise in place to build nuclear reactors for New Brunswick, submarines and mine-sweepers for Ottawa and warships for NATO. "We are always looking for new contracts," says J.K. "That's what this business is all about."

Indeed, if there is one thing that K.C. taught his boys, it is to take nothing for granted. When Arthur says, "You can't stand in one spot," he is stating one of the undeniable truths of the family corporate philosophy. To stand still, for a business enterprise like the Irving family's, is to be complacent; to be complacent in the shark-infested waters of the corporate world is tantamount to writing your own suicide note. So they forge on, searching for an edge and an angle wherever they can find one.

You can see their unrelenting philosophy in operation throughout their empire. For instance, at the mile-long, $1.2-billion refinery, which, with its own streets, sewage system and fire department, is like a futuristic village. There, according to Arthur, "Crude is cooked into the highest-octane gasoline anywhere in the country." Nearby tower the huge tanks that are capable of storing 6 million barrels of crude and 6 million barrels of refined products. That enables the Irvings to take advantage of oil price fluctuations, such as the boom that occurred when Iraq invaded Kuwait, pushing the price of Middle Eastern crude, of which Irving Oil is far and away the largest purchaser in Canada, sky-high.

Their single-minded doctrine is also on display throughout their forest products operations, which span lumbering, pulp, paper and tissue production, serving customers around the globe. At the pinnacle of their forestry arm stands J.D. Irving Ltd., the first family business and the company closest to K.C.'s heart. J.D. Irving looks after the bulk of the 3.4 million acres of forestland that the family owns outright or leases from governments throughout the Maritimes, Quebec and Maine. Irving harvesting techniques, like virtually everything about the empire, are decisively straightforward; usually, huge mechanical harvesters sever and strip whole trees in a single motion. The practice, known as clear-cutting, bares whole swaths of land right to the ground. Each year vast tracts of Irving land are cleared and the harvest trucked to their stable of mills.

The family, however, has never forgotten the early lesson K.C. learned when he was unable to find enough trees to fuel his father's mill in Bouctouche. The Irvings spend some $10 million annually growing millions of seedlings to be planted on their land as part of the reforestation program that K.C. pioneered in 1958. In 1986 they planted their 200-millionth tree. The vast majority of the seedlings are black spruce, which are resilient to the spruce budworm that cyclically attacks spruce and fir. It will be years, decades in some places, before the family realizes profits from reforestation; in other areas the Irvings may never see the benefit of the program. The point is that they are well on the way to turning vast sections of New Brunswick into their own private tree farm; never again, if they can help it, will their mills fall silent because the flow of logs has simply dried up.

Indeed, foresight of this sort is evident throughout the Irving forest products operations, which each year account for roughly $900 million worth of sales. J.D. Irving Ltd.'s showcase sawmill in Saint-Léonard — according to J.K., "absolutely the best mill you will find anywhere" — can produce 400,000 board-feet of lumber daily (enough to build 15,000 houses a year) and is so state-of-the-art that its computers constantly monitor the spot commodity markets and automatically cut boards to the length fetching the highest price at the time.

The Irving vision is even obvious at the gloomily high-tech Irving Pulp & Paper complex, which sits above the foaming chaos of Saint John's Reversing Falls. The mill was producing just 80 tons of pulp daily in the late 1970s. After spending hundreds of millions on new technology, the mill employs 500 and pumps out nearly 900 tons of semi-bleached and bleached kraft pulp every day for delivery to customers as far away as Europe and the Middle East.

The Irvings, of course, always keep an eye out for opportunities for expansion, and through the years they have incessantly sought new markets for their forestry products. For a start there is the Rothesay Paper Ltd. newsprint mill, which they bought from MacMillan Bloedel Ltd. of Vancouver for $145 million in 1981 and immediately began renovating and upgrading. With over 700 employees, the mill spews out 950 tons of newsprint and fine paper on a good day; rolls of Rothesay newsprint are sold as far away as Miami and the Caribbean.

In the late 1980s they stepped into a new direction — finished products. They paid Kimberly-Clark roughly $100 million for their Saint John tissue plant. Later they invested another $30 million in a new plant in Dieppe, outside of Moncton, to turn the tissue made at the Saint John plant into facial and bathroom tissues, paper towels and napkins. Much of the production was destined for the United States, where the Irvings have big plans now that the Canada–United States Free Trade Agreement has removed the barriers on shipments of finished products to the south.

The family prides itself on paying as much attention to small details as to the big picture. For Arthur, this approach is best demonstrated by the Irving restaurants, which are always built beside a family service station and convenience store. Nothing pretentious inside their eateries — just good, plain, home-cooked food. Over lunch, during a brief break in the tour, he proceeds to illustrate.

"See this?" he says, waving a small packet of ketchup. "It is Heinz. The other guy doesn't use Heinz." He points to a container of cream. "See that? Eighteen per cent. The other guy uses 12 per cent."

Then, for final emphasis, he waves a paper napkin. "See this: big napkins. The other guy uses small ones."

Leaning forward, he concludes profoundly: "That's the key to our success: Heinz Ketchup, 18-per-cent cream and big napkins."

They leave nothing to chance. Spend some time watching their organization in action and it becomes apparent that this same unsparing attention to detail marks all aspects of the Irving management style, including their investment decisions. "We like complementary businesses," explains Arthur in an oversized understatement. What he is talking about, of course, is vertical integration, K.C.'s hallmark. To really understand how his sons have transformed this simple business strategy into a high art, it is best to talk specifics — say, a simple tree grown on an acre of Irving land.

When a crew comes to fell the tree, they will be using all Irving products: tools from Thorne's hardware, heavy equipment from Commercial Equipment, even food from Cavendish Farms. The wood goes to an Irving sawmill, where it is cut into lumber or pulpwood. The logs leave the mill on trucks owned by Sunbury Transport Ltd., one of the family's three trucking lines, which run on Irving gasoline and use tires from Irving-owned Maritime Tire Ltd. The driver might stop for lunch at an Irving restaurant. Then he wheels the truckload of timber to one of the Irving pulp mills — where, say, Strescon Ltd., the family's concrete fabrication company, is in the midst of expanding the facilities — to be dissolved into wood pulp. From there, the pulp moves across town to the family's Rothesay newsprint plant, to be transformed into newspaper for the Irving dailies. The papers, of course, get a good chunk of their ad revenues from other Irving companies and are sold in Irving convenience stores. There, as likely as not, they are bought by Irving employees, who get their paycheques from. . . .

And so it goes, on and on and on, through product after product and business after business. Until in the end what exists is an airtight world, where all the businesses feed off one another and where few pennies are spent that don't go back into the Irving coffers. The tissue plant that the family opened in Dieppe in 1990 is a case in point. The only product consumed by the plant that is not provided by an Irving company is the carton used to package the tissue products. Underlining the family's ultimate goal was Robert Irving, who heads up the tissue plant and who said during a rare press conference, "It was always a dream of my grandfather's to be able to complete the vertical integration concept in his forestry operation." The sons seem bent on penetrating all the nooks and crannies of the New Brunswick economy, the tiny crevices where big conglomerates usually don't bother to tread, where they compete against small local businesses struggling to survive in the perennially depressed economy.

One pillar of the Saint John business community, not a fan of the family's, has a theory that each year the three brothers order their companies to present a consolidated statement of expenses by suppliers. Then they run their fingers down the columns to see which companies they paid the most to during the past 12 months, and consider whether they should get into the business themselves. Farfetched as that sounds, there's no denying their penchant for cutting out the middleman by simply supplying their own companies with products and services, instead of paying someone else. Indeed, when a Saint John printing company went bankrupt in early 1989, it blamed its failure on an inability to win Irving business.

"We don't have a monopoly in New Brunswick," counters Arthur. "Anyone is free to come in and set up any business they want." Fine in theory. But the complicated cross-fertilization of Irving outfits makes it difficult, some say impossible, to compete with them in their industries. For one thing, their companies don't have to be strictly profitable. The Irvings can afford to carry a new firm if it doesn't make money at first. There are even companies that are consistent money-losers — the S.M.T. bus line, for one. Yet they keep the outfit going because it helps keep the wheels turning in the rest of the empire.

At the same time, the empire looks after its own. Irving companies buy only from other Irving companies, even if they could pay less by getting their products from an outsider. When, for instance, a newcomer signs a lease to run an Irving service station, he or she agrees to buy "all other merchandise or other products which Irving may from time to time designate." Proprietors of Irving convenience stores regularly receive memos from head office ordering them to do business only through authorized suppliers, almost all of which are other Irving companies. Thorne's hardware, for example, supplies "all hardware, carryout bags, light bulbs, ice, salt, work gloves, Irving garbage bags and kitchen catchers exclusively, barbecues, styrofoam coolers . . . ." Cavendish Farms products "should be carried exclusively." Commercial Equipment provides "car care items and Duracell Batteries." As well, "a good supply of *Atlantic Advocates* [the glossy Irving-owned monthly magazine] is to be kept in a rack beside the cash register at all times."[5]

The Irving organization does not permit any deviation from the rule. A letter from an unidentified employee to Arthur Irving, dated April 6, 1976, and entered as evidence before the 1983 federal inquiry into the oil industry, underscored this. "In the Merri-Milk Mart on Sunday I noticed that panty hose of other brands than Irving Oil were being sold. This is completely ridiculous. We must look into raising Mr. Lamb's [the proprietor's] rent, and in the meantime it shows bad supervision on our part and bad thinking on the lessee's part to buy products from a competitor."[6]

When the empire doesn't actually make a product, it plays an intricate game of tit for tat. The upshot is that if you want to sell to the Irvings, your own company had better buy from them. When head office orders convenience store managers to "support" Kingsford Charcoal, it is because "AMCA Food Brokers, distributor of Kingsford Charcoal, supports Irving Oil 100% by giving us all their gas and oil business." Direct competitors, by the same token, get short shrift: store managers were once ordered not to buy from Canada Packers because the McCain family, which competes with Irving's Cavendish Farms products, had purchased a substantial stake in the food company.[7]

Outsiders just don't seem to have much of a chance against the Irving colossus. One example: the independent truckers that compete against the family's trucking lines. According to a 1990 decision by the New Brunswick Motor Carrier Board, Irving-owned Sunbury Transport had a monopoly over freight from Irving companies and was using it to underprice independent trucking companies in the fight for non-Irving freight. "Sunbury is able to charge artificially high rates on the movement of affiliated [Irving] freight," said the board in turning down an application by Sunbury to expand its trucking licence so that it could haul freight anywhere in North America. "This allows Sunbury to cross-subsidize its non-affiliated rates. If the authority applied for is granted, we conclude that it will likely result in abuse of market power through further cross-subsidization and entry-deterrent pricing in the open markets. As independent carriers that have no captive freight are faced with the cross-subsidized prices of Sunbury, they will have to withdraw from the market or sustain continuing losses."[8]

The Irving family plays hardball. A prime target of their wrath over the years has been the Daley family of Saint John, which runs a string of service stations under the logo of Petro-Canada, Arthur Irving's chief nemesis. Whenever and wherever the Daleys apply to build a new station, the Irving lawyers ask the local municipal council to dismiss the bid. Should that fail, the Irving team takes to the courts, if necessary carrying the fight to quash the proposal straight through to the Supreme Court of Canada. Sometimes Irving Oil simply erects its own station across the street from the new Daley operation, whether the site warrants another new station or not. The Daleys say that they have even caught Irving employees in the dark of night trying to take readings from their gas pumps to see how much business a site is doing. "Let's just say they are tough competitors," concludes Tom Daley.

Organized labour has also from time to time found itself in the family's gunsights. One of the family's trucking concerns, RST Industries Ltd., owes its very existence to an effort to thwart a union organizing drive. When Irving Oil's truck drivers showed signs of wanting to unionize in the 1970s, RST was incorporated under the direction of J.D. Irving Ltd. After the Irving Oil drivers walked out, RST simply took over the bulk hauling, virtually ending the strike before it began. In 1990, the Canadian Brotherhood of Railway, Transport and General Workers complained before the Canada Labour Relations Board that the Irving truck companies were using threats and intimidation to stop their drivers from joining the union.[9]

Size isn't a factor in raising the Irving ire. Wayne Murray, a mechanic, had managed an Irving station in tiny Scotsburn, Nova Scotia, for 11 years when he and his father decided to strike out on their own in 1988, because Irving Oil refused to expand the station to meet rising demand for repair service. When they approached the Public Utilities Board (PUB) for a licence to pump gasoline at their new site, the Irving lawyers intervened, eventually persuading the PUB to turn down the application on the grounds that Scotsburn wasn't big enough to warrant another station. Murray approached Irving Oil about rejoining the fold but learned that his service station rent, previously set at $2,000 a year, was going up by another $500 a month. "We had pissed them off and they wanted us out," Wayne Murray declares.

So the Murrays appealed the PUB ruling. They had plenty of support: Scotsburn's citizens organized a boycott of the Irving station, and letters from Cape Breton to Victoria poured in to support David's battle against Goliath. More than 700 people crowded into the Scotsburn fire hall in late 1988 when the PUB finally ruled that the Murrays could compete with Irving Oil after all.

Arthur Irving, for his part, says the whole dispute with Murray simply got out of hand. "It was a misunderstanding," he explains. But even he might have to admit that sometimes he and his brothers go a bit overboard. How else to explain their lawyer's unsuccessful contention that a life insurance salesman should have been agile enough to jump out of the way when an Irving bus hopped the curb and ran over his leg?[10]

Usually the Irvings have better luck in the courts, which they tend to view as simply another vehicle for attaining their corporate goals. "They are extremely litigious," says one Saint John Q.C. who has sat across the table from Irving lawyers on a number of occasions. "They take everything right through to the Supreme Court. They rarely settle." For the big cases they invariably turn to Edgar Sexton, the $300-plus-an-hour partner in the Bay Street firm of Osler Hoskin & Harcourt. He earned the family's undying loyalty for his services during Arthur's messy divorce case. The Irvings also maintain an in-house staff of 20 lawyers in Saint John and keep dozens more on retainer throughout the Maritimes and New England. Over the years the high-priced legal guns have earned their keep — and never more so than in 1988, when Sexton succeeded in his appeal of Ottawa's decision to rule out $142 million in deductions claimed by Irving Oil from 1971 through 1975. The verdict survived Ottawa's counter-appeal in 1991. [11]

The Irving corporate culture mirrors its rulers' no-nonsense nature. They have established an environment of egalitarianism that is unique in Canadian business and bears comparison in North America only to the remarkable culture spawned by the candy-bar-making Mars family, one of America's richest business clans and certainly its most secretive.

Everyone is equal inside the Irving empire. Since they feel that closed doors hinder productivity, virtually no one, with the exception of the most senior managers, enjoys a private office. Traditionally, desks are spread across the floor in bull-pen fashion, with the higher-ranking executives towards the front and their troops behind them. "You wouldn't have a job without those people," Arthur once told an accountant who was unhappy about sitting cheek-by-jowl with the rest of the Irving Oil office staff. Even those rare employees who need isolation for secrecy's sake have to be content with an office bearing large windows, which allow underlings to peer in.

Titles are as rare as privacy. The usual bureaucracy of managers, supervisors, department heads and vice-presidents found in most large corporations is nowhere to be seen within the Irving organization. Business cards carry the holder's name and company, but no title, for the simple reason that no one really has one. There is really no such thing as a job description for an Irving employee. Basically, you do what you are told, and that can be anything; middle managers are routinely ordered to chauffeur the brothers around while they scout for properties to buy. Skilled tradesmen spend the day putting together duck shooting blinds for Arthur's Ducks Unlimited buddies. Head office accountants suit up and work the gasoline pumps during times of labour strife.

Sometimes the tasks are truly bizarre. Arthur once called ten of his service station managers and ordered them to show up one Saturday afternoon at his home, where he was throwing a "Gatsby Days" party for some friends. Another hired hand from Thorne's hardware arrived with a large plastic child's wading pool, a dozen bags of ice and several cases of pop. They pumped up the pool, threw in the ice and filled the whole thing with pop for the enjoyment of partygoers. Then the group of them donned straw boaters and spent the day parking guests' cars.

There is room only for team players in the Irving organization, where everyone is trained to fight tooth and nail for the best price and the best deal, and where they are taught, above all, to keep costs down. Company auditors place expense accounts under the microscope. By the same token, the Irving companies are notorious for leaving payment of their own bills until the last possible moment. The money they save goes into plants and equipment, where only the best that technology can provide will do. The Irving organization remains as obsessed with quality today as in K.C.'s time. "Their service stations are cleaner than most hospitals I've seen," says one competitor. Irving restaurants — with their fresh breads, home-made soups and pies — are consistently some of the best rural restaurants found throughout the Atlantic provinces and Maine. One manager remembers watching in awe as Arthur refused to open up a million-dollar Big Stop service station complex until he had personally checked the shower stalls for the truck drivers, to ensure that they were stocked with big bars of soap, rather than the tiny, hotel-room variety.

To those who work for them, that is just one of the odd things you have to put up with under the Irving brothers' somewhat strange leadership. Another is their no-booze policy, which even extends to expense account dinners with the biggest corporate customers. As a result, Irving managers are forced to pay out of their own pockets if they want to buy a client a cocktail or bottle of wine with dinner. (Once an Irving Oil security officer drove all the way from Saint John to Maine to check up on an executive who had dared to expense a bottle of wine from a dinner with the president of one of Canada's biggest companies.) And with a few rare exceptions, Irving executives are forbidden to be quoted in the press. Information on such mundane matters as service station sites and plant production is a closely guarded secret.

Not everybody fits into this storied culture. To enter the Irving fold you have to fit the mould. This isn't as easy as you might think, even in Saint John, which has a limited white-collar and skilled workforce. To weed out those who don't fit their blueprint, all applicants at the managerial level fill out a multiple-choice quiz in which they are asked to describe themselves and to speculate how others would describe them. The Irvings want a certain type of person: aggressive, confident, hard-working. Most of all they must be team players, untainted by experience within other organizations and malleable enough to learn to do things the Irving way.

Theirs is an old-fashioned organization. Middle- and upper-management types are invariably white, male Anglo-Saxons. The typical Irving executive is family-oriented, clean-cut, restrained and given to wearing tame suits and driving a dark Ford gas-guzzler hand-selected by the Irvings. Adds one young former manager, "They like people who are athletic-looking. If you're upper management you can be fat. But if you're out there meeting the public, they want people who look sharp."

The brothers, when they are so inclined, know how to build loyalty. Salary levels in recent years have been raised to make them comparable with the industries in which they operate. At many companies it is commonplace for managers to receive an annual bonus cheque that makes the yearly take-home pay look puny by comparison. Then there are the little things that bind their people to them: their willingness to fly ailing employees down to the Lahey Clinic in Boston; the university scholarships they provide for employees' children; the annual Irving Days Concerts they sponsor, which include performances by country artists the likes of k. d. lang.

And, of course, there is the J.D. Irving Christmas party, where 2,000 employees per night pour into the Saint John convention centre over four nights to dance to orchestra music and gorge themselves on thousands of pounds of lobster trucked in from the province's north shore. Each night the Irving brothers and their families work the room, shaking hands and passing on their compliments of the season. The boys pull out all the stops: everyone gets free Irving jackets and all the lobster they can eat. No booze, though — that's where they draw the line. Even so, when the convention centre cleaners tidy up after each night's festivities, they find empty rum, rye and scotch mickeys stashed under the tables.

If you work for the Irvings you *work* for the Irvings. That means being on call 24 hours a day, seven days a week, literally 52 weeks a year. Employees sometimes receive pre-dawn telephone calls at their homes, ordering them to be packed and at the airport in a couple of hours for a trip that could take them away for days. One Saint John businessman recalls getting ready to drive at the Riverside Country Club in Rothesay one weekend when the club pro came roaring over the hill in a cart. The pro yelled at the golfer's partner, a high-ranking Irving employee, "Mr. Irving wants you in the office by 11 a.m." The whole workaholic mentality is put into perspective by a former Irving executive who recalls being in one of the family's restaurants in the Nova Scotia countryside. Around 1 p.m. in walked Arthur, Jack and one of their employees, whom he recognized. After a quick coffee, the brothers were up and out the door. "At least you're out of this," groaned the underling as he headed for the car and his chauffeur's duties. "My day is just beginning."

Working for the Irvings, any employee will privately tell you, is life inside a blast-furnace. The brothers are always there, looking over the shoulders of their managers, constantly pressuring them to increase volumes, slash costs and bring in new business. And if you want to see a look akin to pure animal fear, just peer into the eyes of the manager of a small Irving station — as I did — when the three Irving brothers burst through the front doors, large as life, their coats trailing in the wind, on one of their unannounced visits. Arthur greets him by name and starts firing off rapid questions about sales volumes. J.K. and Jack shake hands and then prowl around the store, looking at shelves and inspecting products. Within a matter of minutes they are gone, on to the next destination, leaving the manager nervously chewing his lip and assessing the damage.

The idea, the Irvings themselves say, is to make their employees the best and most productive workers they can be. As Arthur explains, "As long as they are doing their job, they have nothing to worry about." Even so, many former employees complain that they worked in constant fear while in the Irving fold. "They do their best to stir up competition between their employees. When you fail, everyone knows it," says one former employee. Adds another, who spent a decade in their personnel department, "Each week there is some confrontation or some challenge designed to see what your limits are, to see how far you can be pushed."

The family's hard-driving approach is epitomized by the annual Irving Oil sales conference, which could just as well be held in a revival tent as in a downtown Saint John hotel. Each summer hundreds of oil company managers converge on the city for three days of indoctrination by top Irving execs and special inspirational speakers, ranging from super car salesmen to hockey stars, brought in to pump their enthusiasm to a fever pitch. The Irving motivational techniques are far from ordinary; those who attended in 1988 sat in bafflement while an Irving Oil sales manager hopped around on stage in a headband and white karate gi and smashed a bunch of boards bearing the names of Petro-Canada, Esso, Texaco and other Irving Oil competitors. The whole thing culminates in Arthur's stream-of-consciousness closing remarks, which usually build to a crescendo, as they did during a 1980 speech recorded for posterity.

I love getting up in the morning, and I love people and I love to work and no damn fooling about it. We have people, whether they are Saint John or Halifax or Montreal or Sept-Îles or wherever they may be. They can learn if they are prepared to work. If they are prepared to work, we want them. If they are not prepared to work, we don't want them on our team. Let them go work for the federal government or the provincial government or someone else [*loud applause*] . . . or preferably our competition and they've got lots of them. [*more loud applause*] . . . Ninety-five per cent of the people in the room today come from the town where they were born. And they were that big a snowball [*circling thumb and forefinger*] and today they're that big [*spreading his hands a foot or so apart*]. They've got a reputation to earn, and once they earn it they must keep it. And you don't do it by being smart-assed and you don't do it by telling fibs, there's no damn fooling about it. There's no secret to success other than work.

That's what my dad always told me: "Boys, if you're prepared to work, I'll help you. But if you're not prepared to work . . . then, well, let's discuss it."[12]

While life at the executive level is high on stress, it can be correspondingly low on sense of accomplishment. The brothers have never really learned to delegate responsibility well. No Irving Oil employee, it is said, can write a cheque for more than $5,000 unless Arthur or Jack Irving's signature is on it. Normally senior managers only have to be worried about getting results, but Irving managers can be second-guessed at any time by the brothers. J.K., Arthur and Jack say that they are willing to listen to underlings' thoughts about the organization's direction. Yet they don't hesitate to get rid of executives who try to deviate from the Way, a practice that has sparked a number of wrongful dismissal suits by former executives over the years.

Many don't wait to be fired. Despite the dearth of job options in New Brunswick, their staff turns over at an alarming rate. "It is a great stepping-stone," says one former oil company manager who has since moved on. "Working for Irving Oil for four years is like working for anyone else for a decade." Predictably, many simply burn out, unable to stand the workaholic pace, the paranoia and the constant pressure. The moment someone resigns he's gone: a security guard watches while he cleans out his desk and then escorts him out of the office building. Executives who leave the organization are immediately dropped from the small, clubby, work-related social circle, because the other members are petrified that the brothers will find out they are consorting with the enemy. Loyalty, like everything else within the Irving empire, is a matter of extreme gravity.

10

The Hatfields and the McCoys

We're not enemies. We're New Brunswickers.
Neighbours. We're friends, for heaven's sakes.
What is all this stuff about french fry be-
tween the McCains and the Irvings, anyway?
— Wallace McCain

THERE IS ONE point — and perhaps only one — on which the
McCains and the Irvings will agree: if a rivalry exists between their
two families, it is strictly one-sided. "Why, we're the best of friends,"
says J.K. Irving, when asked about New Brunswick's "other business
family." "Look, any bastard who says anything about us and the
McCains is looking for a god-damn punch in the nose. Okay." J.K.
is understandably weary of being asked if there is some sort of backwoods feud between him and his brothers and the McCain boys,
Harrison and Wallace, who are the second most powerful family in
the province. He is equally bored by claims that the Irving Way
is best symbolized by the not always friendly manner in which he
and his brothers treat their "friends."

True, it's been more than a decade since the Irvings broke the
unspoken truce and started selling their own line of frozen food beside
McCain products on supermarket shelves throughout the Maritimes.
And there's no denying that since then the Irvings have steadily es-
calated the war for supremacy in the frozen french fry market, where
the McCains make most of their money. Still, ask any member of
either clan whether they are engaged in a Hatfields-and-McCoys–style
shoot-out, and you will undoubtedly hear the same fierce protests:
Feud, what feud? This is pure, unadulterated free enterprise, they
say. The timeless pursuit of customers and profits, nothing more.

And for a time it was possible to believe them . . . until, that is, the strange events of 1990.

The first thing that Shirley Morris, the deputy mayor of Florenceville, says is that if you're looking for dirt on the McCain boys, you've come to the wrong place. "Don't think that you'll hear any criticism here," she warns. "You certainly won't hear any from me. The McCains have provided a good, clean life for us."

Absolutely. Florenceville, a town of 700 nestled placidly on the banks of the Saint John River about 55 miles northwest of Fredericton amid rolling hills and lush hardwood forests, is one of New Brunswick's beauty spots. Small shops and churches — Anglican, Catholic, United, Baptist and Pentecostal — line the quiet main street. There is a fire hall with a pair of gleaming red fire trucks out front and a local medical clinic that boasts two doctors and a dentist. As she wheels through the town, Morris passes a spotless village park, a public pool, indoor and outdoor tennis courts and the town curling club, which was donated by the McCain family.

Driving across Florenceville's famous covered bridge, the deputy mayor makes it clear that she is proud of her pristine town. Almost as proud as she is of the family that put it on the map. Atop a ridge overlooking the river, Harrison and Wallace McCain live side by side in sprawling splendour, surrounded by their families and their most trusted employees. Harrison, a firm, compact bundle of raw nerves, energy and exuberant purpose, makes his home in a rambling white bungalow, which stands a full football field back from the road. At five-foot-nine and 180 or so pounds, he has a round, almost cherubic face, a bald dome and a ruddy complexion. A reporter once described him as looking like someone "who might fit a tractor seat more comfortably than a corporate swivel chair."[1] The same could be said for Wallace, who is four years Harrison's junior. He sports a shock of white hair and is taller, lankier and less communicative than his older brother, whom he lives next door to in a white-pillared mansion that visitors like to compare to Tara in *Gone With the Wind*.

When the McCain boys look out their picture windows, they see the smoke swirling up from the factory that started it all in 1956. Nowadays the brothers run an empire with more than $2 billion in annual sales, more than 40 factories and 12,500 employees worldwide. Each hour McCain Foods Ltd. plants churn out half a million pounds of potato products plus tons of frozen dinners, desserts, juice, fish, vegetables and pizzas. McCain, moreover, is a global name: only 20 per cent of its sales are made in Canada, another 20 per cent come from its expanding U.S. operations and fully 45 per cent are made in Europe, where the New Brunswick company has become the largest frozen french fry producer on the Continent.[2]

Make no mistake: the McCains don't have to stay in Florenceville. As it is, they already spend half their year flying to plants in Australia, the United States, England, France, Belgium, Spain and the Netherlands. That explains the private mile-long airstrip behind their homes, where two jets sit on permanent stand-by. The brothers contend that operating an international conglomerate from rural New Brunswick actually costs more than, say, running it out of Toronto or some other urban centre. The "Florenceville factor" also makes it difficult to recruit new executive talent to the sleepy backwoods town.

The owners don't seem to care about all the inconvenience. Wallace and Harrison would have you believe that they have never really contemplated living anywhere else. There have been McCains in the area since the 1820s when the family arrived from a farm in Meenahoney, a county one mile northwest of Castlefinne, County Donegal, Ireland. Family lore says that the three McCain brothers, William, Andrew and James, landed at Quebec City, travelled west to Rivière-du-Loup and came into New Brunswick via the Saint John River valley. Eventually they stopped at a small village that had been named for Crimean War heroine Florence Nightingale. Soon the family was making a name in the area as farmers, businessmen and powers in the local Liberal party.

Throughout the 1930s and 1940s Andrew McCain sold seed potatoes overseas. Eventually his two older sons, Robert and Andrew, took over the management of McCain Produce Co. But Harrison and Wallace, the younger boys, seemed to have little interest in the family business. Harrison attended Acadia University, unofficial training ground for almost all prominent New Brunswick businessmen, finished a bachelor of arts degree and then hit the road flogging pharmaceuticals in Ontario and Quebec. Wallace, for his part, chose

Mount Allison University in Sackville, New Brunswick. But by the mid-1950s both found themselves toiling for K.C. Irving.

Harrison, who was the first to join K.C.'s empire, knew the Irving boys from Acadia. "They told their dad I was one helluva salesman," he recalled.[3] Their real apprenticeship began under K.C.'s wing: Harrison managed the chain's service stations in Nova Scotia, Newfoundland and New Brunswick; Wallace managed the Thorne's hardware store chain from Saint John. Though they were rising stars in K.C.'s company, the McCain boys didn't act like typical Irving men. "Jesus, they were wild," recalls one early co-worker. They swore like troopers and loved hard work, long parties and fast cars. They thought nothing of staying up all night and then putting in 16 hours of work the next day.

In many ways they seemed the antithesis of K.C.'s sober and serious brood. But the McCain and Irving boys hit it off. J.K., Arthur and Jack visited the McCain family abode in Florenceville. In fact, Arthur reportedly met his first wife, Joan, at the reception for Wallace's marriage to Margaret Norrie, daughter of a senator from Truro, Nova Scotia. For a time, Arthur, Wallace, Harrison and their wives (Harrison's wife, Marion, was the daughter of J.B. McNair, a former premier of New Brunswick) were part of the same smart young Saint John crowd.

By 1956 the McCains had grown fidgety in the Irving fold. They wanted to stay in business; the question was, What business? They considered buying seats on the Toronto Stock Exchange, opening a department store, even setting up their own dry-cleaning business. The only important criterion, Harrison told journalist Stephen Kimber, was that they "make money, a lot of it."[4] Then their older brother Robert persuaded them to consider the frozen potato business. There seemed to be opportunities there, he said. Wallace and Harrison were intrigued. Start-up capital wasn't a problem: the New Brunswick government agreed to help out, guaranteeing a $420,000 loan to build a potato processing plant. There was also a modest inheritance from their father. So they took their money and set out to build an empire.

Harrison was the visionary and financial genius. Wallace was the details man, the guy who made sure that the plants actually turned out frozen food. The pair worked hard, arriving early in the morning and usually turning the lights off in the office at the end of the day. And they enjoyed one of those rare fraternal partnerships, without jealousy or animosity. Recalls one former executive, "They were lucky in that they brought different strengths to the operation, which enabled them to stay in their separate spheres of influence."

All the jetting around the globe and hobnobbing with the rich and famous is pretty heady stuff, particularly for a couple of guys from Florenceville who crave acceptance from the Canadian establishment and who, it is said, treasure their bank directorships above all other trappings of success. Yet no matter how large their operations grow, no matter how far their reach spreads, nobody could ever accuse the McCains of forgetting their roots. They might dine with prime ministers and sit across the negotiating table from global captains of industry, but back home in Florenceville they are just plain Harrison and Wallace, sponsoring hockey teams and running televised curling tournaments. "Everyone knows them, has known them since they were little children here," says Shirley Morris. "You meet them on the street, at the grocery store, at the gas station or on the tennis courts. Everyone is very comfortable with them."

By the late 1970s people were talking about "them" in the same breathless, awed tones they used to speak of that "other" New Brunswick family. Indeed, there were undeniable parallels between the way the McCains and the Irvings did business: both had started small in downtrodden New Brunswick and built huge, world-class business empires. Both ran secretive, family-directed, family-owned operations (Harrison and Wallace's children would soon be sprinkled throughout the McCain Foods organization). The McCains, like the Irvings, had stubbornly refused to surrender control by issuing shares on the stock market. Instead of dabbling in high tech or high finance, the McCains had also stuck to fundamentals, selling basic, old-fashioned commodities. The McCain brothers even seemed to follow K.C.'s dictum about the importance of growth. Asked by a reporter once what he had learned under the industrialist's tutelage, Harrison replied with a laugh, "Don't ever be satisfied."

In fact, once you get beyond the obvious differences in temper-
ament and personalities, the two families that have carved up most
of the industry in New Brunswick seem much alike. And perhaps
that is where all the troubles started.

The news wafted softly across the Bay of Fundy and into Florenceville. The Irvings, it was said in the summer of 1979, had taken
over C.M. McLean Ltd., Prince Edward Island's biggest potato buyer
and only potato processor. Journalists who tried to confirm the story
ran into the usual Irving stone wall. They had the same lack of
success in pinning down rumours that Irving agents were gobbling
up Island potato land, often for double the going price. Equally tan-
talizing were reports of a massive tree-clearing operation under way
on Irving-owned forestland near Saint-Léonard. There, gossip had
it, they were planning to plant their own spud crop.

Suddenly everyone in the potato business was asking the same
questions: Just what were the Irvings doing? And why were they
moving into McCain territory? The theories proliferated. *Atlantic
Insight* magazine suggested the Irvings might "see a chance to arrange food-for-oil swaps with OPEC countries that had previously
bought Island potatoes."[5] Some Irving-watchers argued that the
Saint John family had invested in McLean (which soon changed its
name to Cavendish Farms Ltd.) for tax reasons. Others claimed that
the Irvings had simply seen the McCains make a good buck in frozen
food and had decided to have a go at it themselves.

Yet there was also intriguing talk about some sort of feud between
the two clans. The first shot was reputedly fired in the early 1970s,
when the McCains decided to drop Irving Oil as their major fuel
supplier. In 1977 the Irvings apparently advanced C.M. McLean
money to expand its processing operations, allowing the P.E.I. company to compete with the McCains for a contract to supply french
fries to the McDonald's hamburger chain. Soon afterwards, the
McCains countered with a direct foray into the Irving domain, helping to restart a bankrupt sawmill at Juniper, New Brunswick, in
1979. Not to be outdone, the Irvings entered trucking, launching
Midland Transport Ltd., a direct competitor to McCain-owned Day
& Ross Inc., already one of the biggest trucking outfits in the Mar-

itimes. At one point, McCain Foods even sued Cavendish Farms for copyright infringement, arguing that the Irving company's packaging closely resembled their own. The action was settled out of court in 1988 and the details were never disclosed. When journalist Stephen Kimber asked Harrison McCain about the rumoured bad blood between the families in 1982, he dismissed the theory out of hand: "If you mean, do I have any vendetta against the Irvings, the answer is no."[6]

No indeed. Competition from a normal adversary would not worry Harrison and Wallace. Cavendish, however, was a different matter altogether. The McCain boys knew too much about the Irving Way to underestimate their drive to win market share. The McCains, according to employees at the time, were livid over the Cavendish purchase. Privately they speculated that the Irvings were running the plant at a loss just to eat into their market. And the subject of Cavendish Farms was the one thing that made Wallace and Harrison lose their professional objectivity. They refused to admit that the P.E.I. plant turned out a product that was comparable, let alone superior, to theirs. When Cavendish products fared better than their own during anonymous taste tests, the McCain brothers turned the air blue with obscenities. "Cavendish Farms," recalls a former executive, "brought out all their venom."

Robert Morrissey had a problem. It was a decade later, in the summer of 1989, and Joe Ghiz's Liberal government had been swept back to power in P.E.I. The young, fresh-faced MLA was the province's new minister of industrial development, which meant he was expected to fulfil Ghiz's campaign promise of creating new jobs and attracting new enterprise to the province. He had an additional mandate: only months before his appointment, the Mulroney government had announced the closing of the Summerside armed forces base as part of its campaign to cut costs. In one fell swoop 1,300 Island jobs would be lost. Summerside, the third-largest centre on P.E.I., would turn into a ghost town unless Morrissey could find a new industry to jump-start the local economy.

New companies were not exactly climbing over one another to set up shop on the Island. The province's gross domestic product —

the total value of everything produced — was a measly $1 billion a year. Outside of government, the Island's single biggest private employer was the Irving family, who each year themselves generated many times as much business as Prince Edward Island. Irving service stations, home and industrial heating fuel companies, bus lines, trucking companies and shipping firms literally and figuratively fuelled the provincial economy. As elsewhere in the Maritimes, they owned convenience stores, restaurants, coffee shops, auto dealerships and appliance stores. More importantly, they owned Cavendish Farms, which until 1991 owned the only potato processing company on spud-dependent P.E.I.

The Irvings were a touchy issue on the Island — had been ever since 1979, when they secretly bought out the McLean family. In theory, that take-over was good news for P.E.I. farmers, who had been stung enough times in the past when McLean's cash-flow problems stopped the company from living up to its obligations to buy potatoes. At the same time, they were well aware of how the Irving family did business in New Brunswick, where they insisted on owning everything from the raw materials to the seller or consumer of the finished product. Farmers were worried that Cavendish, which already bought fully 30 per cent of the province's raw potatoes, would start growing its own crop, driving the little guy out of the business and taking away one of their major markets.

These were legitimate concerns. In February 1980, Prowse Chappell, then agriculture minister in the P.E.I. Tory government, received a letter from the Irvings. Although they already owned 1,400 acres of prime Island farmland, the family wanted to buy another 6,000 acres to grow potatoes for the Cavendish plant. Publicly, the company never directly referred to the possibility of pulling out of the province if its request for more land was denied. Yet the threat seemed implicit in the letter to Chappell, in which Cavendish's vice-president of operations maintained that more land was required to ensure "the long-term viability of its processing operation on Prince Edward Island."[7]

It was a page right out of K.C.'s notebook: set up in a place that desperately needs jobs and tax revenue, ask for concessions, and if the government doesn't come across, threaten to pull out. The government was in a tough position. The plant was critical to the Island economy; but so were the small family farms, owned and operated by local residents. Land ownership is a sensitive subject on P.E.I., which has a long, unhappy history of non-resident ownership. In 1972, after seeing some of the province's choice lots slip away to non-Islanders, the Liberal government passed a law that required cabinet approval before a non-resident individual or corporation could buy more than 10 acres of land or 330 feet of shore frontage. Eight years later, Angus MacLean's Tory government tightened up the absentee ownership laws even further by making cabinet approval a requirement for corporations buying shares in Island companies. So when the Irvings lobbed their hot potato into Prowse Chappell's lap in early 1980, the minister did the Canadian thing: he threw the whole emotional issue into the hands of a special legislative committee, which launched a series of public hearings to decide whether the existing land-owning laws needed further alteration.

As the debate raged, the Irving family refused to sit still. Demonstrating their typical indifference to public opinion, they applied to buy still more farmland and began leasing other acreage, including a 600-acre block for which they signed a five-year agreement without even applying for the proper cabinet approval. It was incredibly bad judgement. The government's new land protection laws, brought in the following year, moved to curb the Irvings' hunger by setting a limit of 1,000 acres per individual and 3,000 per corporation. Cavendish, in fact, never did get around to making an official application for those 6,000 acres. Instead, they took to the courts. Even then they were denied a request to lease an extra 150 acres over the new limits. By the mid-1980s any goodwill that the Irvings had built on the Island by turning around the troubled McLean plant had disappeared. Islanders felt mostly suspicion and hostility towards the New Brunswick family.

All of which made Robert Morrissey a touch uneasy in the long summer of 1989 when he began looking around for companies willing to pour some badly needed cash into the province. He had already approached Harrison and Wallace McCain about setting up their own processing plant on the Island. At the time they were not interested. Neither was Carnation Foods, the British food giant, or the European interests that the P.E.I. government contacted. So

Morrissey decided to make another call, this time to young Robert Irving, the titular manager of Cavendish Farms. He agreed to come to Charlottetown for a chat.

After listening to Morrissey's pitch, K.C.'s 32-year-old grandson was interested enough to return to Moncton and begin drafting a preliminary proposal for a potato processing plant. The more Robert and J.K., his father, looked at the idea, the more they liked it. Morrissey assured them that government funding would be available. Barbara McDougall, his federal counterpart, had already given her word that the government wanted to lessen the pain of the Summerside base closing. Ottawa was adamant on one point: if the province wanted federal funding, it had to come up with a private-sector solution to the Summerside employment dilemma. Now perhaps Morrissey and his government had one.

Soon the Irvings were talking about a new, state-of-the-art processing facility capable of doubling the number of Island potatoes being turned into french fries. This was beyond even the provincial government's expectations. The negotiations between the two sides continued throughout September and October. Finally, in November 1989, everyone was prepared to close the deal: the Irvings were ready to commit to a new $85-million plant, $40 million for which would come from federal government grants. Morrissey, elated that he had fulfilled his mandate so quickly, left on a business trip to Hong Kong, confident that the world was unfolding as it should. And that's when all hell broke loose.

It all started with a simple phone call. Hearing rumours that a new plant was in the works, the P.E.I. Potato Producers Association — the umbrella organization that represents Island potato farmers — called the premier's office and requested a meeting. When the day came, Ghiz was vague, repeatedly stressing that the deal, which would be "worth megabucks," was at "a very delicate stage."[8] In fact, Ghiz had made a fatal mistake in underestimating the depth of the farmers' fear and animosity towards the Irving family. When the meeting ended, Peter van Nieuwenhuizen, chairman of the association, walked over to a telephone, called directory assistance and asked for the number for McCain Foods in Florenceville, New Brunswick.

Since Harrison McCain had heard nothing about the Irving plans, the telephone call came as a shock. The past decade had been good for McCain Foods, but it had been equally good for Cavendish Farms. Hardly a day seemed to pass without a new Irving convenience store popping up in the Maritimes, Quebec or Maine, stocking only Cavendish Farms products and refusing to sell any McCain brands. Soon the Cavendish brands were popular enough that other super-markets had to give their products shelf space. By 1990 Cavendish held a 30-per-cent share of the eastern Canadian french fry market, much of it won at the expense of McCain Foods.

For Harrison and Wallace McCain, news of the new Cavendish plant seemed to indicate that the Irvings were gearing up to battle for a bigger piece of the $3-billion North American french fry market. As the McCain brothers saw things, there was already too much potato processing capacity around; their New Brunswick plants were operating at just over 60-per-cent capacity. They would be running on even fewer cylinders if Cavendish built a new P.E.I. plant.

Then there was the trade matter: if the $40 million in government aid to the Irvings was viewed as a subsidy in the U.S., it could attract countervailing duties, thereby closing down sales into the lucrative American market for the entire Canadian potato industry. Not every-one was worried about this possibility. Certainly not the P.E.I. gov-ernment, which had already been advised by U.S. trade lawyers that American authorities were unlikely to view the aid from Ottawa as a subsidy. Still, as a rationalization for fighting the Irving proposal it would do — even, perhaps, if the real reason Harrison and Wallace wanted to torpedo J.K., Jack and Art's plans had more to do with a personal rivalry than with the vagaries of trade law.

They wanted the thing derailed, plain and simple. When a weary Robert Morrissey stepped off his plane in Charlottetown airport, summoned back from Hong Kong by an urgent fax from Ghiz's of-fice, it looked like their goal was close to reality. By then, the McCain counter-attack was well under way. Using their impeccable political connections, they lobbied every federal cabinet minister and MP they knew, urging them to withdraw support for the government aid pack-age. Although the McCains had fought vigorously against the Free Trade Agreement, they hired Simon Reisman, the belligerent

Canadian trade negotiator, to use his considerable expertise and connections to help fight the "subsidy." They also had an impressive list of unpaid lobbyists, including New Brunswick premier Frank McKenna and his Manitoba counterpart, Gary Filmon, who personally took the McCain case to Prime Minister Mulroney.[9] Providing the Irvings with government aid, they stressed, would end jobs at McCain plants in both their provinces.

The high-powered lobby campaign seemed to be having an impact. Suddenly the federal government was getting nervous about the whole thing. Their commitment to help create jobs in Summerside had left them in a difficult position. "The deal can only be aborted if there is an appropriate alternative," said the feds in a letter to the McCains. So on January 22, 1990, the McCains proposed their own $36-million plant, which would create 169 jobs and require no government assistance. There was a catch: the province had to build a $14.5-million waste treatment facility, for which the plant would pay a user fee. And the McCains would build only if the Ghiz government denied funding for the Irving facility.

Ghiz wasn't budging. The government wanted the Irving deal: it was better planned and more ambitious and would create more jobs than the McCain plant. Besides, the premier had his back up at the attitude of the McCains, who seemed to think that they could come in and dictate their terms to the government. Earlier, the premier exploded after learning that the province's potato farmers had tipped the McCains off to the Irving plans. He called the farmers' association, intent on tearing a strip off Peter van Nieuwenhuizen. When he learned that the association head was out of the office, Ghiz simply lit into a puzzled vice-president who had the misfortune of being in when the call came.

What followed were the most intense negotiations Charlottetown has witnessed since the gathering of the Fathers of Confederation. Under the cloak of darkness, McCain and Irving corporate jets taxied into the tiny Charlottetown airport, where cars waited to whisk the occupants to the government offices of Ghiz and Morrissey. The talks were a contrast in style and personalities. Grimly serious, the Irvings arrived *en masse* — J.K., his sons Jim Jr. and Robert, daughter

Mary Jean, a lawyer and an accountant — in a characteristic dark Ford. Their proposals were extremely detailed. On the way to and from the airport, they stopped for impromptu inspections of their service stations.

As for the McCains — their approach was a bit different. Usually Wallace and Harrison landed in Charlottetown by themselves. Their plan, in contrast to the thorough Irving documents, was extremely light on details. In fact, as the negotiations progressed, it became clear that the McCain brothers really didn't know what type of plant they would build if their bid was accepted. "We'll build a god-damn plant, Joe," Harrison would say. "Don't you worry."[10]

The government wasn't so confident. At one particularly intense moment in the premier's office, Wallace McCain knocked over his briefcase. Blurting "I need my heart pills," he dropped down on all fours and began crawling around on the office floor; his face grew redder and redder while the others in the room watched in growing alarm. Finally he found his pills, gobbled one and sat back down again. "I'm glad you found those," said Morrissey. "I think you'll need them before this is over."[11]

The province, though, suffered the first set-back. The context of the negotiations changed dramatically when Ottawa pulled its funding for the Irving proposal. Left without a firm commitment from either the Irvings or the McCains, Morrissey and Ghiz started to scramble. By now, outside eyes were focused on the strange events on P.E.I. Newspapers and television stations throughout North America were covering the "Great French Fry War." Morrissey even got a call from Simplot Inc., a giant U.S. potato processing outfit, wondering what kind of government assistance they could hope for if they were willing to build a french fry plant on the Island.

Then Morrissey got some good news: the Irvings agreed to go ahead anyway. Cavendish's newest proposal was far more modest — a $35-million facility with a single production line, employing about 160 people. Still, if markets improved, a second $37-million phase might be built, involving two more production lines. Ghiz promised that not a cent of provincial government money would go into the project. But the government did agree to build a $10-million sewage treatment centre at the plant site, which would then be leased to Cavendish. "The Irvings have their act together," Morrissey told reporters at the parsimonious Cavendish press conference — $72.25 worth of tepid coffee and bran muffins — announcing the project.

The ink was barely dry on the Cavendish deal before Ghiz was back on the phone with Wallace McCain, calling on him to live up to the earlier promise to build a plant, now that both the province and Ottawa had bowed out of the Irving project. Lo and behold, he agreed. A few days later Ghiz and Morrissey stepped off the plane at the McCain airstrip in Florenceville and got into Wallace's green Jaguar. They stopped for a short chat at the McCain headquarters, then motored across the covered bridge to Wallace's house for a few drinks and further discussions. When they boarded the aircraft to return to Charlottetown, the Island politicians were happy men, their spirits buoyed by the liquor and a firm commitment from the McCain family. Maybe this, thought Morrissey, would quiet the angry farmers who questioned the government's wisdom in accepting the original Irving deal.

Many of those farmers were present in Charlottetown on February 1 when Wallace McCain officially announced the new plant. Unlike the austere Irving reception, the spread put on by the McCains pulled out all the stops: smoked salmon, jumbo shrimp, exquisite flower arrangements, linen tablecloths and all the free booze the invitation-only crowd of 200 could drink at the lavish CP Prince Edward Hotel ballroom. Total price tag for the event was $3,450. The guest list was carefully chosen to include most of the Island's big potato producers, a Who's Who of local and national media, and all stripes of politicians, including federal public works minister Elmer MacKay, who jetted in for the reception and quipped, "Nineteen-ninety is going to be one hell of a year for potatoes."

The McCain checkmate took the Irvings somewhat by surprise. Ottawa had already pulled the purse-strings closed. Now McCain was going to be right there on the Island, competing with them for potatoes and markets. Suddenly the whole thing no longer looked so attractive. They began thinking that perhaps an expansion of their existing plant would be a better idea than a whole new facility. Meanwhile the family's popularity among Islanders sank even lower, if such a thing was possible. A spring 1990 survey of Islanders' attitudes towards the two competing families, conducted by Baseline Market

Research, a Fredericton polling company, showed only 18 per cent felt the Irvings would act in the Island's best interests, while 69 per cent thought the McCains would do so. The same poll showed that a whopping 82 per cent of those surveyed favoured further limiting Irving land ownership.[12]

And just when it seemed that things couldn't get any worse for the Irvings, they did.

It was a bizarre twist, even for this strange story. At the centre of it stood the unlikely figure of Mary Jean Irving, K.C.'s blonde grand-daughter, who had arrived on P.E.I. in the late 1980s with her husband, Stewart Dockendorff, a Christian fundamentalist minister who grew up in a family of Island mussel farmers. They met at Acadia University, married and moved to P.E.I., they said, because they wanted to start a farm. Ordinary farmers, though, they were not. In late April 1990, news leaked out that Mary Jean and her husband had recently spent $10 million to buy 4,000 acres of farmland on the western part of the province, as individuals and through a company called Indian River Farms Inc.

Farmers were outraged at what appeared to be an attempt to get around the province's land ownership limits. Marching to the premier's office, they informed Ghiz that some 20,000 acres of the province's best potato land was now Irving-controlled or -owned. Perhaps best expressing the farmers' sentiments was a young women who shivered in the April cold outside the P.E.I. government buildings, shouldering a handwritten sign that read "Prince Irving Island."[13]

Ghiz, whether he liked it or not, had to act. Technically there was no corporate connection between Indian River Farms and Cavendish Farms. Finally Ghiz wrote to Indian River Farms, demanding information on the corporation's ownership and ordering Mary Jean to reduce its holdings if they exceeded the legal limits. In the twilight hours of the April legislative session, the government passed new laws prohibiting corporations from buying more than five acres of land without the government's okay. Then the premier sat back and waited for the Irvings to respond.

For six months he waited. Then, just days before the province's lawyers were scheduled to take Mary Jean and her company to court, she notified the government that Indian Farms would comply with the order to reduce its land holdings. "The reason I chose not to pursue this matter through the courts is because the legal proceedings against me would be used to explore other private aspects of the Irving family's business interests," she said during a hastily called press conference.[14]

By then, though, the Irvings had taken the war with the McCains to a new level altogether. In late September 1990, Cavendish announced that it would erect a new potato processing plant in New Brunswick — in Grand Falls, at a site right across the Trans-Canada Highway from the McCains' flagship Florenceville plant.

The McCains responded with another bout of free trade flag-waving. Enlisting their usual array of legal advisers, high-profile trade consultants and even some high-profile New England politicians, they bombarded Ottawa and the media with dire predictions of crippling trade wars if the new Cavendish plant went through. This time, though, the Irvings had covered their flank. New Brunswick's deputy minister of commerce and technology had personally put together the deal. Ottawa and the province had agreed to provide the Grand Falls plant with $14.5 million worth of pollution control equipment, a $10.5-million investment tax credit and $4 million in funding for employee training. Archie McLean, a McCain senior vice-president, told anyone who would listen that the deal was "put together on the back of an envelope." But, as much as they complained, it was hard for the McCains to argue that the government aid package amounted to an unfair subsidy when it was exactly what they were receiving for their own new P.E.I. plant.

Typically, both families downplayed the latest offensive in the escalating war. Cavendish's public relations man, Robert Bonnell, said "the Irving family's only interest is in doing business in the proper way and expanding their markets."[15] Archie McLean, who spoke publicly for the McCains throughout the débâcle, shot back that his outfit "bears no malice against any of its competitors." By then, the words had a familiar ring.[16]

11

The Last Fiefdom

A prince need trouble little about conspiracies
when the people are well disposed, but when they
are hostile and hold him in hatred, then he must
fear everything and everybody.
　　　　　　　　— *The Prince*, Niccolo Machiavelli

"IT IS NOT MY intention to spend a great deal of time tonight telling you how often the Irving ox is gored, and how we feel about being bashed and about those who bash us," J.K. Irving was saying at a conference room in a Saint John hotel. "But I do want to say it is a rare day when the Irvings are not accused of something, some dire or devious or destructive act."[1] J.K., the unlikely spokesman for the empire, enjoys making speeches about as much as he likes a good dose of stomach flu. The head of the Saint John Board of Trade had expected the usual response when asking him to give the keynote speech at their annual dinner in May 1990; an Irving, as far as anyone could remember, had never addressed, or even attended, a Board of Trade meeting. But J.K. accepted, mainly because he had had enough of the "Irving-bashers," the name he gives to his family's most persistent critics.

"Some of the criticism we undoubtedly deserve. Some of it may even do some good. But I do want to say this. There are only about a half a dozen of us: Art and Jack, myself and some sons who are now active in various branches of the business. There are, in fact, hardly enough Irvings to go around — hardly enough to satisfy all those who would tar and feather us every day of the week and twice on Sundays."

The Irving skin is thin; they don't like criticism. Incredible as it might seem, the Irvings dismiss any talk about their power and influence in New Brunswick affairs as simply another myth that has sprung up around them. And it is characteristic of this attitude that, speaking to a group that included the owners of dozens of small businesses that compete against the Irvings, J.K. would try to cast his lot with the underdogs. "Welcome to the club," he barked. "We learned a long time ago there is always someone bigger, someone with more business clout, someone with greater financial resources."

Maybe. Maybe there are a few families in North America who are worth more. Maybe there are some who can muster more resources. Still it is inconceivable that any business organization could wield more raw, unadulterated power and influence than J.K. and his family do over New Brunswick. Corporate concentration is a way of life in the perennially depressed Atlantic provinces, where government after government has struggled to attract big outside investors to plunder their raw resources, and where a handful of homegrown families have emerged to exercise almost feudal control in their spheres of influence. In addition to the Irvings there are families like the Jodreys and the Sobeys, who, in unofficial partnership, hold sway over Nova Scotia, and the McCain clan. But the Irving empire is the black hole of the Maritime universe — so powerful that it determines the path of all the other objects in its realm, yet so deep and dark that it remains inaccessible to the outside world.

To what ends the empire directs this influence is another matter entirely.

Power brings respect, sometimes fear, rarely love. And it is as dangerous for rulers to breed hostility among the vassals today as it was in Machiavelli's time. The Irvings understand this implicitly. In recent years they have launched a slick (at least, by their standards) campaign to improve the empire's public image. Suddenly J.K. is making speeches on everything from free trade to the environment, he is being quoted in the family's newspapers, he has even started popping up on the occasional provincial government committee. After a bankrupt Saint John printing company blamed its failure on inability to win Irving business in 1989, the Irvings ran a series of half-page newspaper ads urging companies interested in becoming suppliers to contact them. Instead of their usual brand of quiet philanthropy, the family name has begun appearing with increasing frequency on large public donations. "We are not a huge multinational company which makes its money here and then sends everything back to the parent company in New York," J.K. declares. "When we make money, the dividends stay here. The people of New Brunswick benefit from that and we think they appreciate it."

Well, it's not quite that simple. In New Brunswick, feelings about the Irving family run the gamut, from total devotion to absolute fear. Among the people who work for them, and even among those who don't, there's stubborn pride in their amazing accomplishments: the huge fortune they have amassed; the way they take on competitors from bigger, more prosperous areas of the country; their steadfast willingness to tackle the U.S. market. Plainly, everyone welcomes the jobs they create and the dollars they send percolating through the provincial economy. New Brunswick, which is saddled with one of the highest unemployment rates and one of the lowest levels of per-capita income in the country, needs every cent. Everyone knows that without the Irving enterprises, which directly or indirectly provide one in five New Brunswick private-sector jobs, the province would sink even deeper. Everyone knows that the Irving companies have repatriated New Brunswick industries that were previously controlled by big outside interests concerned solely with exploiting the province's natural resources for the profit of their shareholders.

Yet even among their avowed fans, the family name doesn't exactly engender warmth. To their harshest critics — the union leaders who call for national boycotts of all Irving products, the environmentalists who demand that some of their operations be shut down, the business competitors who say the Irvings drive them into bankruptcy, the government officials who accuse them of controlling the media — they are akin to feudal landlords who parcel out their land to tenants in return for absolute allegiance and service. Indeed, if these were medieval times, the family might fear armed revolt.

In midtown Saint John, Pat Landers, the energetic city councillor and persistent thorn in the Irving side, swings her car around a street corner and declares that they are nothing less than "plantation owners." Landers, who first ran for council on an environmental platform, says that the Irvings are unconcerned with what is good for the local people. In her view, "the people of Saint John have been reduced to the status of cotton-pickers in the Deep South. They are frightened of their own freedom."

In a nearby building, a man who once sat in the mayor's chair but now watches the Irvings operate from the vantage point of the private sector protests that, despite all the jobs they create, they are not good corporate citizens. "They grew rich because of Saint John and its people, not in spite of them. They have a moral responsibility to this city, and they haven't made a meaningful contribution back into the community." In his view, "what they do best is get government grants and tax concessions from the city and province."

Across town, in a Catholic parish in the midst of one of the poorest parts of Saint John, Father Ralph McQuaid, a white-haired Barry Fitzgerald look-alike, fears for the souls of the Irving family. "As they see it, there is one thing, and that is the accumulation of more capital, to the extent that it appears to be an addiction. I am unsure of the degree to which they are free to make their own decisions. We can become obsessed by all manner of things, and when we do there is never enough — never enough land, never enough lumber, never enough money — all of those things which would be used to accumulate capital and control."

These attitudes exasperate Elsie Wayne, the mayor of Saint John, who stares out into the mist over the harbour from her city hall office. Fiftysomething and compactly built with short, white hair and an open, friendly face, Her Worship is the biggest booster of Saint John, which she likes to call "the best little city in the east." Her cheerleading has won her three consecutive terms in office as well as her quota of critics, who dismiss her as an Irving apologist who has failed to show the leadership needed to solve the city's deepening problems.

Wayne doesn't have much time for negativism about Saint John or, for that matter, about the Irving family. "There is more that they could do, there is more that they should do and more that they would do if they thought that the city appreciated their presence," she declares. She adds in irritation, "If the Irvings were somewhere other than Saint John, the locals would be bragging about them." This attitude is predictable enough, since any mayor of Saint John knows knocking the Irvings won't get you anywhere. Yet Wayne, who went to grade school with Arthur and Jack Irving, contends it all comes down to one painfully simple question: "Where would we be without them?"

That's a common lament. In Saint John, a prominent businessman compares the city's relationship with the Irvings to Canada's rapport with the U.S. — "It gets uncomfortable from time to time, but we cannot do without it." The same note was echoed by Richard Hatfield, the former premier of New Brunswick. Interviewed in his modest Fredericton bungalow less than a year before his death in 1991, he declared that he resented the notion that "K.C. Irving is the king of New Brunswick." He maintained that "the power and influence of the Irvings and the other great pulp and paper companies was contained by the great powers the province assumed in 1967." Hatfield, who was appointed to the Senate in 1990, explained that K.C. Irving is very much like his own entrepreneurial father, who made a fortune in the potato business and "had a very strong belief that the greatest contribution he could make to New Brunswick was to create jobs." Besides, he said, "there is no question that on balance the Irvings have been a positive force for New Brunswick."

In his messy, overcrowded Saint John office, Colin Mackay, the lean, bristly former president of the University of New Brunswick, remembers growing up in Saint John during the 1930s and watching businesses close down, one after the other. "Are the Irvings good for the province? There's your answer," he boomed, gesturing to an old black-and-white photograph of downtown Saint John, showing the dock that Mackay's family then owned — and the empty street leading down to it. "That is broad noon on King Street in 1936!"

Revisit King Street in 1990 and you find that the city has transfigured itself; the acres of decrepit housing have been ripped out. Market Square, the $100-million waterfront development that opened in 1983, has risen from among the historic brick and stone waterfront buildings. Nearby there's a modern convention centre, a Hilton hotel, a Delta Inn and a $9-million Aquatics Centre built to house the 1985

Canada Summer Games. High-speed expressways have replaced the old, choked streets. A handful of fine eateries have sprouted up around town, including a chic French restaurant and a place to sample spicy gumbo cooked by a former Trappist monk and his New Orleans–born wife. Hints of the city's past still exist: the thriving city market, first opened in 1876; the century-old movie theatre that is being transformed into a showcase for local and touring talent by public and private money; the old Victorian homes in the downtown core being spruced up by young, upwardly mobile types. Even so, the old sits side by side with the new. Everywhere the wheels of industry seem to be turning, at the Labatt's and Moosehead breweries and the Atlantic sugar refinery and particularly at the Irving enterprises — the pulp and paper mills, oil refinery and shipyard.

On the surface, it is a stunning transformation. After spinning through Saint John in the fall of 1990, *Toronto Globe and Mail* columnist Jeffrey Simpson christened the city "one of Canada's best-kept urban secrets."[2] All the same, paint, glass and brave talk only tell part of the story, for beneath the signs of prosperity something is plainly amiss. Numbers hint at the problem. Saint John is in decline, compared with other Maritime centres: from 1976 to 1986, the city centre lost 10,000 people, or more than 12 per cent of its population. Moncton and Halifax, Saint John's long-time commercial rivals, had stable populations during that period. Throughout the decade the metropolitan Saint John area did manage to gain 8,000 people, a 7-per-cent increase. But that was dwarfed by the population boom in metropolitan Moncton, which added 24,000, a 32-per-cent rise, and the Halifax area, which gained 28,000 — another 10 per cent.[3]

At the same time, even though Saint John's economy hasn't been this visibly vibrant in 20 years, the unemployment rate continues to hover stubbornly above the 10-per-cent mark. Elsie Wayne blames some nasty labour confrontations for the city's deep-rooted problems: "Saint John is seen as an industrial city with a militant workforce. New firms just don't want to locate here."

There are other possible explanations. In an office not far from Mayor Wayne's, an anonymous city hall official explains that the real reason for Saint John's alarming population loss is that "people are scared to come here." One possible cause of this fear, says the city hall employee, is the "Irving factor." The dilemma was underscored by management consultants who prepared a 1989 development plan for the city. They concluded that the size of the Irving holdings and their penchant for maximum vertical integration were keeping new businesses from testing the waters in Saint John. "[Vertical integration] has pushed a lot of competitors into corners, and in some cases out of the market," said Denis Collart, the Price Waterhouse consultant who prepared the study. "They are formidable competitors, and people are afraid to compete with them."[4]

While new businesses are reluctant to set up in the Irving family's backyard, another less quantifiable trend is even more worrisome. "None of the small companies already in business want to show their full potential," declares the anonymous city hall official. "They are scared that they will attract the Irvings to their little niche, and they will either buy them out or drive them out of business."

As far-fetched as this sounds, Maurice Mandale, an economist with the Atlantic Provinces Economic Council, says the upshot is "a dulling of the entrepreneurial edge." So while Moncton thrives, Saint John, with a $7-billion industrial empire in its midst, suffers a steady exodus of citizens, driven out by the city's high cost of living, lack of jobs and heavy pollution. No one in Saint John is immune to the brain and labour drain. Not even the Irvings, who are having trouble finding enough skilled workers to meet their own needs and are shifting some of their own operations to Moncton.

This is not how things are supposed to work in the free market, where competition, the great equalizer, is expected to keep capitalism's excesses in check. But in Canada, where economic power has been steadily flowing into the hands of fewer individuals, free market competition is declining by the day. The Royal Commission on Corporate Concentration concluded in 1978 that concentration was both a fact of life and a necessity in a country the size and nature of Canada. For decades, Canada has been warned that if this march of increased concentration continues, the result will be a national oligarchy, in which a few dozen businesspeople bargain about the economic future of millions. In New Brunswick, where just the presence of the Irving colossus is enough to scare off most competitors, that day seems to be here already.

Much as the Irvings disclaim any great authority or power, much as they insist that they are weak and really don't have any more economic clout than anyone else, the reality is that they have the first and last word on an estimated $7 billion in assets — which means that a decision by the family to expand or cut back means joy or despair for thousands of New Brunswickers in their own companies, as well as other firms who depend upon the Irving operations for most of their business.

Economic power of the sort they wield means the ability to organize markets to their advantage by influencing prices for the raw materials they buy and the products they sell. For instance, the way Irving Oil and the other big oil companies dominate gasoline prices is well documented. The most recent example occurred in 1986, when New Brunswickers, who already suffered from the second-highest prices in the country, were for months deprived of the benefits of collapsing world oil prices. But there are other examples of their ability to affect markets, such as the heating oil industry, where the Irvings, as virtually the only large supplier in the province, enjoy the power to set prices, regardless of the forces of supply and demand.

In truth, full-fledged competition only rarely breaks out in New Brunswick in many sectors in which the Irving companies are involved. The tragedy for New Brunswick is that instead of a lively, competitive marketplace yielding jobs, innovations and opportunities, the province remains locked in a time warp with a single family producing all kinds of goods and services and most of the wealth. Ultimately, New Brunswick will never know the answer to Mayor Elsie Wayne's question: *Where would we be without them?*

On certain days the first and last thing you notice about Saint John is the smell, like rotten eggs; it wells up in your nostrils when the wind shifts enough to blow the smoke billowing from the Irving pulp mill across the city. Local residents have been living with the stink for more than 30 years. The smell of the smoke pouring from the Irving pulp mill has been one of the things that defined the city, psychologically as well as physically. It is, after all, hard to feel positive about living in a place that smells as badly as Saint John — a city that is so polluted that you have a 45-per-cent higher chance of dying of a respiratory ailment here than virtually anywhere else in the province.[5] By the same token, it is natural to feel anger towards the corporation which is the most noticeable source of the rotten-egg odour fouling the air.

Saint John is an environmentalist's nightmare, and by no means just because of the Irving presence.[6] Sulphur dioxide, nitrogen oxide, ash and carbon particles spew from the Irving pulp plant on the west side of the city, billow from the refinery to the east and pour from the nearby Rothesay newsprint plant. But far larger quantities of poison escape into the air from the east-side stacks of the city's electrical generating stations, run by the provincially owned New Brunswick Power Co. The situation is tolerable on windy days when the emissions are blown out over the Bay of Fundy. But during rainy or foggy weather, or when the cold wind blowing off the bay traps the polluted air close to the ground, Saint John is blanketed in a cloud of contaminant that hangs miserably overhead for days at a time.

Saint John's harbour once jumped with salmon, shad, gaspereaux, pollock, cod, eel, sturgeon, smelt, herring, hake, lobsters and clams. Now, all but the shad, salmon and gaspereaux are gone. Not surprising, considering that each day millions of gallons of city sewage pours untreated into the waters, including 27 million gallons of liquid waste from the Irving pulp mill which in 1988 entered the harbour within clear view of the dozens of tourists who daily visit the lookout over the Reversing Falls.

To really see what industry has done to the quality of life in Saint John, you just have to drive out to Champlain Heights, a subdivision on the city's east side, where the fresh, clear water from the Little River tumbles down a small waterfall. A half-mile downstream the water runs by the Irving refinery. Here it is a different story: each day 3.6 million gallons of oil, grease, sulphur and other refinery wastes flow into the river. A few hundred yards farther, 9 million gallons of wood fibres and chemicals from Rothesay Paper pour into the once-sparkling water. Finally, just as the river is about to flow into the harbour, it gets another dose of toxin, 250,000 gallons a day from the Courtenay Bay Generating Station, owned by the provincial electrical utility.

"By now it is a chemical soup," explains Pat Landers. "It is completely dead." Landers's husband, Mike, is a former Liberal MP who still holds a grudge against Arthur Irving for telling his Irving Oil employees to vote against him in the 1980 federal election. Mike Landers, in fact, once tried to start a citywide boycott of all Irving products. There are those who say that Pat's one-woman campaign to clean up Saint John is really an extension of her husband's vendetta against the Irving family. Not so, says the councillor, who claims, "I'm not anti-Irving, I'm anti-pollution."

As she tells it, the bad blood started in 1987, when she awoke and found that her car, like 600 or so others on the city's north side, was covered in a sticky white coating left after the scrubbers at the Irving pulp plant had broken down the previous night. The Irving officials never actually admitted to being the source of the problem, but they offered a free car wash to anyone whose car was covered in salt cake. "The whole thing made me so angry," she recalled. "I decided to find out if anyone was as upset as I was. If they take all the credit for employment, they have to be willing to take the blame for the pollution that their industries cause. Even the richest man in the world doesn't own the air and the water."

A decade or so ago that sort of statement would have sounded traitorous. Jobs have always won out over clean air and water in Saint John, where people have spent lifetimes grousing about the pollution while sitting around the kitchen table, but seldom raising the issue in public. People simply feared that if the air was cleaned up, the Irvings would shut down. Even if Saint John's citizens wanted to do something about the pollution, there was really little they could do to change things; until the provincial government altered the legislation in 1979, the old pollution protection clauses that K.C. and others had wangled from the provincial government protected the mill and a handful of other New Brunswick industries from nuisance suits over pollution.

The 1980s brought change. The environmental wave that rolled over the rest of North America eventually swept into blue-collar, industry-oriented Saint John. Suddenly people were fed up. So much so that when Pat Landers started up a group for citizens concerned about the environment in Saint John in 1987, she received 6,000 signatures. With cries of outrage ringing in its ears, the Liberal government of Frank McKenna, which came into power the same year, jumped on the environmental bandwagon. Vaughn Blaney, the provincial environment minister, actually called for closing the Irving pulp mill unless the odour could not be reduced. The call soon stopped, but the province still launched a bunch of environmental initiatives, including fines of up to $1 million and even jail sentences for industrial violators. In spring 1990, a provincially appointed committee empowered to examine Saint John's environmental problems said what previously would have been unutterable: "The stink from an industrial plant is not the smell of money; if it is a stink that can be controlled, it is the smell of shortsighted thinking that has no place in modern society. The idea of environment versus jobs should be recognized for what it is: a concept based on misguided thought."[7]

They would get little argument on that point from Dr. Robert Beveridge, the earnest young head of emergency services at Saint John Regional Hospital. In 1989 Beveridge began his own independent study into the effects of Saint John's environmental problems on respiratory ailments in the city. "There had been so much propaganda from either side that it was impossible to know who was telling the truth," he explains. His preliminary results were startling: Saint John, for instance, has three times as many hospital admissions for respiratory ailments as smoke-spewing Hamilton, Ontario. Moreover, the city's rate of deaths due to respiratory ailments is 93 for every 100,000 people, compared with 63 per 100,000 in Moncton and 74 per 100,000 in Fredericton.[8]

All of which made the public more than a little sceptical when J.K. Irving told one of the family newspapers in 1990, "I like to think of myself as an environmentalist." Rightly or wrongly, much of the discontent over Saint John's pollution problems has focused on the Irvings and their environmental track record, which, no matter how you look at it, is dismal. Through the years Irving Oil has been repeatedly charged for not reporting oil spills and for underground gasoline leaks. Even today, the *Irving Whale* oil tanker, which sank with its cargo of 4,100 tons of bunker fuel oil in 1970, remains a submerged environmental time bomb that periodically releases a slick of oil onto P.E.I.'s pristine beaches, continuously signalling what lies below.

The Irving pulp mill's reputation is well established. In 1976 it was acquitted on charges of polluting the Saint John River, even though rainbow trout died within three minutes of being dropped into the liquids flowing from it.[9] After the mill's recovery boiler operation broke down in 1978, there was a rash of complaints from residents living near the mill who were suffering from nausea, vomiting and sore throats.[10] A decade later, Environment Canada reported that Rothesay Paper and Lake Utopia Paper Ltd., also Irving-owned, were among the six New Brunswick pulp and paper mills that were still discharging toxins that killed fish in nearby waterways.[11]

The Irvings have got the message. The $30 million they've spent on scrubbers and other anti-pollution equipment since 1983 has enabled them to slash pulp mill emissions from 800 to a mere 8 pounds every 60 minutes. By December 1989, according to a national survey by the Canadian Pulp and Paper Association, the effluent discharged by the mill into the Reversing Falls was dioxin-free.[12] Nonetheless, in 1991 J.D. Irving Ltd. promised to spend another $60 million over the next decade to improve treatment of the effluent from its two mills in Saint John. All in all the provincial government maintains that the Irvings have become much more sensitive to complaints from the worried public. Nowadays they are said to diligently report every spill or accident that affects the environment. As one provincial environment official, who declined to be identified, explained: "They realize that it is bad for the public image for a company selling directly to the consumer to be viewed to be neglecting the environment. It is a lot easier dealing with them than with the other corporations. They haven't received enough credit for what they have done."

No doubt. But the cautious praise with which their decision to go green has been received is a measure of the wariness that many New Brunswickers continue to feel towards the Irvings. If they can control the very air that people breathe, the reasoning goes, then they can control virtually anything. Like politics, for one thing. The Irvings, along with most Canadian corporate rich, have never shown much interest in running for public office. There is, however, a type of political power that operates behind the scenes, the power to pull the right levers, whether they be in Ottawa, Fredericton or Saint John, with a quiet word here, a telephone call there. And the Irvings have this power, even if J.K. argues that the family has no more influence than anyone else in New Brunswick. "I get one vote, Jack gets one, Arthur gets one. Same as anybody else."

The brothers have never blatantly abused their political clout, as K.C. did when he tried to mount a campaign to usurp Louis Robichaud. Richard Hatfield said that during his 17 years in power the Irving family "made their case persuasively, but never once did I sense a threat or even the suggestion of one." Fair enough. But the family's political influence is still considerable, even if these days they apply it in much more subtle fashion than their father did.

Campaign contributions, obviously, are the easiest way to try to curry political favour.[13] In the 1984 federal election, for instance, Saint John Shipbuilding made the single largest contribution — $5,000 — to Gerald Merrithew's successful bid for the Saint John East seat. Five years later, during the next federal election, Merrithew got another $5,000, again his largest single donation, from J.D. Irving Ltd.

Provincially, the Irvings are known as "60-40 people" — 60 per cent of their contributions go to the party in power and 40 per cent to the opposition. Until 1991 there was a $9,000 cap on political party donations from a single source, imposing severe limits on how much they could hand over to a provincial party. (In 1991 the cap was lowered to $6,000.) Still, in 1987, J.D. Irving Ltd. contributed $6,000 to Frank McKenna's victorious Liberals, one of the McKenna campaign's largest single contributions.

Even in the patronage-ridden Maritimes, campaign contributions don't normally allow businesses to dictate the actions of elected officials. But politicians who plan to stay in power, here or anywhere, generally try to avoid antagonizing those who have contributed or might someday contribute mightily to their efforts — particularly if those contributors are fairly open about flexing their muscles to attain their political goals, as the Irvings are. They demonstrated that they are not beneath playing politics during the 1980 federal election. Arthur, still apoplectic over the Trudeau Liberals' National Energy Program, told his employees to vote Tory. [14]

The brothers aren't political partisans. Politics, in their view, is just another facet of doing business. Like their father, they understand the importance of staying on hospitable terms with government. Good relations certainly came in handy during the Hatfield administration when Department of Environment officials repeatedly failed to persuade the government to charge Irving companies with polluting. [15] Being on good terms helped when the Hatfield government passed a special law declaring their refinery's oil storage tanks non-taxable, after the courts had ruled otherwise. [16] More recently, federal Tory cabinet minister Gerald Merrithew, who has enjoyed the family's financial support, helped Saint John Shipbuilding win both frigate contracts and emerged as one of the strongest proponents of building a second nuclear power plant at Point Lepreau, New Brunswick, which would bring more work to the Irving shipyard.

The family has also built a good rapport with Liberal premier Frank McKenna, who, according to one of his former top aides, is "impressed and intimidated by the Irvings." Critics say that McKenna's Liberals have shown themselves most willing to lend a helping hand to the province's most powerful citizens, whether it is by providing provincial funding for a new french fry plant or changing regulations to allow the Rothesay paper mill to avoid buying wood from the province's small woodlot owners. That is not really surprising, since what is good for the Irving family is also, by definition, good for New Brunswick — even if the Irvings themselves have always gained the most from this symbiotic relationship.

Even now, many critics are reluctant to give public voice to their complaints about the Irving family. Most of the province's business or political élite need their support. The New Brunswick press, owned almost entirely by the Irving family, is understandably reluctant to criticize its proprietors. The family, to this day, steers clear of influencing editorial policy. However, this does not mean that you are likely to see the Irvings pilloried in the pages of the *Moncton Times-Transcript* or the *Fredericton Daily Gleaner.* "We print everything about the Irving family, be it good or bad," Tom Crowther, publisher of the Fredericton paper, contends. "We are pro–New Brunswick and pro-industry in terms of jobs for our young people. But we don't treat the Irvings any differently than we treat anyone else. We have a tough but fair editorial policy."

As publisher of the *Saint John Telegraph-Journal*, then one of the best dailies in the Maritimes, Paul Wilcocks echoed a similar theme. "We try not to be any more or less rigorous with them than with other companies," he explained in an interview in early 1989. "We aren't treated any differently than anyone else by the Irvings. They don't talk to us either."

In fact, with Wilcocks in the publisher's chair, the *Telegraph-Journal* actually broke new ground in Irving journalism, pursuing environmental stories involving the family enterprises with such fervour that it shocked long-time readers — and perhaps the three brothers as well. When Wilcocks resigned to run an Ontario daily in the spring of 1990, the publisher's chair was filled by Arthur Doyle, former director of alumni affairs at the University of New Brunswick, who was said to be destined for a job as the family's public relations director before the publisher's spot opened up. Since then, even the newspaper's employees admit that the paper has lost its edge.

Who, then, is keeping tabs on the empire? Mainly the financially strapped CBC. But there are definite limits to how much they can do in the only province where they lack an English-language television station. Since 1979, the sole CBC content in New Brunswick has been a locally produced suppertime news show and some national programming, carried by Irving-owned CHSJ-TV. The CBC has long sought to remove this embarrassing gap in its national service. In 1984 a solution seemed at hand, after the CBC discovered that a few vacant television wavelengths, which no one previously knew existed, were available.[17] As the Mother Corp. cobbled together a proposal for the CRTC, word of the newly discovered frequencies leaked out to Irving television executives. Coincidentally, they were well along on a plan to launch a new television system, to be called MITV, to span New Brunswick, Nova Scotia and Prince Edward Island.

Both the CBC and CHSJ-TV presented plans to the CRTC. The federal regulator chose the more thorough Irving proposal. There was a caveat to the licence: CHSJ-TV has to give up one of its frequencies when the CBC is finally ready to put a station on the air in New Brunswick. The Crown corporation had planned to have a proposal in hand when the next set of licence applications comes up in 1994. But the 1990 wave of austerity measures within the CBC may prevent that happening. Indeed, in late 1990 J.K. and Arthur Irving privately told Prime Minister Mulroney that they were interested in selling CHSJ-TV to the CBC. J.K. later told a Canadian Press reporter that he was "surprised at the CBC's apparent lack of interest."

12

Strange New Worlds

*It is even more grim and wild than you had
anticipated. . . . These are not the artificial forests
of an English king — a royal preserve merely. Here
prevail no forest laws, but those of nature.*
— *The Maine Woods*, Henry David Thoreau

THE BEARDED customs guard walks around to the driver's side of
the green, mud-splattered van and waits for the man at the wheel
to roll down his window. "What brings you to Maine?" he asks per-
functorily, his breath forming small puffs of steam in the cold air.
Sitting in the passenger seat, I watch as J.K. Irving replies flatly,
"For business. We're just looking at a piece of property." The guard
waves us through and J.K. slowly manoeuvres the vehicle down the
slushy, pot-holed road in Van Buren, Maine, just inside the New
Brunswick–Maine border. After several blocks Arthur Irving, seated
in the back with his brother Jack, directs J.K. to a small parking
lot in front of an abandoned liquor store. "Well, where is it?" asks
a puzzled J.K. "We're parked on it," Arthur replies. "We've got 600
feet on the main street." The three brothers step out of the van and
walk down the sidewalk, shivering with cold in spite of their beaver
hats, standard-issue rubber galoshes and thick winter coats. For 20
minutes, three of the richest men in North America tramp up and
down the muddy pavement as Arthur describes in loving detail how
he would level the standing buildings and erect a shiny new Irving
service station and convenience store.

Arthur Irving has a vision, and when he talks about the United
States his eyes burn with the fever of a man who has seen the future.
The Canada–United States Free Trade Agreement, he says, back in

the warmth of the van, "is the best thing that ever happened to Canada. The Maritimes are closer to New York and Boston than to Toronto. The richest market in the world is in the northeastern seaboard of the United States. That is the natural way for us to go." Arthur makes no bones about it: his family "plans to go right down to Florida," he tells just about anyone who will listen. And this is more than just tough talk from K.C.'s wilful son.

Entering the 1990s, the empire K.C. Irving's three sons inherited is a clanking, hissing, fire-stoked industrial machine the likes of which Canada has never seen before. The inertial force of the empire is enormous. Even if the Irvings do nothing, their businesses will continue to roll on for years, perhaps even decades to come. But the empire must never stop striving. When K.C. said he likes "to see wheels turn," he underlined a pragmatic reality about the empire he built, as well as intoning his personal philosophy.

Industry begets industry; the wheels, no matter what else happens, have to keep turning. Not simply out of greed or ego — K.C.'s sons and grandsons suffer from neither malady. Expansion is important because corporate entities develop critical mass. An organization the size and scope of the Irving empire is like a huge roaring furnace that needs to have ever-larger quantities of coal shovelled into it from now until eternity. No matter what happens, the Irvings constantly need to find new work and new customers, to develop new products, to do whatever it takes to keep fuelling the insatiable furnace. For if they stop growing, the fire will go out.

Expanding is no easy matter when you're the size of the Irving empire. They own so much of New Brunswick that opportunities for further growth within the province are limited. Where, for instance, will they find the wood to feed their pulp, paper and lumber mills? How will they keep their refinery running on all cylinders? Where are the new customers for their service stations, restaurants and convenience stores? These are not theoretical questions. Their ability to push further into the other Maritime provinces is also reaching its outer limits: the P.E.I. government has passed legislation designed to stop the Irvings from gobbling up more land on the Island; even Nova Scotia's Tory government, never known to stand in the way of big business, has been making worrisome noises about expropriating Irving holdings. Likewise, opportunities for expansion are limited in Quebec, where the tide has again turned against English business.

Of course, they could always look further west. But the Irvings have normally steered clear of the crowded Ontario market, where they have limited their efforts to owning a few service stations and maintaining their lumber, pulp and paper customers. Since they own no oil exploration and production arm, and they obtain their crude oil from inexpensive offshore sources, Alberta holds little allure, although they have invested in Chevron's drilling programs there. They have stayed away from the west coast, too, even though there seem to be obvious opportunities for their lumber companies in the British Columbia interior.

Truth is, they have always liked the view better to the south, in New England, which for two centuries has been a rich market for timber from New Brunswick, salt fish from Newfoundland and Nova Scotia and potatoes from Prince Edward Island. The Irvings, in a way, are throw-backs to a particularly stubborn breed of Maritimer. Born with Loyalist roots and harbouring a deep historical suspicion of what used to be known as Upper Canada, these Maritimers have always felt a greater affinity with the hard-headed Yankees of Maine, Vermont, New Hampshire and Massachusetts than with the polished businessmen of Ontario.

Maine, a mirror image of New Brunswick with its untapped forests, rural, unsophisticated economy and clannish citizens, is the natural place to begin an assault on New England. And the Irvings are breathtaking in their assurance that they can repeat their Canadian success in America. Their expansion has run into resistance, perhaps more than they had bargained for, certainly more than they are used to at home. But their drive is relentless: since they are hemmed in within Canada, Maine is nothing less than the family's springboard into the United States, and into the future. In the final years of the 1980s, they spent hundreds of millions of dollars to expand and modernize their facilities to garner a bigger chunk of the American market for their product lines. What is being played out in Maine will determine not just how they fare in one New England state but also whether the sons of K.C. Irving have the stuff to fully transform their regional fiefdom into an international power. They proved themselves in the difficult 1970s and 1980s. Now they must face the 1990s and the challenge of competing in a global economy, which even K.C. might have found unnerving.

"Except the few burnt lands, the narrow intervals on the rivers, the bare tops of the high mountains, and the lakes and streams, the forest is uninterrupted," Thoreau wrote about the Maine woods, and the moment you enter them you understand what he meant. The northern hills and ridges of Maine, nicknamed "the Pine Tree State," are actually carpeted with acre after acre of spruce, fir, maple and birch. The forest stretches on, broken only by an occasional lake, river, logging road or lumber town.

In the Age of Sail, the big pine forests supplied masts, spars and timber for wooden ship hulls. Today the woods are grist for the paper mills' insatiable demand for pulpwood. With annual sales of $4 billion, forestry remains Maine's most important industry. During the 1980s the southern part of Maine prospered, as a wave of high-tech industries took root. The isolated northern region stubbornly clung to its forests. It was the forests, after all, that brought the first white settlers to Maine in search of towering trees to make ship's masts for the British navy. And it was the forests that ultimately brought K.C. Irving to Maine just as the rest of the world was stumbling to its feet from the carnage of World War II.

In 1946, when K.C. bought the Reversing Falls pulp mill in Saint John from the Lacroix clan, one of Maine's most famous lumbering families, he also gained title to a sawmill in Van Buren — once the largest milling operation in New England — and 200,000 acres of timberland in the northwestern corner of the state. In those days K.C.'s priorities lay elsewhere; for years the mill sat idle and local agents looked after his forestland. His first tentative moves came in the mid-1950s, when a few Irving trucks began hauling industrial fuel oil into the state. A decade later he added another sawmill, this time on the Maine–New Hampshire border. When he doubled the capacity of his Saint John refinery in 1969, K.C.'s gaze was fixed firmly on northern New England, where not one refinery existed to fuel the fast-expanding market.

True to form, he was not content to merely supply the service stations of others. In 1972 K.C. and Charlie Van Horne headed down to Tulsa, Oklahoma, to see the good ol' boys at Phillips Petroleum. Facing dire financial problems, Phillips had decided to sell all 152 of its U.S. stations to focus on its foreign assets. K.C. perused the list and found 52 he liked in Maine, New Hampshire, Massachusetts and Vermont. Phillips wanted $3.8 million for the lot. But the stations carried $4.3 million in outstanding mortgages. A compromise was reached: Phillips sold Irving the 52 stations, and the company treasurer handed K.C. a cheque for $500,000.[1]

Throughout the 1970s, Irving Oil sold millions worth of gasoline, oil and industrial heating fuel in New England. The flood became a trickle in 1982 when the U.S. slapped restrictions on refined petroleum products entering the country. Even so, the empire pushed on: in 1985 J.D. Irving Ltd., facing wood shortages in New Brunswick, spent $20 million for 220,000 acres of forestland in Aroostook County — the chunk of northern Maine closest to New Brunswick — pushing the Irving timber holdings in Maine to 500,000 acres. Three years later, they added another sawmill.

Meanwhile, Irving Oil resumed its march. Eager to reinflate its sagging oil export figures, the company approached D.W. Small and Sons, a family-owned operation, and offered to buy their 18 gasoline and convenience stores in 1986. It was a typically thorough Irving deal: a few days after the initial inquiry, J.K., Arthur and Jack arrived at the Small family's doorstep. After examining the company's financial statements, they hopped in a car and spent the next 20 hours inspecting individual service stations, stopping only for a snack at a doughnut shop. Eventually the sale was made.

Now the assault on the Maine oil market began in earnest. Irving Oil's timing was impeccable. Desperate to cut costs, many major oil powers had pulled out of the state altogether, and the spate of mergers and consolidations in the American oil patch left fewer players competing overall. The Irving refinery, which was handier to Maine than any U.S. facility, gave the family strong leverage. Their strategy from the beginning was to buy market share, rather than build it from scratch. The approach was vintage Irving: when they saw a service station location they liked, they bought it, even if it meant paying twice what anyone else would pay. Competition was irrelevant: red-white-and-blue signs announced the Irving presence not just once, but up to six times in small towns along Interstate 95. Giving new meaning to the term "market saturation," they bought two or three service stations within blocks of one another. To complement their industrial and retail gasoline operations, the family snapped up small home-heating companies in strategic markets around the province.

Irving Oil Corp., the U.S. subsidiary, now owns about 130 service stations in Maine and controls 25 per cent of the state's $600-million gasoline industry, approximately 60 per cent of the industrial fuels market and 75 per cent of the asphalt business. Their Mainway and Big Stop convenience stores are running neck and neck with Cumberland Farms, the state's perennial market leader. They have a strategic foothold in the home heating oil industry. Irving trucks — they have fuel licences for more than 500 — dominate the Maine highways. Often the trucks carry loads of timber from their Maine forestlands across the border to their state-of-the-art sawmill in Saint-Léonard, which has 30 per cent more capacity than any mill in northern Maine. They even have a real estate arm, East Coast Properties, which is quietly buying and banking property along the rocky Maine coast.[2]

By now the Irving name is mentioned as a potential buyer whenever large tracts of forestland come up for sale. Irving Oil, which has clustered its stations mainly in the northern part of the province, is soliciting independent dealers in southern Maine with ads promising "prestige, quality product, competitive pricing, credit cards and financial assistance." All the while, the company is investigating new properties to the south in Massachusetts and to the west in New Hampshire and Vermont, where they already own some service stations. Still, not everything is going smoothly.

Mainers have never exactly cottoned to "people from away." As citizens of the most northern territory in the mainland U.S., they are known as resourceful and independent, and as laconic, deadpan masters of the "put-on" and the "put-down." There's scepticism towards all foreigners, but no one is more suspect than people from neighbouring New Brunswick. In 1839, the American state and the Canadian province almost went to war over a long-festering dispute about the precise boundary line separating them. In 1907 century-old trouble between Canadian and American lumbermen flared into violence, and only the hasty appointment of an international commission prevented the situation from deteriorating into open warfare. Since then New Brunswickers and Mainers have skirmished over everything from the ownership of a few tiny islands to the control of huge fishing banks.

Not surprising, then, that from the backwoods of Aroostook County to the halls of the state legislature in Augusta, Mainers have been talking about the Irving family. About how clusters of Irving service station signs are appearing on street corners in Maine towns. About how the highways are teeming with their bright yellow Sunbury, green Midland and red Land and Sea trucks.

The inevitable legends — as unverifiable as the ones back in New Brunswick — have sprung up around the family: how Irving companies try to cut costs by refusing to put radios and air conditioning in the cars driven by their executives; how Arthur orders his underlings not to hire employees with red hair, beards, moustaches or excess weight.[3]

Not everyone is leery of them. In the state's southern reaches, where the Irvings have yet to become a household name and are known mainly for their clean stations, superior service and good-quality restaurants, their growing presence raises hardly an eyebrow. In the counties closest to the New Brunswick border, they are lauded for their job-creating powers and the way their presence has brought competition to the stagnant local economy, long one of the weakest in the land.

As P.D. Merrill, of Merrill Transport, explains, "Irving's presence has stimulated a lot of activity. We're a better trucking company as a result of it."[4] Adds former governor Kenneth Curtis, who served a stint as U.S. ambassador to Canada and once acted as the Irvings' lawyer in Maine, "The Irvings are very, very sharp, very, very, tough negotiators. But they are honest. They still do business on a handshake. With them, that's as good as any contract. But you'd better be sure that you really want to do what you shake hands on, for they'll hold you to it."[5]

Yet as the Irving attack on Maine gathers force, it is becoming hard to hear the scattered praise above the din from their detractors, the business owners — who wonder how they can compete against the Irvings' awesome vertical integration and huge financial clout — as well as the ordinary citizens, who decry the family's desire to buy up more and more of their state.

Pockets of resistance have sprung up. In one notable example Irving Oil wanted to build a 24-hour gas station and convenience store in historic Hallowell, a bedroom community for the state capital, Augusta, where the streets are lined with restored homes from the 1700s and 1800s. After the locals resisted, the Irvings backed off. But they demonstrated their usual tenacity when the townspeople of Dover-Foxcroft argued against allowing the construction of an Irving gas station and convenience store operation near a nursing home on the town's main street. Irving officials argued that a moratorium of that sort would be seen as anti-business. In the end, the town's planning board narrowly approved the plan.

Their forest management techniques have also generated opposition. Usually their strategy is to clear-cut the land and then replant with insect-resistant black spruce. Mainers do not take kindly to outsiders coming in and changing the landscape they have known all their lives.

The uproar has been loudest in Aroostook County, a huge chunk of land in the northern part of the state, which is so wild and unpopulated that, heading north from Bangor, you drive for two hours through dense, unbroken woods before hitting civilization. Aroostook is rural, remote and economically depressed, and its people are the very epitome of conservative, opinionated, hard-headed Mainers. In the town of Westmanland, locals reacted with dismay, fear and anger when the Irvings stripped several hundred acres of woodland down to the roadside. Banding together, they passed an ordinance forbidding clear-cutting within 100 feet of any roadside. A number of nearby towns followed suit, instituting their own clear-cutting bans.

But the bitterness remains in the area around Madawaska Lake, a popular Aroostook vacation spot that in the late 1980s began to be plagued by summer "algae blooms," caused by too much nutrient pouring into the water from the land. Faulty septic systems were partially to blame for the problem. Still, much of the anger focused on the Irving clear-cuts, which allowed the nutrient-laden soil to be washed into the lake. Roger Harpine, a restaurant and bar owner on the lake who has a sideline selling T-shirts emblazoned with "Keep Aroostook Green, Send Irving Back to Canada," leaves no confusion about who he blames for ruining the lake's inlets and coves: "Irving is destroying everything we've got up here," he complains, adding, "I hate to see Canadians control my country. I could accept a Saudi Arabian quicker than I would a Canadian."[6]

Their defensiveness is entirely predictable. After spending a lifetime across the border from the Irving fortress, the people of Aroostook County have found themselves on the front line in the New Brunswick family's incursion into the U.S. It is all pretty overwhelming. When a typical Aroostook contractor now picks up a load of lumber, chances are that the wood he's hauling, the truck he's driving, the fuel he's using, even the asphalt he's driving on were made or are owned by the Irvings. What the people of Aroostook County want most to know is how far the Irvings intend to go. "Arthur Irving is going to take over the state of Maine," muses Dean Brown, manager of a rival Exxon station in Calais. "You cannot beat him. He's got too much money."[7]

True as that may be, the Irvings have quickly discovered that Maine is not New Brunswick, and the old rules no longer apply. When they try to get tough, people notice, as they did when the Irvings attempted to buy out a lucrative truck stop outside Bangor. When the owners refused, the Irvings tried to locate a station on the adjacent lot. Failing to round up enough land, they had to settle with building a stop miles down the road. The press in Maine also plays a different game, and suddenly the Irvings' critics have equal opportunity to voice their complaints. "Maine is Becoming Part of a Foreign-Owned Empire," screams one newspaper headline, while another declares, "Canadian Family Combine Reaps Maine Harvest."

Phyllis Austin, a reporter with the award-winning weekly *Maine Times*, uncovered alleged somewhat questionable business practices by Irving companies, including selling at or below cost in an effort to wipe out competition in the asphalt business and so-called tie-in sales, in which contracts go to companies that agree to purchase related Irving products. (The Irving brothers refuted the allegations during a short, antagonistic interview with Austin.[8]) "Suddenly we find a huge, closely held, unaccountable conglomerate dominating parts of the state's economic life," the *Times* editorialized. "There is no reason to believe that Irving will stop where it is; members of the family have made no secret of their interest in further expansion. As Irving continues to weave its web across Maine, we should be asking ourselves if this is what we really want."[9]

The lawmakers have shown interest. When Texaco put 12 Maine stations up for auction in the fall of 1988, Irving Oil offered twice as much as their appraised value, a move designed to thwart the stations' existing leaseholders, who had the right to match any offer by the highest bidder. Outraged members of the Maine legislature briefly toyed with legislating Irving Oil completely out of the state. Instead, they drafted a bill that would have made it illegal for firms owning refineries to sell gasoline directly to the public. That was eventually withdrawn in favour of a resolution directing the state attorney general to investigate "the trade practices of the motor fuels industry." In early 1990 the legislature passed a bill forcing anyone buying gas stations to notify the attorney general 30 days before the deal or face a $10,000 fine — a law unabashedly aimed at keeping state lawyers abreast of Irving Oil's ever-increasing market share.

Considering the locals' deep-seated suspicion of outsiders, the Irvings were probably guaranteed a cool welcome no matter how they acted. "People saw this foreign giant with unlimited resources swooping in and buying up everything in sight," Helen Tupper, a Republican member of the Maine legislature, explained. "It upset a lot of people."[10] Bruce Ellison, a business writer with *Kennebec Journal*, concluded that the real blame lies with Mainers themselves. "The problem with much of Maine is that we have become comfortable as we are, and many of us have adopted the attitude that since we are up here in an isolated corner of the nation we are exempt — and can remain exempt — from the trends and events that affect the rest of the nation. That is simply untrue. . . . We should watch the Irvings and learn from them."[11]

The Irvings themselves are plainly learning from their experience. Scrambling to disguise its foreign origins, Irving Oil has taken great pains to declare itself "a U.S.A. corporation." The corporate logo, mostly white in Canada, has become predominantly blue and red in the United States. Giant U.S. flags fly over the biggest Irving truck stops, and most of the convenience stores sell patriotic-looking Irving U.S.A. hats.

The family has mounted a public relations effort of sorts, donating $100,000 to the YMCA building fund in Ellsworth, home of Irving Oil's U.S. headquarters, and also emerging as a major corporate sponsor of Maine Public Broadcasting. Whenever possible they trumpet the fact that any profits made in Maine are reinvested in the state. They have flown reporters and some politicians to New Brunswick to have a look at their forestry practices. After the early PR set-backs, they have assiduously skirted controversy, steering clear of the state courts, even though Portland's most august law firm has been retained to represent them.

Through it all, the Irvings themselves are as invisible as ever. Occasionally, one of them is seen at Sugarloaf Mountain, the state's most popular ski hill, where they own a chalet. As always, they make few public appearances or statements, leaving what little communication emanates from their American operations to their top lieutenants.

But back in their Saint John headquarters, Maine — or, more accurately, what it symbolizes — is never far from their thoughts. For they have glimpsed the future, and what they see is a day when their trucks will roll down U.S. highways, past Irving service stations, convenience stores and restaurants, hauling loads of their own gasoline, lumber, newsprint, home furnishings and frozen food right to the tip of Florida.

Can they succeed? Conquering Maine, New Hampshire and Vermont, with their small, rural populations, presents virtually the same degree of difficulty as dominating the Maritimes. In the more heavily industrialized states to the south, where a service station costs many times more than one in New England, it is a different matter altogether. Eventually, they may run up against U.S. antitrust laws, which are much more stringent than those in Canada.

Storming that fortress may be beyond the wits or lifetime of the three men who now pull the levers back in Saint John. Time may be against them. It took their father a lifetime to trace his remarkable image across the land. K.C.'s sons have spent their days widening the scope of the vision they too believe in so fervently. All the same, one day soon a new generation will step forward to claim their inheritance. It is their mission to ensure that K.C.'s vision lives on.

EPILOGUE

An Epic Inheritance

*Through the years, a man peoples a space with im-
ages of provinces, kingdoms, mountains, bays,
ships, islands, fishes, rooms, tools, stars, horses
and people. Shortly before his death, he discovers
that the patient labyrinth of lines traces the image
of his own face.*
    — *A Personal Anthology*, Jorge Luis Borges

FROM CHILDHOOD on, they understood that they were different.
They could see it in how people looked at them, could hear it in
the voices of the men and women who worked for their fathers, could
feel it in the way that a room suddenly went silent when they entered.
This was part of their mixed birthright. For, along with the billions,
the Irving name has also conferred extraordinary resentment and
expectations.

Whether in their private or professional lives, the newest generation
must always measure up to their famous family name. Being Irvings
means that they must live cleaner, more responsible and productive
lives than most people. They must work harder than ordinary folk
in order to win respect and credibility, both from the average man
on the street and from their demanding parents. Carrying the Irving
name has always meant being judged by a different, harsher standard
than the rest of the world. That has never been truer than for the
cousins, the 12 grandchildren of K.C. Irving, who will eventually
inherit the family fortune and the huge responsibilities that go with
it.

No dynasty remains on top forever. Some decline in fortunes is
inevitable for all rich families who have enjoyed steady growth only

to see their operations became mature corporations in saturated markets. In Canada even the most powerful business empires expand for only a few generations before they grind to a halt, break up or are eclipsed by others. Some succumb to a revolution in which managers, not entrepreneurs, take over the controls, turning what was once a highly efficient corporation into a giant bureaucracy. In others the founder dies and the male heirs have little or no interest in the business affairs of their companies. Sometimes the new generation falls victim to the inevitable friction that occurs when succession takes place; one of the scions decides to cash out and go his or her own way — meaning the sale of a major holding, the first step in the dissolution of the empire.

In the end it often comes down to demographics. It is, after all, a demographic inevitability that most families, even the richest ones, become larger and more tangled with each passing generation. Family unity is usually not a problem for the first few generations. As long as the founder or his wife is alive, there is little difficulty in maintaining clan unity. Even in the second generation, the task of maintaining some semblance of family harmony is not hard, because usually the siblings share the sense of affinity common among brothers and sisters. By the time the third generation rolls around, however, kinship is less important. The members of this wave, many of whom are only first cousins to one another, do not hold the same unity and sense of common purpose that existed among their parents. Then, usually, the first cracks appear.

Until now, no fractures have split the Irving family's united front. Entering the third generation (the fourth if you count James Dergavel as the real clan patriarch), the organization has remained free of bureaucratic sloth and has maintained its entrepreneurial bent. The family has been able to finance growth from retained earnings and debt, and has avoided issuing common stock to the public. And the newest Irvings are showing no signs of relinquishing hands-on control; not just for duty's sake and to protect their own personal investments, but also because they feel compelled to make their own mark.

But questions remain. Are the grandchildren committed enough to K.C.'s creed to withstand the inevitable divergence in their aims and ambitions? Do they have the right stuff to lead the empire into the uncertain century that lies ahead? These will be the key themes in the next chapter of the Irving story, the part where they are confronted with the elusive challenge of ensuring that their family enjoys prolonged prosperity instead of beginning the long decline that plagues most dynasties.

These billionaire children have always known where they stood. The Irvings are fond of naming male progeny after their illustrious forebears. J.K. christened his first son James Jr., making him the namesake of K.C.'s own father and of the family forestry company he started, J.D. Irving Ltd. In the same tradition, Arthur called his first child Kenneth and his second boy Arthur Leigh. Jack, for his part, named his sons John Jr. and Colin.

Each of the children realized early on that the family character obscured their personal identities. They have led remarkably parallel lives. Growing up at their family homes in Saint John, the cousins saw enough of one another to forge a common character and attachment. Virtually all attended private schools: J.K.'s sons went to Rothesay Collegiate and Hyde School, a controversial institution in Bath, Maine, that caters mainly to gilded youth from wealthy families, and his daughters went to Stony Brook School in Long Island, New York. Arthur's sons attended Lakefield College School, the alma mater of Prince Andrew of the British royal family. From there, on to university, where they became the first generation of Irvings to actually graduate with degrees. Then, usually, into the family businesses, where they began learning the Way.

Jim Jr., J.K.'s oldest son, is the best known and most powerful in the new wave of Irvings to come forward. He looks the part: over six feet tall, with a sturdy build, strong features and a headful of straight blond hair, he has "an almost regal bearing," according to one of his employees. As the oldest son of the oldest son in a family where seniority counts for a lot, Jim Jr. has always been one of K.C.'s favourites. After university he joined J.D. Irving Ltd., the business closest to K.C.'s heart. Today he runs the day-to-day operations at the family forestry company and has responsibility for a number of associated companies, including Kent Homes, the prefabricated-home building company, and Sunbury Transport, one of the trucking concerns.

So far, reviews of his stewardship have been decidedly mixed: like his father, he is "all business," a sober and serious workaholic who values the businesses above all else. "My grandfather started this program," he once told a reporter touring the J.D. Irving tree plantations. "My father believes in it. I believe in it."[1] That is about as chatty as Jim Jr. gets. Even the most loyal employees say that he is aloof, has a temper and occasionally displays a touch of arrogance not in evidence in his father's personality.

If there is a "people person" on J.K.'s side of the family, it is Robert, now in his mid-30s, who runs Cavendish Farms, a tissue company and two trucking lines from his offices in Moncton. Short, balding and prone to put on weight, he lacks Jim Jr.'s gravity but compensates through enthusiasm and sheer likeability. At Acadia University he was a regular guy who liked to hoist a weekend beer with the boys. Even a decade within the family businesses has not drained all the good humour from him.

Still, as unassuming as he looks, Robert has ambitions: a sibling rivalry is rumoured to exist between he and Jim Jr., perhaps not surprising given the Irving penchant for spurring internal competition among their managers. Cavendish's high-profile shoot-out with McCain Foods pushed Robert into the public spotlight more than any other member of the new generation.

J.K.'s daughters have also remained close to home and the heart of the family empire. Mary Jean, the youngest, has disappeared from public sight after playing a pivotal role in the family's bid to buy up more Prince Edward Island potato farmland. Judith, a congenial mother of two, runs a clothing shop and her own photographic studio in Saint John. She says she started both without the financial help of her family. "That's just the way we were brought up," she once said. "You have to be able to stand on your own two feet. And that's the way I hope my family will look on things."[2] Perhaps more likely to play a major role in the family business eventually is Judith's husband, Paul Zed, an ambitious Saint John corporate lawyer with a degree from the London School of Economics and strong connections within the federal Liberal party.

Arthur's children are also moving up the line. Kenneth, his handsome, tall, older son, spent his university summers working for the Kent Line shipping company and after graduation received a management trainee's exposure to all the Irving Oil divisions, from home heating to convenience stores. Life was not easy under his father's watchful eye. "Arthur was determined that he was going to make Kenneth an Irving if it killed him. He was twice as hard on him as the other employees," recalls a former Irving Oil executive. Kenneth, in his early 30s, is learning the ropes at the refinery and earning a reputation for quiet competence.

Still, some say his abilities pale in comparison with his younger brother, Arthur Leigh, who helps run Les Pétroles Inc., their Quebec oil business. In his mid-20s, Arthur Leigh is likeable, full of energy and a superb salesman. "He always seems to be three feet off the ground," one former Irving official says about Arthur's lean, sandy-haired son.

Who will succeed Arthur Sr. to the top Irving Oil job? In most family-controlled corporations, the management of the company is passed from father to son, which means that men from other branches of the family rarely have the same chance of being chosen to serve as president. All the same, Arthur's sons may have competition for their father's office from cousin John Jr., Jack Irving's oldest son. He has an MBA from Harvard — he decided to upgrade his education after four years at Irving Oil — and is apprenticing at a number of Irving Oil divisions. Underlings find him smart and capable, but his ready temper and sometimes difficult personality have made him a few enemies among employees and within the extended family.

In that, he could not be more different from his younger brother, Colin, the loose cog in the well-oiled Irving machine. He studied acting at university in California. Since serving the obligatory apprenticeship, he has stayed far away from Saint John and the empire as much as possible, working as a ski instructor, model, actor, apprentice film producer and, most recently, a producer at an Ontario radio station.

Some say he is the first crack in the foundation, the first sign that the resolve of the new generation is weakening. Control, however, has always mattered more in this corporate family than in most.

Rather than worrying about "blowing it," this generation of Irvings seem mainly determined to outdo their celebrated fathers. Like many heirs, they need to prove to themselves that they're still breathing by undertaking extraordinary challenges. No matter who emerges behind the controls, the demands will be immense. They must find a way to reconcile the Irving Way with the huge changes occurring in the world. They must manage to keep the empire intact in the face of the powerful stresses from within and without. They must find new ways to grow and new markets to conquer.

And if they succeed in all of that, one day soon they too must begin preparing a new generation to continue to give life to the diamond gleam of their great-grandfather's vision.

They are well positioned to face the future. The Irving empire is better placed than virtually any other Canadian organization to walk the world stage. K.C. and his progeny have forged an organization that, in style and substance, looks less like a traditional North American conglomerate and more like one of the Japanese *keiretsu* industrial organizations, which strike fear into the heart of corporations everywhere in the world.[3] *Keiretsu* literally means a "lining up" of companies. These global powerhouses — among them Mitsubishi Corp. and Toyota Motor Corp. — are loosely formed alliances of financial and industrial firms that are linked by cross-ownership of one another's stock; they share resources in order to strengthen the competitive abilities of each member of the group. Though somewhat smaller, the Irving empire shares a similar structure: an almost seamless web of cross-owned companies spanning a wide range of industries and products with the financial clout to be a major player in any market in which it chooses to compete. The values that hold sway in the *keiretsu* — long-term planning and a sharing of resources among affiliates — closely mirror the way K.C. and his sons have always run things.

The Japanese approach has not always translated well to Canada, even though huge amounts of the country's corporate wealth are secured in a few hands. The most obvious failure of a home-grown Canadian *keiretsu* organization is the Edper industrial conglomerate controlled by Peter and Edward Bronfman. The stock market value of the more than 360 Edper companies approached $100 billion before the market softened in 1990. Their activities span the corporate world. But, as David Olive wrote in *Report on Business Magazine*, "the sun is setting on the Edper complex, and none too soon." According to Olive, Edper's managers assembled a hodge-podge of companies that never developed the "synergistic" sharing of resources that would have enabled them to strengthen one another's competitive positions at home and abroad. Added Olive, "The real penalty to the economy of such convoluted constructions as Edper is that, in the hands of a different set of managers, this collection of great companies could have amounted to something on the world stage. As it is, the empire will eventually be dismantled so that the Bronfmans' hired hands can cash in their chips."[4]

The Irving organization is different. Whereas the Edper group and other conglomerates were hastily assembled over the past decade, the Irving group fermented from within over a period of 70 years. As it is, the Irving organization may be the only Canadian corporate complex with the financial might and unflinching commitment to long-term planning necessary to compete with the likes of the Japanese *keiretsu*, the Korean *chaebols*, the American conglomerates and the German-style *Konzern*. That, in the end, may be the ultimate testament to the dream that K.C. had so long ago in the tiny village of Bouctouche.

As for the patriarch himself, now that K.C. has entered his 90s, he is seldom seen in public any more. The last significant public speech he made was in 1979, after accepting membership in the Canadian Business Hall of Fame. "On occasions such as this," he told his Upper Canadian audience, "invariably someone recites the nice things I have done — or the nice things I'm now alleged to have done — and very kindly omits all the terrible things I used to be accused of doing. I must confess I like it much better this way, and if I had realized what a fine fellow I would become simply by growing old I might well have done it much sooner."[5] Today, even on those rare occasions when he accompanies his sons to corporate functions, he rarely speaks, adding conviction to the persistent rumours that his powers are not what they once were.

Still, it is said that he remains keenly interested in the empire. He makes his regular sojourns to Bouctouche to visit old friends. He likes to sit in one of the family airplanes and lazily circle his forestlands. Each year he appears on J.D. Irving Ltd.'s corporate calendar, sporting a red-and-black Hudson's Bay–style winter coat and grey fedora, measuring a tree he planted years ago to show how much it has grown. Often he can be glimpsed on the Bridge, looking down upon what he has built and on the descendants who have taken up his handiwork. If he is pleased or saddened by what he sees, no one really knows; who can say whether someone is pleased or saddened by his own reflection. The only thing truly certain is that when K.C. Irving peers down from the summit, he sees his own image traced over the landscape for as far as the eye can see.

NOTES

Prologue: The Autumn of the Patriarch

1. Newsprint production: author's interview with J.K. Irving.

2. Irving timberland holdings: New Brunswick Department of Natural Resources, Nova Scotia Department of Lands and Forest and Maine Bureau of Forestry.

3. Number of Irving service stations: author's interview with Arthur Irving.

4. On Irving security force: New Brunswick police and RCMP estimates.

5. Diane Francis, "K.C. and His Sunshine Band Are Just Soaking Up the Oil," *Toronto Star* (Nov. 16, 1984).

6. Estimates that follow are the author's, based on a variety of sources including the New Brunswick government, Statistics Canada, Irving officials and industry sources.

7. National Film Board and CBC, producers, *I Like to See Wheels Turn*, 1981, Giles Walker, director.

Chapter One: The Baron of Bouctouche

1. Antonine Maillet, introduction to Pierre Cormier, *Bouctouche of the Past* (Lunenburg, N.S.: Lunenburg County Print, 1984), p. 9.

2. For the past and recent history of Bouctouche that follows, I have relied on interviews with Laurie Boucher and Pierre Cormier, as well as Cormier's book *Bouctouche of the Past*; and Chris Wood, "Bouctouche, N.B.," *Atlantic Insight* (Apr. 1984), pp. 43-45.

3. The early history of the Irving family comes from Robert Bonnell, *K.C. Irving*, printed privately by the family in 1980, and on interviews with Pierre Cormier and Willie Duplessis of Bouctouche.

4. Antonine Maillet, *La Sagouine* (Toronto: Simon & Pierre, 1979), p. 19.

5. Michael Bliss, *Northern Enterprise: Five Centuries of Canadian Business* (Toronto: McClelland & Stewart, 1987), p. 287.

6. Account of Bouctouche at the turn of the century is based upon Cormier, *Bouctouche of the Past*, p. 60.

7. Michael Wardell, "K.C. Irving: The Amazing Creator of Millions," *Atlantic Advocate* (Mar. 1959), pp. 21-22.

8. National Film Board and CBC, producers, *I Like to See Wheels Turn*, 1981, Giles Walker, director.

9. David Pickard, "Stay-at-Home Success," *Canadian Business* (Feb. 1948), p. 24.

10. John Kenneth Galbraith, *The Scotch* (Toronto: Macmillan of Canada, 1964), p. 27.

11. Wardell, "K.C. Irving," p. 19.

12. Ibid.

13. "At 85, K.C. Irving One of Youngest at the Reunion," *Saint John Telegraph-Journal* (June 9, 1984).

14. Ralph Allen, "The Art of Wielding Power," *Maclean's* (May 16, 1964), p. 50.

15. James Dykes, *Canada's Automotive Industry* (Toronto: McGraw-Hill, 1970), p. 31.

16. Pickard, "Stay-at-Home Success," p. 25.

17. Nowlan's rumrunning exploits are chronicled in B.J. Grant, *When Rum Was King* (Fredericton, N.B.: Fiddlehead Poetry Books, 1984), pp. 167-71. His relationship with Irving is noted in David MacDonald, "The Wrong Way to Make Millions," *Maclean's* (Aug. 15, 1953), p. 44, and in Cyril Robinson, "Tycoon of the Maritimes," *Montreal Standard Magazine* (June 25, 1949), p. 14.

18. Robinson, "Tycoon of the Maritimes," p. 14.

Chapter Two: A Visionary Gleam

Epigraph: Charles Lynch, "Saint John: A City Reborn on Its 200th Birthday," *Canadian Geographic* (Nov. 1983), p. 10.

1. On early history of Saint John: George Schuyler, *Saint John: Scenes from a Popular History* (Halifax, N.S.: Petheric Press, 1984), and Schuyler, *Saint John: Two Hundred Years Proud* (Windsor Publications [Canada] Ltd., 1984).

2. Schuyler, *Saint John: Two Hundred Years Proud*, p. 96.

3. Lynch, "Saint John: A City Reborn," p. 10.

4. Schuyler, *Saint John: Two Hundred Years Proud*, p. 110.

5. Ibid.

6. Bonnie Kulak, "Developer of the Year," *Atlantic Advocate* (Nov. 1975), p. 36.

7. Harry Bruce, *R.A.: The Story of R.A. Jodrey* (Toronto: McClelland & Stewart, 1981), p. 64.

8. A.E. Wetchford, "Irving's New Power Punch," *Atlantic Advocate* (July 1960), p. 57.

9. Stock Prospectus for Irving Oil Company Limited — $125,000 6% Cumulative Sinking Fund Participating Preference Shares Par Value $50 — April 16, 1930, p. 2. Private collection.

10. Ibid.

11. Edward Cowan, "One-Man Conglomerate," *New York Times* (June 20, 1971).

Chapter Three: Darkness and Daylight

1. David Pickard, "Stay-at-Home Success," *Canadian Business* (Feb. 1948), p. 84.

2. National Film Board and CBC, producers, *I Like to See Wheels Turn*, 1981, Giles Walker, director.

3. Last will and testament of James D. Irving, registered at 4:00 p.m., Nov. 6, 1933, by Fred S. Sayre, Registrar, Kent County.

4. Pickard, "Stay-at-Home Success," p. 84.

5. Author's interview with Edward Byrne, who was told this by Irving when the two men were both living in Bermuda during the 1970s and 1980s.

6. Pickard, "Stay-at-Home Success," p. 84.

7. Irving Oil financial results, *Financial Post* (June 22, 1935).

8. Michael Wardell, "K.C. Irving: The Amazing Creator of Millions," *Atlantic Advocate* (Mar. 1959), p. 23.

9. Russell Hunt and Robert Campbell, *K.C. Irving: The Art of the Industrialist* (Toronto: McClelland & Stewart, 1973), p. 92.

10. Report of the New Brunswick Motor Carrier Board for the year ending Dec. 31, 1937.

11. This account of the battle over the Saint John bus franchise is based mainly on Hunt and Campbell, *K.C. Irving*, pp. 53-88.

12. Ibid., pp. 60-61.

13. Ibid., p. 82.

14. Harry Bruce, *R.A.: The Story of R.A. Jodrey* (Toronto: McClelland & Stewart, 1981), p. 208.

15. A.J.P. Taylor, *Beaverbrook* (New York: Simon & Schuster, 1972), p. 414.

16. Hunt and Campbell, *K.C. Irving*, p. 100.

17. The story of the Mosquito fighter comes from Fred Hotson, *The De Havilland Canada Story* (Toronto: Canav Books, 1983).

18. On Canada Veneers and its transformation: Author's interview with Art McNair.

19. Hunt and Campbell, *K.C. Irving*, p. 101.

20. C. Martin Sharp, *DH: The Story of De Havilland* (Shrewsbury, England: Airlife Publishing Ltd., 1982), pp. 188-189.

21. Wardell, "K.C. Irving," p. 23.

22. Reports of the New Brunswick Motor Carrier Board for the years ending Dec. 31, 1943, and Dec. 31, 1946.

23. Irving Oil financial results, *Financial Post* (June 19, 1948).

24. "New Brunswick Railway Company Acquired by Irving Interests," *Saint John Evening Times-Globe* (Apr. 10, 1945), p. 1.

25. "Port Royal Pulp & Paper Co. Changes Hands," *Saint John Evening Times-Globe* (Mar. 2, 1946), p. 1.

26. Irving Oil Co. Ltd. prospectus: $6-million 5 1/4% Sinking Fund Debentures, Series A, Mar. 31, 1952. From private collection.

27. Byron Fisher, "Mystery King of the Maritimes," *Liberty* (1954 [?]), p. 72.

Chapter Four: Citizen Irving

1. Cited in Cyril Robinson, "Tycoon of the Maritimes," *Montreal Standard Magazine* (June 25, 1949), p. 9.

2. Cited in David MacDonald, "The Wrong Way to Make Millions," *Maclean's* (Aug. 15, 1953), p. 23.

3. Harry Bruce, *Down Home: Notes of a Native Son* (Toronto: Key Porter, 1988), p. 95.

4. MacDonald, "The Wrong Way," p. 23.

5. Author's interview with Colin Mackay.

6. MacDonald, "The Wrong Way," p. 42.

7. Ralph Allen, "A Tour of the Irving Empire with the Irvings," *Maclean's* (Apr. 18, 1964), p. 52.

8. Ralph Allen, "The Art of Wielding Power," *Maclean's* (May 16, 1964), p. 49.

9. MacDonald, "The Wrong Way," p. 42.

10. Bruce, *Down Home*, p. 195.

11. Author's interview with Charlie Van Horne.

12. Author's interview with Charlie Van Horne.

13. MacDonald, "The Wrong Way," p. 46.

14. MacDonald, "The Wrong Way," p. 46.

15. Ibid., p. 43.

16. Allen, "The Art," p. 42.

17. Ibid., p. 45.

18. MacDonald, "The Wrong Way," p. 44.

19. Royal Commission on Corporate Concentration, Study No. 16, *The Irving Group* (Feb. 1978), p. 14.

20. Irving Oil financial results, *Financial Post* (Mar. 1, 1958).

21. Allen, "The Art," pp. 45-46.

22. "Irving: Gas Pump $200,000,000 Empire," *Toronto Star* (Oct. 31, 1959), p. 10.

23. Anthony Sampson, *The Seven Sisters* (New York: Bantam Books, 1973), p. 7.

24. The account that follows of Socal's involvement with Irving Oil comes from "Reasons for Judgement," filed March 4, 1988, in the archives of the Federal Court of Canada. The case, *Irving Oil Limited v. The Queen*, is reported as 88 Dominion Tax Cases 6138 (F.C.T.D) and as [1988] 1 Canadian Tax Cases 263 (F.C.T.D.).

25. Account of the opening of the Irving refinery comes from stories in the *Saint John Evening Times-Globe* (July 21, 1960).

Chapter Five: The Knight Errant

1. Author's interview with Ed Byrne.

2. Russell Hunt and Robert Campbell, *K.C. Irving: The Art of the Industrialist* (Toronto: McClelland & Stewart, 1973), p. 121.

3. John Edward Belliveau, *Little Louis and the Giant K.C.* (Hantsport, N.S.: Lancelot Press, 1980), p. 35.

4. Letter from K.C. Irving to Hugh John Flemming, Apr. 11, 1959, filed with New Brunswick Archives, Fredericton, N.B., as part of Flemming's private papers.

5. Della Stanley, *Louis Robichaud: A Decade of Power* (Halifax: Nimbus Publications, 1984), p. 50.

6. Ibid., p. 49.

7. Ibid., p. 50.

8. Ibid., p. 70.

9. Author's interview with Ed Byrne.

10. Letter from Boylen to Hugh John Flemming, Nov. 18, 1959, filed in New Brunswick Archives, Fredericton, N.B., as part of Flemming's private papers.

11. John Braddock, "Irving Joins Boylen," *Atlantic Advocate* (July 1964), p. 52.

12. Charles McElman, Senate of Canada *Debates*, Mar. 11, 1971.

13. Author's interview with Ed Byrne.

14. Stanley, *Louis Robichaud*, p. 139.

15. Agreements between Irving Oil Co. and Irving Pulp & Paper Co. and City of Saint John. Archives of the City of Saint John.

16. Langevin Coté, "King Irving and the Revolutionary," *Toronto Globe and Mail* (Mar. 15, 1966).

17. Russell Hunt and Robert Campbell, *K.C. Irving: The Art of the Industrialist* (Toronto: McClelland & Stewart, 1973), pp. 140-141.

18. Brunswick Mining and Smelting accounts payable, Oct. 31, 1966, filed in Robichaud's private correspondence in New Brunswick Archives, Fredericton, N.B.

19. Letter from Louis Robichaud to K.C. Irving, Aug. 1, 1964, filed in Robichaud's private correspondence in New Brunswick Archives, Fredericton, N.B.

20. Charles McElman, Senate of Canada *Debates*, Mar. 11, 1971.

21. "Brunswick Now in Noranda Bailiwick," *Financial Post* (July 8, 1967).

22. Author's interview with Alf Powis.

23. J.B. Burgoyne, "Brunswick Mining Meeting Erupts," *Saint John Telegraph-Journal* (May 7, 1969), p. 1.

24. Author's interview with Louis Robichaud.

25. Cited in Richard Starr, *Richard Hatfield: The Seventeen-Year Saga* (Halifax: Formac, 1988), p. 33.

26. Ibid., p. 29.

27. Ibid., p. 37.

28. Stanley, *Louis Robichaud*, p. 172.

29. Walter Stewart, "Portrait of a Political Storm Centre," *Toronto Star Weekly* (Oct. 21, 1967), p. 2.

30. Belliveau, *Little Louis and the Giant K.C.*, p. 97.

31. Author's interview with Louis Robichaud.

32. Author's interview with Richard Hatfield.

Chapter Six: The Fourth Estate

1. Charles McElman, Senate of Canada *Debates*, Mar. 11, 1969.

2. "Control of the Gleaner," *Fredericton Daily Gleaner* (Mar. 13, 1969), p. 1.

3. Ibid.

4. On the *Citizen*: author's interview with Charles Lynch.

5. Author's interview with Charles Lynch. William March in his authorized history of the Halifax papers, *Red Line: The Chronicle-Herald, the Mail Star, 1875-1954* (Halifax: Chebucto Agencies Ltd., 1986), p. 355, wrote that control of the papers never fell into Irving's hands.

6. Ralph Costello, "Costello: Saying Goodbye Was the Hard Part," *Saint John Telegraph-Journal* (Mar. 19, 1988), p. 13.

7. Alden Nowlan, in *Canadian Newspapers: The Inside Story* (Edmonton: Hurtig, 1980), p. 70.

8. Jon Everett, "Thoughts on the Chairman of Good Old Irving Oil," *Atlantic Insight* (Apr. 1980), p. 20.

9. Ibid., p. 20.

10. On Wardell's life: his obituary, *Saint John Evening Times-Globe* (May 1, 1978), p. 1.

11. Charles McElman, Senate of Canada *Debates*, March 10, 1971.

12. Kenneth Bagnell, "Does the News Belong to K.C. Irving?" *Globe Magazine* (June 14, 1969), p. 7.

13. William Wardell, "Irving Charges Bias," *Montreal Star* (Dec. 17, 1969).

14. Hearings of the Senate Special Committee on Mass Media, Dec. 16, 1969.

15. Ibid.

16. Ibid.

17. Ibid.

18. Ibid.

19. *The Uncertain Mirror: Report of the Special Senate Committee on Mass Media* (Ottawa: 1971), p. 70.

20. Ibid., p. 84.

21. Senate of Canada *Debates*, Mar. 10, 1971.

22. Charles McElman, Senate of Canada *Debates*, Mar. 11, 1971.

23. "Former Publisher Replies to Senator," *Toronto Star* (Mar. 12, 1971).

24. "Irving Says: 'Read Matthew,'" *Saint John Telegraph-Journal* (Mar. 15, 1971), p. 1.

25. "Irving Quits N.B., Leaves Empire to His 3 Sons," *Toronto Star* (Jan. 19, 1972).

26. Ibid.

27. *Saint John Telegraph-Journal* (Jan. 21, 1972).

28. "Irving Says He Let Papers Run Without Interference," *Toronto Star* (Oct. 18, 1972).

29. "Irving Considered Giving Papers to Foundation, Trial Told," *Toronto Globe and Mail* (Oct. 25, 1972).

30. Dal Warrington, "Big Improvement Made in Irving Papers — Camp," *Ottawa Citizen* (Nov. 15, 1972), p. 36.

31. Royal Commission on Newspapers, *Final Report* (Ottawa: 1981), p. 58.

Chapter Seven: The Changing of the Guard

1. Letter from K.C. Irving to R.G. Follis, chairman of Standard Oil Co. of California, dated Sept. 4, 1962. Arthur Irving subsequently testified in court that the letter was never actually sent.

2. Ibid.

3. Irving Oil financial statements for years ending Jan. 31, 1962, Jan. 31, 1963, and Jan 31, 1964. From private collection.

4. On the negotiations between Socal and the Irvings: see *Irving Oil Limited v. The Queen*, 88 Dominion Tax Cases 6138 (F.C.T.D.) and [1988] 1 Canadian Tax Cases 263 (F.C.T.D.).

5. John Blair, *The Control of Oil* (New York: Pantheon Books, 1976), p. 48.

6. Testimony of Otto Miller, as quoted in "Respondent's Memorandum of Fact and Law," in the archives of the Federal Court of Appeal. The federal appeal, *The Queen v. Irving Oil Limited*, is reported as 91 Dominion Tax Cases 5106 (F.C.A.) (Feb. 18, 1991).

7. "Reasons for Judgement" in *Irving Oil Limited v. The Queen*, filed Mar. 4, 1988, in the archives of the Federal Court of Canada, p. 30.

8. Ibid., p. 40.

9. "Appellant's Memorandum of Fact and Law" in *The Queen v. Irving Oil Limited*, in the archives of the Federal Court of Appeal, p. 35.

10. Ibid., p. 30.

11. Irving Oil financial statements: from private collection (Dec. 31, 1971, Dec. 31, 1972); filed in archives of the Federal Court of Canada (Dec. 31, 1974, Dec. 31, 1975), in reference to *Irving Oil Limited v. The Queen*.

12. Statistics Canada, *External Trade, Exports by Countries*, Jan.–Dec. 1977 and Jan.–Dec. 1978. (Irving Oil is the only exporter of refined petroleum from New Brunswick into the United States.)

13. Ross Henderson, "The Rotterdam Connection in Oil," *Toronto Globe and Mail* (July 11, 1979).

14. Statistics Canada, *External Trade, Domestic Exports*, Jan.–Dec. 1979 and Jan.–Dec. 1980.

15. Exhibit I-256, Petroleum Inquiry Hearings, Restrictive Trade Practices Commission, 1983. Profits from Irving Oil Company, Ltd. Report and Financial Statement, May 31, 1981.

16. John Honderich, "$500-Million Exports Slip Should Boost Canadian Dollar," *Toronto Star* (Nov. 15, 1979).

17. "Considered Suit Against K.C. Irving," *Financial Post* (May 20, 1978).

18. Royal Commission on Corporate Concentration, Study No. 16, *The Irving Group* (Feb. 1978).

19. Ibid.

20. On the Bertrand inquiry: *Canada's Oil Monopoly: Highlights from "The State of Competition in the Canadian Petroleum Industry"* (Toronto: James Lorimer and Company, 1981).

21. *Royal Commission on Newspapers* (1981), p. 95.

22. Statistics Canada, *External Trade, Domestic Exports*, Jan.–Dec. 1981, Jan.–Dec. 1982.

23. Andrew McArthur was interviewed by James Bagnall, *Financial Post* (Oct. 1982).

24. On the ceremony awarding the shipyard contract: "Special Report," *Saint John Telegraph-Journal* (May 19, 1988).

Chapter Eight: Gassy, Grease and Oily

1. Rothesay Collegiate School Yearbook, 1946.

2. Author's interview with Ian Doig.

3. On inherited wealth, see Alan Farnham, "The Children of the Rich and Famous," *Fortune* (Sept. 10, 1990), pp. 112-128.

4. Alexander Ross, "It's Tough to Be the Boss's Son," *Maclean's* (June 1968), p. 16.

5. Author's interview with Donald Savoie.

6. Ross, "It's Tough," p. 16.

7. Alan Freeman and John Urquhart, "All in the Family: Hard-Working Irvings Maintain Tight Control in a Canadian Province," *Wall Street Journal* (Nov. 1, 1983), p. 1.

Chapter Nine: The Irving Way

1. Alfred D. Chandler, Jr., *Scale and Scope: The Dynamics of Industrial Capitalism* (Cambridge, Mass.: Belknap/Harvard University Press, 1990).

2. Exhibit M-594 (1), Petroleum Inquiry Hearings, Restrictive Trade Practices Commission, 1983.

3. Confidential figures from the Retail Gasoline Dealers Association of New Brunswick and the Retail Gasoline Dealers Association of Nova Scotia.

4. James Bagnall, "Ships of State," *Financial Times of Canada* (Sept. 10, 1990), pp. 10-12.

5. 1986 memo from Irving Oil head office to Irving Oil stores (from private collection).

6. Exhibit M-595, Petroleum Inquiry Hearings, Restrictive Trade Practices Commission, 1983.

7. July 20, 1983, memo from Irving Oil head office to Irving Oil stores. Private collection.

8. Robert Jones, "Irvings Lose Truck Licensing Bid," *Toronto Globe and Mail* (Oct. 25, 1989), p. B1.

9. Charles Perry, "Renewed Fight with Irving Truck Firms," *Moncton Times-Transcript* (Jan. 25, 1991), p. 1.

10. *Chinnery v. Smith and City Transit Ltd.* (1977) 19 New Brunswick Reports (2d) 81 (Q.B.).

11. "Court Clears Irving Oil," *Toronto Globe and Mail* (Feb. 20, 1991), p. B3.

12. National Film Board and CBC, producers, *I Like to See Wheels Turn*, 1981, Giles Walker, director.

Chapter Ten: The Hatfields and the McCoys

1. Chris Morris, "McCains Run the Business from NB Because They 'Like It Here,'" *Saint John Evening Times-Globe* (Nov. 27, 1984), p. 15.

2. Gordon Pitts, "Chipwagon to the World," *Financial Post* (Jan. 15, 1990), p. 9.

3. John Godfrey, "Harrison McCain (Canada's CEO of the Year)," *Financial Post Magazine* (Dec. 1990), p. 10.

4. Stephen Kimber, "Spud Wars," *Canadian Business* (Sept. 1982), p. 83.

5. Kennedy Wells, "Irving and Potatoes? Rumours Are Flying," *Atlantic Insight* (Mar. 1980), p. 10.

6. Kimber, "Spud Wars," p. 83.

7. "Can See No Conflict, Jackson Tells Meeting," *Charlottetown Guardian-Patriot* (Apr. 9, 1981).

8. Author's interview with Peter van Nieuwenhuizen.

9. Author's interview with Archie McLean, senior vice-president, McCain Foods.

10. Author's interview with Robert Morrissey.

11. Author's interview with Robert Morrissey.

12. "Islanders' Views on the Irving and McCain Companies' activities in P.E.I." Baseline Market Research Ltd. (June 22, 1990).

13. Author's interview with Prince Edward Island journalist Barbara McAndrew.

14. John DeMont, "Old Rivals, New Wars," *Maclean's* (Nov. 12, 1990), p. 52.

15. Ibid.

16. Ibid.

Chapter Eleven: The Last Fiefdom

1. J.K. Irving's address to the Saint John Board of Trade was reprinted in *Saint John Today* (June 1990), p. 1.

2. Jeffrey Simpson, "Saint John Revisited — and Found to Be Refurbished and Vital," *Toronto Globe and Mail* (Sept. 19, 1990), p. A16.

3. Statistics Canada, 1986 Census of Canada.

4. George Nikides, "Many Think Irvings Key to Prosperity," *Saint John Telegraph-Journal* (Feb. 22, 1990), p. C1.

5. Author's interview with Dr. Robert Beveridge, head of emergency services, Saint John Regional Hospital.

6. On Saint John's environmental problems: *A View of the City*, Final Report of the Saint John Environmental Consultation Committee, May 1, 1990.

7. Ibid., p. 49.

8. Author's interview with Dr. Robert Beveridge.

9. "Trial Told Fish Died After Test," *Saint John Evening Times-Globe* (Aug. 25, 1976).

10. "Will Consider Allowing Nuisance Suits Against Polluters, N.B. Says," *Toronto Globe and Mail* (Oct. 28, 1978).

11. Elaine Bateman, "Report States Pulp Mills Continue to Pollute Province," *Saint John Telegraph-Journal* (Nov. 19, 1988), p. 4.

12. Mac Trueman, "National Survey Finds Mill Dioxin-Free," *Saint John Evening Times-Globe* (Dec. 13, 1989), p. C1.

13. On Irving political contributions: campaign financial returns.

14. Author's interview with former MP Michael Landers.

15. Author's interview with officials in New Brunswick Environment Department.

16. David Folster, "Tax Credits by the Tankful," *Maclean's* (Aug 4, 1980), pp. 18-19.

17. Author's interview with Michael Daigneault, Manager, English Service Television in New Brunswick, for the Canadian Broadcasting Corporation.

Chapter Twelve: Strange New Worlds

1. Author's interview with Charlie Van Horne.

2. Irving market shares: based on estimates of competitors and industry experts.

3. Phyllis Austin, "A Canadian Conglomerate Muscles In on Maine," *Maine Times* (Dec. 4, 1987), p. 4A.

4. Denise Goodman, "Irving Stirs Fear in New England," *Boston Globe*, as reprinted in *Saint John Citizen* (Nov. 29, 1988), p. 3.

5. Bruce Ellison, "Curtis: Irving Filled Need for Oil Supplier," *Portland Press Herald* (Dec. 9, 1987), p. 23.

6. Interview by Phyllis Austin with Roger Harpine.

7. Goodman, "Irving Stirs Fear," p. 1.

8. Austin, "A Canadian Conglomerate," pp. 2A-9A.

9. "Should Maine Be Vertically Integrated?" *Maine Times* (Dec. 4, 1987), p. 10A.

10. Robert Jones, "Irving Expansion Plans Slowed by Wary Maine Townspeople," *Toronto Globe and Mail* (Jan. 5, 1990), p. 10.

11. Bruce Ellison, "The Irving Clan: No Evil Empire," *Portland Press-Herald* (Dec. 10, 1989).

Epilogue: An Epic Inheritance

1. Jennifer Henderson, "New Generation of Irvings Moving Up," *Financial Post* (June 13, 1988).

2. Ibid.

3. For *Keiretsu*, see Charles McMillan, *Services: Japan's 21st-Century Challenge* (Canada-Japan Trade Council, 1991); and David Olive, "The Edper Complex," *Report on Business Magazine* (May 1991), pp. 7-8.

4. Olive, "The Edper Complex."

5. As quoted in Robert Bonnell, *K.C. Irving*, printed privately by the family in 1980.

INDEX

The author is grateful for the permission to include the following previously copyright material:

Excerpt from *Don Quixote* by Cervantes, translated by J.M. Cohen copyright © J.M. Cohen 1950 (Penguin Books, 1950). Reprinted by permission.

Excerpt from *Down Home: Notes of a Martime Son*, copyright © 1988 Harry Bruce (Key Porter Books, Toronto, 1988). Reprinted by permission.

Excerpt from"Tiger in the Dublin Zoo" from *Between Tears and Laughter*, copyright © Alden Nowlan (Stoddart Publishing Co. Ltd., Ontario). Reprinted by permission.

Excerpt from *A Personal Anthology*, copyright Jorge Luis Borges (Grove Press Inc., New York). Reprinted by permission.

Excerpts from *La Sagouine*, copyright © 1985 by Antonine Maillet, translation by Luis de Cêspedes (Simon & Pierre Publishing Co. Ltd.). Reprinted by permission.

Excerpts from *Bouctouche of the Past*, by Pierre Cormier, published by the Town Council of Bouctouche. Reprinted by permission.

Excerpt from *Louis Robichaud: A Decade of Power,* by Della Stanley, copyright © 1984 (Nimbus Publications, Halifax, Nova Scotia). Reprinted by permission.

Excerpt from *The Seven Sisters* copyright © Anthony Sampson (Bantam Books, New York). Permission applied for.